Jesus Christ understood the conce[barcode D1002432] had, you are going to have to do something you sses, our universities, our school systems, and yes, designed to get the results we are currently getting. If you don't like those results, then something must change. Today, there are more people on this planet than have ever been here at one time before, and for the first time, the body of Christ is in decline. The church SHOULD be growing exponentially, but we are not… that is why change is called for, and that change can be found in discovering relevant ways to impact culture. Because participation and interests in leisure activities is at an all-time high, sports and recreation ministry done the right way, for the right reasons has been found to be that agent of change to reach the masses with the message of salvation through Christ. That is what this book is about. The body of Christ must be diligent in seeking out ever-changing ways to share a never-changing message. This book will provide all the basic tools needed for any church to use recreation and sports ministry as a dynamic way to share the eternal truth of the gospel. I highly recommend it, not for every church library, but for every desk at every church.

—*Caz McCaslin, Founder and President*
Upward Unlimited

This intellectually invigorating edition of *Recreation and Sports Ministry* should be mandatory reading for anyone using sports and recreation to spread the Gospel. John Garner continues to engage sports ministers with insightful information by utilizing years of experience combined with research to provide educational and practical information for all. This comprehensive history and analysis of recreation ministry provide the reader with insight into the theological underpinnings, modern trends, and cultural implications. *Recreation and Sports Ministry* is exactly the tool needed to motivate those with years of experience and to train the next generation to intentionally use recreation and sports to glorify God.

—*Chad Payn, Assistant Professor of Sports and Recreation*
Oklahoma Baptist University

John Garner's *Recreation and Sports Ministry* has been the gold standard, guiding church sports outreach ministries since first published in 2003. I have recommended this book to many churches, and it is required reading for my sports ministry students at Azusa Pacific University.

Many takeaways from the original edition are incorporated into my teaching and my sports ministry. To name a few, Linville's concept of viewing "opponents" as "co-competitors;" Oswald's "Mandate, Means, and Method;" and Garner's "eight reasons for a church to employ sports." I'm so excited for this revision. Thank you, John, and contributing authors.

—*Steve Quatro*
Founder, Sports Outreach Los Angeles
Professor, Azusa Pacific University

"Recreation and Sports Ministry: Impacting Postmodern Culture," is filled with wisdom and practical application from outstanding leaders in sports ministry. They provide solid insights into reaching this culture with the message of Jesus Christ through the avenue of sports. This resource gives practical A to Z guidance on how to develop a biblical foundation for sports ministry, cast vision and implement effective sports ministry that touches, evangelizes, and disciples all ages and stages of life in your local community. A bonus to this second edition is the final chapter on discipleship through sports ministry. If you are looking for ways to impact your community, this is a must read for every church leader.

—*Dr. Ken Thomas*
President, Connect Ministries, Inc.
Senior Director of WinShape Camps

If you feel that God is calling you into recreation and sports ministry or you are already serving in that role, this book is a must read for you. Even if you are a volunteer or lay person serving in your church or simply someone who wants to know more about this type of ministry, you will find a wealth of information on how to use leisure activities in a church setting to reach a lost and dying world. "Recreation and Sports Ministry: Impacting the Post-Modern Culture" gives you a blueprint for starting and leading a successful recreation ministry. You will learn everything from the foundations of recreation ministry to how to effectively plan, program, and administrate a ministry so that it reaches its maximum potential.

As you read through this book, I pray God will open your eyes to the wealth of information that it contains, and may you find the resources needed to make your ministry the most effective that it can be for God's Kingdom. Read, pray, and play and use what God gives you here to reach your community through sports, recreation, and leisure activities.

—*David Maki, Associate Pastor, Sports and Recreation*
First Baptist Church, Carrollton, TX

Recreation and Sports Ministry: Impacting the Postmodern Culture

2nd Edition

Written and Edited by
John Garner

Recreation and Sports Ministry: Impacting Postmodern Culture
2nd Edition

ISBN 13: 978-0-9976828-2-3
Library of Congress Control Number: 2017941364

Author Contact Info:
John Garner
Twitter: @jgarner71
john.garner71@gmail.com

Lynchburg, VA

PRESS
Liberty.edu/LibertyUniversityPress

Contents

APPENDIXES

Acknowledgements

To my wife, Judy. You caught the vision in high school. You believed in the Lord and you believed in me. As my wife, you told me I had to stay in college and seminary when I wanted to quit. Later, you spent many evenings alone with our boys while I was at the church gym or the field and you hung in there. Now all these years later, you are still there, encouraging, helping, and praying—O, how you pray! You are God's precious gift to me. I would not have been able to accomplish what I have done, be the person I am, or do what I do today without you.

This work is also dedicated to the men and women who are called to use recreation and sports ministry as tools to reach people. Your work is other people's play. You toil tirelessly to capture the imagination of a leisure oriented culture to share the gospel. I honor you. Your ministry methods and tools are often misunderstood by church members and leaders alike. But on you march, seeking to point people to Christ during their leisure, holding high the banner of salvation through Christ alone. May God bless you richly and give you and your families a balanced life and the restful leisure you so desperately need and richly deserve as you practice what you preach. Never give up on the pursuit of excellence, never give in to mediocrity in what you set out to do, and never lose faith in the God who is faithful to you.

I would especially like to acknowledge the staff at Liberty University Press. Thank you to: Cheryl Job, Press Manager, who put up with my emails, questions, and change requests with much patience. To editors Heather Bradley and Kerry Hogan who had some great editorial suggestions. To graphic designer Danielle Heitzman for the eye-catching cover design. To Makayla Millington who took on the difficult job of formatting my submissions and did a phenomenal job of editing and interior layout. All of you are givers of grace and have the hearts of servants. I am indebted to each of you.

— John Garner, author and general editor, 2016

Preface

He was a middle school boy whose family had just moved to town. They went to church, but that was about it—little or no involvement in any other ministry. Then the knock at the door came; a knock that would change one kid's destiny. The education minister, Henry Love from First Baptist Church in Shreveport, LA, was out to visit new move-ins. The lady of the house opened the door, and he introduced himself. He was telling her about the church when he saw the middle schooler with his younger brother in the background. "Hey, guys I'm Henry," he said. Then he began to ask the boys questions: "Do you like to play basketball? Do you like to play ping pong? Do you like to roller skate? How about bowling, do you like that?" The boys readily answered yes to all except the last question, "Do you like to shoot pool?" They had never shot pool, but they said, "We think we would." Then Henry said something that was unbelievable to them: "We have a place at the church where you can do all of that in our recreation building." He had totally captured the middle schooler's imagination! Wow, a place at a church to play basketball, to play ping pong, to skate! They even had a bowling alley and pool tables! In the boy's mind, he could see himself doing all those things—especially on the court, with the clock ticking down, 5, 4, 3, 2, swish, winning at the buzzer!

That day, Henry Love told the mom and her boys how to be involved not only in the recreation and sports program, but also the youth Sunday school, music program, and missions program. He gave an invitation to come the next Sunday and excused himself. The boys said, "Momma, we don't know where you are going to church, but we know where we are going!"

That was how I was introduced to involvement in church which would lead to my salvation and my calling. I began to get involved in the recreation and sports program, the Sunday School ministry, the youth ministry and yes, even the choir ministry. From that home visit, a destiny was changed, a calling would be issued by God, and a life of ministry would be born. I am the product of a sports and recreation ministry.

This book reflects the influence the men and women who used sports and recreation as tools to influence my life. It is written as a tribute to FBC

Shreveport and the first recreation minister I ever knew, Elmin Howell, under whose ministry I came to know the Lord. He would later open the door to my first ministry position out of college. It reflects the influence of Bobby Shows, the Minister of Recreation who took me under his wing when I was in the 10th grade and allowed me to learn the ropes. He later led to Christ the young lady who eventually became my wife. I am deeply indebted to you Bob for your investment in my life in so many ways. This text is reflective of the pastors of churches I served: Maurice Clayton at my college church, Hillcrest, in Jackson, MS, the first truly expository preacher I sat under (he used golf as a ministry tool); Dr. Dalton Havard at FBC Texas City, TX, who hired a green kid out of college to start a "new" ministry in his church not knowing if it would work or not; and Dr. Ronald Prince at FBC Minden, LA, who came to Christ because of a recreation program as a teenager at a church in downtown Boston, MA in the 1930's. He invited me to begin a ministry that would eventually host two and half times the population of our town at ministry events. These pastors had faith in me and supported and encouraged me. They believed that recreation and sports ministry could be a tool to reach people. And, to my astonishment, allowed me to lead their churches in this area. I am grateful and thankful for each of these important men of God.

Later I was privileged to work with "heroes" of the recreation and sports ministry at The Sunday School Board's Church Recreation Department, later to become LifeWay Christian Resources Recreation and Sports Ministry. Heroes like Frank Hart "Pogo" Smith, the best social recreation leader in the nation; Don Mattingly, the creator of a recreation based international youth camp called Centrifuge; Wendell Newman, "Mr. Facilities design and programming;" Deane Hartzell, the creator of CrossPoint, a sports camp for children; and Ray Conner, the department director who gave the okay for me to be hired. I honor those who have gone to glory and those who still encourage and influence me even now!

My life, my marriage, my children, and now grandchildren have all been impacted by this little known, misunderstood and often misused area of ministry. May God grant his favor on the readers and "capture your imagination," the way he did mine.

Contributors

The following authors are competent and accomplished practitioners and teachers. Any one of them could have compiled this work or written it outright themselves. It is hoped that each reader will make him/her self aware of who these leaders are and learn from their experience. —J. G.

DALE ADKINS, BA, RE.D.

K. Dale Adkins is Department Chairperson Appalachian State University, Boone, North Carolina Department of Recreation Management and Physical Education. He received his doctor of recreation from Indiana University. He has presented at the state, regional, national, and international levels, and has published numerous articles and abstracts. Dr. Adkins is past president of the American Association for Leisure and Recreation within the American Alliance for Health, Physical Education, Recreation, and Dance. Dale also has served on the board of directors for the American Camping Association.

DALE CONNALLY, PH.D., CPRP

Dale Connally is Professor and Assistant Department Chair, and the director of the Recreation and Leisure Services Program at Baylor University in Waco, Texas. Dale received his doctorate in education from the University of New Mexico where he majored in parks and recreation management. Dale has published articles, abstracts, and ministry resources for use in the church. He lectures and teaches extensively in the field of recreation and leisure services and has presented papers at various outdoor and leisure service symposiums. He is the author of Games with a Purpose 2 and is actively involved in the Outdoor Network. Dr. Connally is author of: "Boots On the Ground: Case Studies in Hunting Ministries" in God, Nimrod, and the World: Exploring Christian Perspectives on Sports Hunting.

JOHN GARNER, BS, MRE

John is former director of Recreation and Sports Ministry at LifeWay Christian Resources. He has been working in recreation and sports ministry for 40 plus years and is the author of more than 100 articles in ministry related newsletters, theological journals, ministry magazines, and blogs. He is author/editor of the Guidebook for Planning Recreation Centers and the Operating Manual for Recreation Centers. John is currently pastor of Belmont Heights Baptist Church in Nashville, TN. He also lectures in an adjunct capacity at several seminaries and colleges.

JUDI JACKSON, BA, MRE, PH.D.

Judi is a pastor's wife, professor, writer, conference leader, and women's ministry leader based in Atlanta, GA. She graduated from Louisiana State University with a degree in journalism and from New Orleans Baptist Theological Seminary with an MRE in youth education and Ph.D in Christian Education. Judi serves as a faculty member at New Orleans Baptist Theological Seminary, teaching in the division of Christian Education Ministries. She coauthored The Retreat Notebook 2 with her husband Allen.

GREG LINVILLE, BA, M. DIV., D. DIV., D. MIN.

Dr. Greg Linville was one of the founding members of the association of Church Sports and Recreation Ministers (CSRM) and has served as the Executive Director since 2000. He has experience as a local church sports and recreation minister through First Friends Church in Canton, OH. Greg served as chaplain for various professional, collegiate and scholastic sports teams and was the chaplain for the Akron Aeros, an AA affiliate of the Cleveland Indians. He also served on the urban staff of the YMCA and Young Life in Canton, OH where he ministered to center city kids and gangs through sports and recreation. Greg is married and the father of two teenage children.

RODGER OSWALD, BA, MA

A graduate of Multnomah Biblical Seminary and College, Rodger is former executive director of Church Sports International in San Jose,

CA. He earned his bachelor and master's degrees from California State University in San Jose. He has served as Christian Education, Missions, and Sports pastor at several California churches. Rodger was instrumental in designing curriculum for an undergraduate degree in sports ministry and establishing a sports ministry department at the Master's College. Roger has written extensively on the use of recreation and sports ministry. He lectures and teaches in an adjunct capacity at colleges and seminaries.

PAUL STUTZ, BS, MARE, PH.D.

Paul is Assistant Professor of Administration and Church Recreation and Associate Dean for Master's Program at Southwestern Baptist Theological Seminary. He is also adjunct faculty at Dallas Baptist University. He is former director of the Recreation/Aerobic Center at Southwestern. He teaches extensively in the camping and outdoor education field. Paul has served several churches in Texas as a minister of recreation. Paul has served on the Recreation and Sports Ministry Leadership Team for LifeWay Christian Resources and is a lecturer at Rec Lab: The International Conference on Recreation and Sports Ministry and RecSpo.

BRAD WESNER, BA, MA, MS, PH.D.

Brad has served in higher education since 2002. He is currently Dean at ITT Technical Institute, North Charleston, SC. He has worked in Christian camping and served churches in various capacities since 1984. He has had extensive writing and editing experience for educational journals such as Play and Culture and has written more than 50 articles for various religious and nonreligious publications, including magazines such as Parks and Recreation, Church Recreation, and Church Administration. Brad's doctoral work focused on the history of recreation in the American church. Brad's leisure is centered on creative writing, cartooning, model railroading, and his family.

Introduction

This book is an introduction to the who, why, when, where, and how of recreation and sports ministry. I have endeavored to bring together some of the brightest minds in the field to share their hearts and skills with a new generation. The reader will gain practical knowledge from these leaders who have put on paper some key concepts they have learned and employed in the use of recreation and sports as ministry tools.

As an introduction, it is by no means definitive. There are many other books and writers who go into much depth and detail on the topics we only have room to glance over on these pages. The reader is referred to the "Books Worth Reading" selected bibliography at the end of the work.

This work is a second edition ministry overview of a work published in 2003. The substance of the first edition, though hopefully clarified and amplified, has not been changed. Language and statistics have been updated to speak to a new generation of leaders. Although each chapter can stand alone, the reader will see a continuity in the overall scope of the work as each chapter supports, reinforces, and expands the others. I am indebted to the authors for their consistency and hard work as they have examined and explored this ministry area from their chapters' point of view.

Second Edition
© 2017 by John Garner
Published by Liberty University Press
Lynchburg, Virginia

I have become all things to all people, so that I may by all means save some. Now I do all this because of the gospel, that I may become a partner in its benefits.
1 Corinthians 9:22b–23

1

Introduction to Recreation and Sports Ministry

John Garner

"Opportunities abound in America to use sports to reach people."

Every church from the smallest mission point to the largest mega church uses recreation and sports—every church. They may have a highly organized staff with a huge sports complex with indoor and outdoor facilities, or they may rely on a small committee of three volunteers using a large room, parking lot, grassy area, or nearby park for activities. It matters not the size of the staff or facility nor the tools they have to use. What matters is that activities are planned and carried out with the intent of making God's name and salvation through His Son known as the church shares the gospel, makes disciples, and strengthens the church.

In 1927 the first issue of *Church Administration* magazine had an interesting lead article. The title was "The Modern Movement for Better Rural Church Buildings." America was in the midst of prosperity—not knowing that the Great Depression was just around the corner. Most of the country was rural. There was a new rural prosperity. Travel was becoming easier. Soldiers had returned from the "Great War." Public schools were being built in rural areas. Churches were doing new ministry actions. Indeed, churches were the center of community life—everything was done there, from worship to socials that gathered folks in their communities.

The interesting part of that article (outline, really) was in section three. In that section, "Some co-ordinate equipment," the listing went like this:

- A well-kept church lawn
- A pastor's home
- A few acres of land
- Part for the pastor's use
- Part for athletic fields
- Garage containing Ford car
- Private light and water system
- A building for community social life[1]

Here was a major denominational publication recommending that a church provide places for athletics and social life. The church was using sports and recreation (socials) to reach people because that was what people were involved and interested in.

In 1889 James Naismith applied to be a student at the YMCA Training School at Springfield. One of the questions asked on the application was, "What is the work of a YMCA Physical Director?" He answered, "To win men for the Master through the gym." In December 1891 Dr. Naismith created the game of basketball. Naismith's invention came during that winter when his supervisor asked him to come up with an indoor game to attract young men during the harsh New England winters—in order to share the gospel on a year-round basis. "Using a soccer ball, two empty peach baskets, a ladder and ten handwritten rules, Naismith introduced his game that would become the most watched and played indoor sport in the world."[2]

In the early twentieth century, famous sports figures were using their sports platform to gather a crowd to share the gospel: The Olympic champion known as the Flying Scotsman, Eric Liddell, was using sports as a platform for gathering a crowd and sharing the gospel in 1924. C. T. Studd used his status as a well-known cricket player in England. In America, Billy Sunday, former professional baseball player, became an evangelist and reached millions. Sports and recreation have been used since biblical times to share the message of salvation through knowing Christ as Savior. This was especially evident in the post World War II era as a product of evangelical youth rallies, particularly those connected to the Youth for Christ (YFC) organization. In the 1940s and '50s, YFC discovered what it called "the sports appeal" in attracting an audience—especially among adolescent males—to hear an evangelistic message. On Memorial Day 1945, for example, 65,000 young people came to a YFC rally at Soldier Field in Chicago to hear a gospel message and listen to America's reigning indoor mile champion, Gil Dodds, give a testimony to his faith in Jesus.... By the late 1960s, sports evangelism and ministry was coming to the college campus as athletes and coaches commanded respect as Christ followers. Not only do athletes come to Christian college campuses to play and compete, but many of them also come because they perceive athletic participation as a means to ministry—both during and possibly following their days of intercollegiate competition.[3]

This has continued in the 21st century as Christian athletes continue to draw crowds of men and women who want to "hear their story" about how they learned to live the Christian life as a high profile athlete in sometimes difficult circumstances. Athletes and leaders like former football quarterback and ESPN commentator, Tim Tebow, surfer, Bethany Hamilton, college coach Dabo Swiney, and others who are/were in the college ranks speak to tens of thousands about what Christ meant to them in college and what that means in their lives today.

If it worked then, how much more open to recreation and sports is our culture now? Popular culture today is saturated with both, thanks in large part to the media. The Olympics, Super Bowl, World Series, X-Games, Iron Man events, the Final Four in college basketball, and the playoff series in professional basketball capture the imaginations of millions of people in America. Social media and live streaming makes keeping up with and watching events, teams and scores a normal part of the season no mater where you are or what time it is. Instantly, we can know scores, stats, outcomes, injury reports and become "super-fans." Sporting events are available 24/7/365 and our culture is "all in".

Culture is there. The question is, where is the church and how is the church using these tools to reach people? Or perhaps a better question is, will the church see the opportunity to use recreation and sports as ministry tools? The fact is that most churches are not reaching the postmodern culture. Most churches are being ignored and often marginalized by an increasingly non-Christian American culture because people do not see the church as relevant to their lives. But the culture does see relevance in leisure activities that they pursue at breakneck speed and often at great cost. The church must learn to capture the imagination of a world that is passing it by. If the church can capture people's imaginations, it can get their attention. If a church can gain people's attention, it has access to their minds. If a church has access to a person's mind, it can reach his heart. If a person's heart is reached and the message of the love of God through His Son is conveyed, a life can be changed for eternity. As an open group (whoever comes at anytime will fit in), open door (all are invited) strategy to reach people, recreation and sports ministry, done intentionally, can offer a non-threatening first touch in lives of all ages.

SNAPSHOT OF AMERICAN CULTURE

We live in a leisure-oriented, competition-driven, unseeded culture. In the 1990s it was thought that people would be working shorter hours and have longer weekends to pursue leisure activities. In fact, just the opposite is true. "While four in 10 workers put in a standard 40-hour work week, many others toil longer than that, including nearly one in five (18%) who work a grueling 60 hours or more. That translates into 12-hour days from Monday to Friday—or into shorter weekdays with lots of time spent working on the weekends."[4] "The tools that were supposed to free us from the shackles of our desks have bound us to our jobs in ways unimaginable just a decade ago. They are electronic umbilical cords to the workplace."[5] People are working longer hours not just from home, but on the commute to and from work, at home in the evenings, and on weekends. They feel the need to be more productive as the competition has gotten more intense and the job market tightens.

Work is pervasive. The "electronic umbilical chords" mentioned above of laptop computers, smart phones, and tablets, have sparked an entirely new life-paradigm. These seemingly indispensable items that have given rise to ever-present Email, text messages, Twitter, GroupMe, Snapchat, instant messaging, and apps that have yet to be invented mean that some people never get away from their work. They take work home and on vacation. For many Americans, work has become an addiction. Millennials often blur the lines between work and leisure with 24/7 use of media that can keep them in constant contact with co-workers. This makes one's leisure time a valued commodity.

Even though work consumes so much of their time, Americans prize their leisure above almost everything. It is not uncommon for workers to negotiate more time off even if they give up some salary to get it. People's time has become more valuable than money. Many Americans no longer work for food, shelter, clothing, and transportation; these are givens for most Boomers, Gen-Xers, and Millennials. They work for the weekend, for time off when they can do what they want to do. They will spend considerable time and money in pursuit of fun at the lake or on the golf course; camping; going to baseball, football, or basketball games; mountain biking; jogging; or engaging in a hobby that brings fulfillment to their lives. Billions of dollars are spent on leisure activities each year. The number one retailer of sporting goods sold $9.6 billion worth of sporting goods equipment in a recent year. In American culture, leisure is a fact of life. Leisure is an expected commodity that is sought, bought, and bargained for. It is important to people in all walks and stages of life, and all indications are that it will continue to grow in importance in the coming years.

In the 1990s and early 2000s, "The top four activities of all Americans [were] watching television, reading, socializing with friends and family, and shopping.... Americans [were] spending less time in front of the tube, less time reading and more time hanging out with friends and going shopping."[6] Since then there has been a fundamental shift in use of leisure time. "Four of the most popular five leisure activities for both Millennials, Gen-Xers (Ed: And now Gen-Z) take place on a screen: watching TV, computer/internet, watching/going to the movies, playing video games and computer/internet games."[7] This change over what was reported in the 1990s has huge implications for leisure service providers—be they church or secular. It is interesting to note that "hanging out with friends" is number four on the list. This indicates that the sense of "community" with Millennials and Gen-Xers is important. Recreation and sports ministry has an open door to these two generations as this ministry area fosters fellowship and community if done intentionally. (For more on recreation and culture, see Appendix 2: "Recreation and Sports Ministry: Positioning for Impact.")

FROM WORK ETHIC TO LEISURE ETHIC

Gordon Dahl, in "Emergence of a Leisure Ethic," states: "We are beginning to discern the emergence of a leisure ethic....It is an alternative that is being chosen by thousands of today's Americans."[8] Indeed America has moved from a work ethic to a leisure ethic. Most churches and church leaders have not recognized this fundamental shift in our culture. This shift has changed everything except the way the church interacts with culture.

Every Sunday people by the millions pass by the church on their way to the lake, the golf course, the hunting trip, the soccer field, the amateur or professional sporting event, or any number of other leisure pursuits available today. Churches are trying to gather a crowd by doing the same things in the same ways they have always done them, and they wonder why people are not responding.

A Gallup survey tells us 90% of Americans read about sports (the sports page, magazines, online, etc.), watch sports (attend events, watch events and newscast via TV and on streamed media), and participate in sports (from Horseshoes to basketball) on a monthly basis. On a weekly basis it is 70%. With the advent of "Fantasy Leagues" and all things streamed 24/7 those numbers are even higher. Sports promoters, advertisers, and athletes have captured the imaginations of most of our culture. They keep the sports engine running at full speed. People are "doing their own thing," and this "thing" is all about leisure and sports. Most often, the way people choose to use their discretionary time does not include the church.

Dahl goes on to say, "Instead of worrying over the hazards of [people] doing their own thing...Christians ought to be discovering its opportunities. In other words, we should confidently and consciously affirm the leisure ethic in an audacious exercise of the freedom we possess in Christ, and make our 'thing' the deeds of love, joy and peace which spring from spirits freed of sin and guilt and promised abundance of life."[8] Here you have a view of believers in Christ living the abundant life that Christ said was available. As this abundant life is lived out during leisure, it will be attractive to the world. The leisure ethic lifestyle is both an avenue of abundant life and a laboratory in living for the Christian. The church has relegated itself to "sit on the sidelines," as it were, acting as if recreation and sports were a minor-league event, when in actuality, sports is a giant steamroller seeking to consume every person and every dollar those people have. The shift from work ethic to leisure ethic is well understood by upcoming generations. Churches must begin to see the value of offering events and teaching opportunities that appeal to the leisure mindset. One view is that "the church whose life and destiny have always transcended particular times...should be one of the institutions best prepared to adapt and flourish in the world of change and variety."[9]

COMPETITIVENESS IS EVERYTHING

Competition on the job has led us to become more conscious of productivity. If I am competitive in my job and produce more services or goods, then I'm often rewarded with more time to use as I see fit. The more competitive I can become and the more products or services I produce in a shorter amount of time give me more time to spend doing what I want to do. Being competitive has it rewards.

College and business school graduates are foregoing jobs with higher paying salaries and taking jobs that will allow them more time off. Time is becoming a new form of currency as increasingly time is more valuable than money to workers. When people of this leisure ethic mindset work, they work hard and are competitive. When they play, they play hard and expect to have the time they need to play. As the one of the most affluent

	FROM	TO
Work	went to work and came home for R&R	24/7; work everywhere — home, car, plane, hotel
Community	place to sleep and eat, friends and neighbors	place to live and belong, cyber communities
Family Vacation	two weeks of togetherness	two days tacked on to a business trip
Childhood Summers	neighborhood fun and pickup games at the park	daycare like, structured or highly specialized
Socialization	participate in recreational leagues seasonally	chat rooms, tv talk shows or play dates
Physical Activities	traditional team sports (softball, baseball, volleyball, or football)	individual activities, youth adventure (inline skating and snowboarding), mature fitness pursuits (walking, gym workouts)
Play	teams and clubs, fun and relaxation, status and socialization	individual focus, well being, self definition

Dr. Ellen O'Sullivan, *Parks and Recreation* magazine

Figure 1-1: Signals of a Shift

cultures in the world, Americans have the money, and they expect to have the time to do what they want to do with their time.

Competition often creeps into the leisure activities. Some Little League teams now require parents to take classes to curb the overly competitive spirit that parents often bring with them to games. Parents are pushing their children to be more competitive so they can win a tournament or a scholarship to college (statistics tell us the odds of this happening are astronomical). The joy of participation has given way to the pressure of competition. In one instance, fans and players of a losing team physically beat referees at a high school boy's basketball game. The police had to be called. In a well publicized instance, a father was convicted of murder for killing another boy's father over a hockey practice. Unfortunately, parental misconduct is one reason children quit playing sports.

Competition cannot be eliminated. Indeed, competition can bring out the best in us. In Romans Paul wrote about the athlete preparing for competition and "running the race." Elements of competition are found everywhere. From sibling rivalries, to corporate boardrooms, to sandlot football games, competition is a part of life. It can bring out the best in us, physically, emotionally, and mentally. Games, sports, art shows, bike rodeos, talent shows, and checkers have elements of competition. Life is full of competition. One cannot have a game without competition.

The problem with competition is when it becomes the driving force in the participant's life. Competition can be a powerful motivator, or it can be an all-consuming force that can ruin the participatory experience for the competitor as well as for those who are watching.

The church has a part in teaching the role of competition in a balanced life. The church needs to offer creative alternatives encouraging participation, developing skills, and fostering a love of sports. By seizing the arena of competition and channeling it to be something that builds lives instead of tearing relationships apart, the church can influence this powerful force.

Competition is neither right nor wrong. In fact, competition makes us strive to be better at whatever we do. It is how individuals handle competition that makes the difference. The church can and should teach participants in church leagues to handle competition in a new way to make a difference. (See Linville's chapter "The Ethics of Competition in a Church Setting" for an in-depth look at a biblical view of competition.)

REACHING AN UNSEEDED GENERATION WITH INTENTIONALITY

We live in a culture that is unseeded with the Word of God. People do not know the Word of God, have not read the Word of God, and are afraid of the Word of God. Perhaps most of you reading this grew up hearing, memorizing, singing, or reading God's Word. Many, if not most, of the Gen-X and Millennial populations know practically nothing about it. They have been told in the media and culture that if you study the Bible, you might go off the deep end. Children are not being taught the wonderful stories and Bible verses that can impress on their hearts the

CHURCH AND CHURCH EVENT ATTENDANCE: A MATTER OF PERCEIVED VALUE

According to the Bureau of Labor Statistics on an average day Americans age 25-54 slept about 87.7 hours, spent 2.5 hours on leisure and sports activities, worked for 8.9 hours, and spent one hour doing household activities. The remaining hours were spent in a choosing from variety of other activities, including eating, educational activities, and shopping. Our days are packed with activity and this impacts time we allocate to discretionary activities like attendance at church/religious activity. Combining leisure and "other activities" gives Americans about 20 hours of leisure a week counting Saturdays and Sundays to choose what to do.

Implications for the Church

If Americans' time is at a premium, that says a lot to the church as it endeavors to impact our culture. Here are several observations:

1. If we spend half our time at work, the twenty hours of leisure are magnified in importance.
2. Going to church/church sponsored events happens in a person's leisure time as a "chosen" activity.
3. Time has a value of its own.
4. People expect certain quality (perceived value) in what they spend their time on. The perception is that if this activity is not going to enhance my life with something of quality/value, I will not spend the time to participate/attend.
5. If going to church is a personal leisure activity, what happens at church must be of the highest quality for people to get their perceived value for the time spent.
6. Churches who offer perceived quality and value (personal, family, financial, social, relationship, recreation, etc.) are going to attract and have effective ministry opportunities.

love of God and the salvation brought by Jesus Christ. Churches realize this and are trying to teach the Word of God, but families are too busy going to soccer tournaments, camping, or simply being at leisure to attend Bible study. Because parents will seek to get their children to quality sports and recreation events, churches must seize the opportunity to use quality recreation and sports to teach the living word of God—Scripture. If we believe the Word of God is alive, and if we believe it will not return void, when or where or how we teach it will not matter. What does matter is that we use people's interest in sports, leisure, and recreation to "intentionally" reach an unseeded generation.

The dictionary defines intentionality this way: "From intent, which suggests greater deliberateness; a more settled determination that requires a more carefully calculated plan. Done by intention or design." Intentionality in the recreation and sports ministry context is the purposeful inclusion of sharing the gospel during recreation and sports ministry events. At one time in the history of recreation and sports ministry, a ministry was seen as successful if it had numerous teams or many people involved in recreation classes. This concept was characterized by activity. Activities became ends in themselves, and recreation and sports ministry became activity for activities' sake. Most churches had no strategy for intentional ministry to happen. If someone came to Christ, that was good. If no one came to Christ, the ministry was considered successful simply because the activity was held.

As recreation and sports ministry has matured, intent has changed. The days of rolling out a basketball and having pickup games are over. Intentional programming is the key. Intentional programming is planned with the intention of sharing the gospel by creating events with built in evangelism opportunities. This type of programming is done with or without a facility. Success does not mean having a facility—recreation and sports ministry can be done effectively without a facility. Successful recreation and sports ministry is characterized by people coming to Christ and believers discipled. (See "Recreation and Sports Ministry" for programming info).

No longer are churches satisfied with being activity driven. More and more churches are seeking to be intentional in their recreation and sports ministries.

They are planning their ministries to be intentional by:

- Reaching people by sharing the gospel at every opportunity.
- Maturing believers by discipling them.

- Multiplying ministering Christians by providing avenues for ministry participation.

By designing deliberate but natural touch points for ministry to take place during recreation and sports ministry events, as relationships are built, churches will find that this leisure-oriented generation will respond. The use of sports and recreation activities can be an open door to reach this generation. It is a natural.

How is the church to respond to this leisure-oriented, unseeded, sports crazy culture? Do we continue with business as usual? If we do, we will have little positive force in the community. Or do we do as Bob Briner suggests in his book Roaring Lambs: "Instead of hanging around the fringes of our culture, we need to be right smack dab in the middle of it."[10] Paul put it this way: "To the weak I became weak, in order to win the weak. I have become all things to all people, so that I may by all means save some. Now I do all this because of the gospel, that I may become a partner in its benefits" (1 Cor. 9:22–23).

RECREATION AND SPORTS MINISTRY DEFINED

There are as many manifestations of recreation and sports ministry as there are churches that have either recreation ministry or sports ministry. The term recreation and sports ministry has only recently been used in churches. For some denominations, church recreation was the term used since the 1940s. For other denominations, sports ministry has been the preferred terminology. Individual churches may have used the term recreation ministry or activities ministry to describe the work in their settings. Whatever a church chooses to call this area of work, its nature involves elements of pure recreation and elements of sport—hence the combination of terms in modern times to recreation and sports ministry.

For the purposes of this text, the terms shall be defined as recreation/ sports, any competitive/noncompetitive activity or action that takes place during the leisure time of a group or an individual; and ministry, helping people understand their relationship with God, his daily role in their lives, and their need to move from where they are to where they need to be in a right relationship to him. Combining the two results in the following definition:

> Recreation and sports ministry: Activity that takes place during leisure time with the stated purpose or intention of helping people become aware of their need for a relationship with God, his daily role in their lives, and their place in his kingdom work. This definition, while not specific as to activities involved, encompasses four of the concepts of leisure: (1) time, (2) activity, (3) a state of mind, and (4) as holistic process. (These concepts are discussed later in this chapter.)

WHY USE RECREATION AND SPORTS MINISTRY?

We've discussed the need to use recreation and sports ministry. Now it is important to understand why this ministry should be used.

Recreation and Sports Events Are Gathering Places for People

Because people are comfortable with recreation and sporting events, they naturally gather at these events. Who isn't familiar with the crowds at basketball and football games? Festivals of all kinds draw huge crowds of people. People understand the nature and action of recreation events. They may not understand what goes on in a church worship service, but they know what happens at a basketball game. By offering recreation and sporting events, the church has a non-threatening avenue to attract people. Parents will bring their children to the "Fourth of July Extravaganza," which features family-oriented activities, fun, food, and perhaps fireworks. This is a natural way for the church to introduce itself to the community and impact the community for Christ.

Other gathering places are sporting events—amateur and professional. Churches are taking Jesus' example and going where the people are. Christian volunteers often help event professionals by offering to work behind the scenes as parking lot attendees, errand runners, or office workers. Churches are endeavoring to be salt and light in the world, looking for a chance to share the gospel.

Recreation and Sports Events Bridge Cultural and Racial Barriers, Building Fellowship

Sports is one of the most universal languages. Every country, every culture plays sports. Christians who use these tools find open doors and multiple opportunities to share the gospel with people from around the world.

Opportunities abound in America to use sports to reach people. Many churches are hosting sports camps and clinics in their neighborhoods or taking teams on the road to play in prisons, being intentional to share the gospel as they go. People will gather for the event. People will listen to the players' testimonies afterward. People will respond to the message of salvation shared in a genuine way.

Here we see the church being what Christ said it should be, unified into one body. The Scripture says, "By this all people will know that you are My disciples, if you have love for one another" (John 13:35).

Recreation and sports ministry can unify and facilitate fellowship and community within the church. As church members fellowship together, they get to know one another better, barriers are broken down, and lasting relationships and a sense of belonging are built. Churches that exhibit fellowship and genuine concern find that people want to be a part of such a group. Everyone wants to be more than a number. Recreation events are relationship and community builders that personalize the church in people's lives.

Sports and Recreation Ministry Offers Ways for Christians to Live Out Their Abilities, Interests, Talents, and Spiritual Giftedness

Each Christian is gifted by the Holy Spirit for service. Each Christian also has natural abilities, talents, and interests. God brings all of these together to make us who we are. As we learn about our spiritual gifts, we can learn how our personality, natural abilities, talents, and interests complement one another. A person may know how to coach softball but have no idea about their spiritual gifts. Through coaching the church softball team, that person can come to understand that the church is using softball to reach and disciple people. Through leading the team by coaching and ministering to spiritual needs, that person is being prepared for other leadership responsibilities within the church.

Sports and recreation ministry is ministry. It is:

- An outreach to nonbelievers.
- A place of discipleship for maturing Christians.
- A training ground for new leaders.

Sports and Recreation Ministry Offers an Avenue to Gain Visibility in the Community

Through sports and recreation, churches are finding ways to make their presence in the community known. One church wanted the community to know who they were and where they were in case someone ever had a need. They decided to do a large event that involved the entire church. They involved businessmen in the community. They advertised in every media outlet. They moved church from Sunday to Saturday so the event would afford the best opportunity for people to attend—on Sunday. When the event took place, they had thousands of people on their church grounds—in a part of the country that is not known for church attendance! One new start-up church used a parking lot to host a "Food Truck Festival". The stated purpose was to raise money to help a local school—which they did. The purpose was to help introduce the new church to the community—which they also did. One church was a mega church, one a small new start, but both churches found ways to share the gospel as people left the events using printed material thus strategically "getting the message out" while providing a fun and engaging the community around them. Both churches gained visibility in their respective communities and shared Christ in a non-threatening way with each adult. Any church can use sports and recreation to gain visibility in the community. This is possible because in our leisure-oriented culture events help gain visibility as people respond. This has implications for the quality of the events and their perceived value to people.

Sports and Recreation Ministry Offers a Way to an Abundant Balanced Life

People are looking for something to fill the void in their lives. Recreation and sports ministry is often the first touch in a person's life with the church. This ministry area offers a way to develop a relationship with people and to introduce them to the life of the church and a relationship with Jesus Christ. Jesus said, "I have come that they might have life and have it in abundance" (John 10:10).

Sports and Recreation Ministry Provides a Catalyst for Outreach

A catalyst is a compound added to a chemical that causes the chemical to change its molecular structure while the catalyst remains the same. As a catalyst, recreation and sports activities open doors and enable a church to reach out into a community in non-threatening ways. Lives are changed, and relationships are developed with the intentionality of ministry action.

Sports and Recreation Ministry Provides an Environment for Fellowship

Recreation and sports events provide informal times of interaction. This leads to a deepening of relationships between participants. These events often are held in a nonreligious setting (ex. basketball court, party, camping, etc.), putting guests at ease. As fellowship is strengthened and relationships are developed, doors open for witness and ministry. Among believers, fellowship is a foundation for building respect, unity, and loyalty in the church.

In 1937, Dr. T. B. Maston, a professor of social ethics, wrote in his book *A Handbook for Church Recreation Leaders*, "Churches need to promote play because of what it can contribute to the church as an institution. Play builds the spirit of friendliness and good fellowship. It unifies the group and contributes to a sense of solidarity and loyalty....It [play] erases artificial, superficial differences and divisions in the group."[11]

Sports and Recreation Ministry Becomes a Tool for Teaching Leadership Skills

Helping people develop leadership skills often starts with their involvement in familiar settings: coaching a team, leading an exercise class, or teaching a crafts class. With training and encouragement, leadership and ministry skills are developed that can also be used while serving on a committee or teaching a Bible study. This is a part of the ministry team's strategy of multiplying ministers.

A LOOK AT LEISURE

Recreation and sports ministry takes place during leisure, when people are not working. This look at leisure considers five perspectives: leisure as time, leisure as activity, leisure as state of mind, leisure as an indictor of social status, and the integration of leisure in a holistic process. Each of these has implications for the church.

Leisure Viewed as Time

During the agricultural age, work centered around producing food and providing life's necessities. Time was spent meeting the demands of daily existence and getting ready for the next harvest. During the industrial revolution, views of work and time began to change. Industrialization brought about automation. Automation brought about higher productivity; more goods could be produced in less time. Work weeks were shortened, and people found that they had more free time.

This newfound leisure was fraught with challenges for culture and the church. The children of working parents needed care. Adults began to spend leisure hours at places that were not reputable in the eyes of the church. Time became something to fill with activity that could be either good or bad. Civic organizations, private businesses, government entities, and churches began to provide for constructive uses for leisure. During this period, playgrounds and national, state, and local parks began to be developed. Churches and YMCAs began to provide places to spend leisure time.

In the Christian context, leisure viewed as time has an element of stewardship. Dahl put it this way: "To a Christian, all of his time is free—his life has been given and redeemed by God—whether it is spent working or playing."[12] Ecclesiastes states that there is a time and a purpose to everything, even leisure time. The Christian has an obligation to be a good steward of leisure time.

Brightbill explains this concept thusly: "Leisure, then, is a block of unoccupied time, spare time, or free time when we are free to rest or do what we choose. Leisure is time beyond that which is required for existence... It is discretionary time, the time to be used according to our own judgment or choice."[13] Brightbill's definition is secular to be sure. But it is the essence of leisure viewed as time. For the Christian, what is done with time is a moral choice.

Carlton, Deppe, and MacLean state, "Our cultural, moral, and spiritual development is dependent, in large measure, upon uses of leisure." These writers point out that what we do with leisure is more important than perhaps our culture realizes: "The moral and spiritual forces of our country do not lose ground in the hours we are on our jobs; their battle is during the time of leisure."[14]

Most crime does not take place while people work but when they have time on their hands. The church has a responsibility to provide creative alternatives for the use of leisure time. Paul exhorts us to "redeem the time," to use all time wisely. The church should take seriously the matter of leisure time and use it to bring people to a knowledge of Christ or into a closer walk with him.

Leisure as Activity

What is leisure activity may be work to others thus blurring lines between work and leisure activity. Leisure can also be viewed as activities that people engage in during their free time—activities that are not work oriented or that do not involve life maintenance tasks such as housecleaning or sleeping. Leisure as activity encompasses the activities that we engage in for reasons as varied as relaxation, competition, or growth and may include reading for pleasure, meditating, painting, and participating in sports. This definition gives no heed to how a person feels while doing the activity; it simply states that certain activities qualify as leisure because they take place during time away from work and are not engaged in for existence.[15]

Listing all the activities that one could do in leisure is impossible. Separating what some consider work and others consider leisure is equally impossible. The lines between work and leisure are blurred. Some people will use the Internet for work; others use it for leisure. The same is true for music, crafts, and other activities. As mentioned earlier, laptop computers and smart phones allow people to take work home, further blurring the lines between work and leisure.

Geoffrey Godbey put it this way: "In the Christian life, leisure activities should be of a positive nature, be socially acceptable and contribute to healthy personal adjustment, relaxation or enjoyment."[16] He said that whatever we do as Christians in our leisure should contribute to our overall wellbeing as a person. Paul says it this way: "Whatever you do, do everything for God's glory" (1 Cor. 10:31). Christians should live out their leisure lives as unto God, seeking to please him in every activity. The church should endeavor to provide activities that draw out the best in people and bring them closer to God.

Leisure as a State of Mind

Going back to the Latin root for "leisure," licere meaning "to be permitted or absence of restraint," we see that this view of leisure is not associated with time, work, or location. Leisure is viewed as how one's mind perceives the experience. Leisure can take place anywhere, at anytime, with anyone—at home, at work, or at an event. The state of mind is the focus.

American culture is increasingly experiential in its orientation to leisure. Increasingly our culture reflects leisure as a state of mind. This concept carries both positive and negative connotations. On the positive side, one may see any leisure experience—whether sports, picnics, or worship—as wonderful. One may say afterward, "I really got a lot out of that." On the negative side, being preoccupied may cause one to have ambivalent feelings about the experience. A person might not "enjoy" the leisure experience because of distractions. This view has nothing to do with location or time. It is the experience that counts, and the mind dictates the quality of the experience.

For the church the implications of this view are important. As a state of mind, worship could be viewed as leisure—engaging the body, mind, and spirit to bring refreshment and recreation. In this view, worship changes our state of mind as we focus on God. Worship becomes a state-of-mind leisure choice. One could argue that worship is the ultimate leisure choice activity. True worship brings about a recreativity of mind and spirit.

In the purely recreational setting, this view says that the experience is everything. Millennials and Gen-Xers are looking for the next experience. Interactive media's proliferation, the growth of recreational risk activities, and the growing popularity of virtual reality experiences are evidence of this. If a recreation and sports ministry wants to attract people, it should provide interactive experiences that engage the body, mind, and spirit.

Leisure as an Indicator of Social Status

Throughout history leisure activities indicate social rank. The working class took their leisure where and when they could find it, usually after long hours in the fields or factories. Country clubs were for the rich who could afford the fees. Travel was for the well-to-do who could afford both the time away and the money for tickets, accommodations, and food. The working class, worried about the next crop or whether they would be laid off, rarely spent money or time on leisure pursuits.

Today the division of class by leisure pursuit is still evident. While most people have access to some form of leisure activity, the differences between the upper, middle, and lower classes are real. Distinctions are made by everything from the brand of athletic shoe, to the symbol on a shirt, to the events one attends during leisure and the vacation spots one picks. Some can afford four star accommodations while others seek campgrounds. Status and image are fostered on society by Madison Avenue as they tell us what to wear, where to dine, and what sports beverage to drink. People seek to convey an image as they choose their leisure pursuits.

Churches in general are impacted by indicators of status. Churches often build recreation and sports complexes for the wrong reasons: to keep up with another church, to keep the kids off the street, or to cure all their financial problems. Churches who do this may hurt themselves in the long run. While properly planned, staffed, and programmed recreation centers can be a valuable tool to facilitate ministry, the church should seek to provide recreation and sports ministry that meets the expressed needs of the people and fulfills the mission of that church. The church should provide events and activities that people can afford and that will help that church live out its mission. Churches must be careful not to foster a "country club" attitude in the use of their facilities or programming.

Leisure Seen as a Holistic Process

This view sees leisure as an integrative whole encompassing all that a person is, experiences, and desires in recreation experiences. This view considers the totality of a person's life—work, family, church, education, and other elements that represent a balanced life. The holistic approach perhaps best fits the biblical model of man; life is lived in relationship to others and the world around us. A Christian worldview of this holistic model of leisure would hold that man does not live a compartmentalized life of disjointed events and activities, but that in God's plan for our lives, we are made up of the sum of our experiences. We are formed by God with a specific set of natural talents, interests, and abilities that make us who we are. And because we are all different, God chooses to give us spiritual gifts to complement our natural abilities and interests for his glory. We use the total of all that we are as stewards of leisure to bring glory to God.

RECREATION AND SPORTS MINISTRY
VIEWED AS A DISCIPLESHIP PROCESS

Instead of recreation and sports ministry, perhaps what we need to talk about is being a kingdom people doing a kingdom work as the body of Christ. Otherwise we may become so wrapped up in trying one new method after another that we lose sight of our God given direction.

Methods are important, but they never can take the place of following the clear biblical commands to be God's people. We know who we are in Christ and by what he has called us and gifted us to do. The means of doing recreation and sports ministry as kingdom work is not to become more important than the lost persons we are trying to reach or the new Christians we are trying to disciple.

Alan Raughton, of LifeWay Christian Resources, says:

> The existence and activity of the church are rooted in God's purposes to bring His kingdom to fulfillment. The kingdom is present wherever the will and reign of God are established in people's lives through the presence of Jesus Christ. Therefore, a biblically sound understanding of church ministry is one with a kingdom focus. It is one where believers see themselves on a kingdom mission: to make disciples of the spiritually lost by bringing them into a right relationship with God through Jesus Christ.

The outcome of faithful obedience will be kingdom growth. Growth becomes God's supernatural work through His people to accomplish His kingdom's purposes. It is the result of God's people obeying His will and His Word in the world in relationship to evangelizing the spiritually lost.[17]

Defining a Kingdom Focused Discipleship Process

Biblical principles identify the primary teachings from Scripture that give direction to the scope and work of the church in relationship to its efforts to lead an unbeliever from the condition of being lost without Christ to service as an obedient maturing disciple of Christ.

The One Great Commission (Matt. 28:18–20)—The Great Commission defines God's mission for the church, for recreation and sports ministry, and for individual believers. Without the driving force of the Great Commission, any attempt at recreation and sports ministry will be little more than a misguided attempt to use new techniques.

The Five Church Functions (Acts 2:38–47)—Recreation and sports ministry acts as a support in the life of the church, or it can act as a lead ministry at times as a part of the following five functions.

1. *Evangelism* (Acts 2:38–41)—In recreation and sports ministry, evangelism must be an intentional element of each event, class, seminar, or workshop. Christian evangelism is the process of sharing the gospel with lost persons and winning people to Christ. In the case of recreation and sports ministry, leaders must be intentional at every point for effective evangelism to take place. Recreation and sports ministry offers the church culturally relevant tools to impact people.

2. *Discipleship* (Acts 2:42–43)—Recreation and sports ministry offers avenues of teaching new Christians about their response to God in love, trust, and obedience, and how to win and train others to do the same.

3. *Ministry* (Acts 2:44–45)—Recreation and sports ministry offers a natural way for Christians to use their gifts, talents, abilities, and interests in ministry to others.

4. *Fellowship* (Acts 2:42, 46–47)—Recreation and sports ministry is a means to facilitate fellowship in the church formally and informally.

5. *Worship* (Acts 2:46–47)—Recreation and sports ministry can facilitate worship that transforms by helping believers to encounter God in worship. This can be done as participants are guided to church worship settings or as worship is facilitated on a retreat, at a camp, at a fellowship event, or on the soccer field.

Relationship to Spiritual Transformation—Recreation and sports ministry, through its strategies and methodologies, addresses three stages of spiritual transformation in the life of a believer:

1. Making disciples represents the efforts to win the lost.

2. Maturing believers represents the efforts to disciple new believers and members.

3. Multiplying ministries represents providing opportunities for service and missions.

Ministry Practice Strategies

Church ministry practice strategies are the clear and deliberate intentions and plans of action that are necessary if a church or any ministry area is to achieve its ministry objectives. While primarily seen as a part of a ministry team strategy, a well balanced recreation and sports ministry will seek to impact all four foundational strategies of corporate worship, small groups, discipleship groups, and ministry teams.

A *corporate worship strategy* exists to celebrate God's grace and mercy, to proclaim God's truth, and to evangelize the lost. The corporate worship service is a large group strategy involving believers and unbelievers. Recreation and sports ministry complements worship as it directs participants to worship or as it provides worship opportunities at recreation events. (See Acts 2:46–47.)

A *small group strategy* exists to lead nonbelievers to faith in the Lord Jesus Christ and to build on-mission Christians by providing ongoing, evangelistic Bible study units. Recreation and sports ministry seeks to build relationships between Christians in small groups and nonbelievers for the purpose of getting the nonbelievers into a small group (some call it Sunday School) Bible study. Paul sets the example in Acts 17:10–12.

A *discipleship group strategy* exists to build kingdom leaders and to equip believers to serve by engaging people in discipleship that moves them toward spiritual maturity. Recreation and sports ministry impacts discipleship groups as it provides an atmosphere of relational fellowship and ministry opportunities. Priscilla and Aquila model this strategy in instructing Apollos in Acts 18:24–28.

A *ministry team strategy* exists to build up the body of Christ to accomplish the work of service within the church and to be involved in missions and service outside the church. Recreation and sports ministry fits the ministry team strategy as it seeks to provide opportunities for Christian growth and intentionally evangelistic serving ministry using recreation and sports as tools. Examples of these two ministry team concepts—one internal, another external—can be seen in Acts 6:1–3 and 13:1–3.

From a practical point of view, effective recreation and sports ministry strategies are implemented through an ongoing process involving ten essential actions that guide its development. These actions take place in the context of a comprehensive church-wide process rather than as independent actions. This approach underscores the value of developing a holistic plan, the interrelationship of the four church practice strategies, and the collaborative spirit needed by recreation and sports ministry leaders for the good of the whole.

Essential actions for effective recreation and sports ministry as a part of an overall church ministry team strategy include:

1. Commit to the recreation and sports ministry as an important group strategy.
2. Minister with purpose.
3. Build ministry leaders through training.
4. Develop soul winners.
5. Intentionally plan to win the lost.
6. Intentionally assimilate new people into small and discipleship groups.
7. Reach out to all age groups and family types.
8. Guide all leaders to lead/teach for life transformation.
9. Set the right team structure to maximize ministry.
10. Multiply leaders and ministry actions.

Methodologies

Each strategy is carried out through methodologies. A methodology becomes the ministry's practical application targeted at specific objectives of the strategy and mission statement of the church.

Balanced programming in recreation and sports ministry is essential for effectiveness. The programming becomes the way methodologies are carried out. For example, programming for a basketball league or a crafts class becomes a methodology for carrying out the ministry team strategy. Methodologies need to be dynamic (changeable) as determined by surveys, needs of the church, and opportunities afforded by the local church context and culture.

Kingdom Results

Four kinds of growth result when a church implements ministry through worship, small groups, discipleship groups, and ministry teams. The kingdom results are numerical growth, spiritual maturation, ministry expansion, and kingdom advance.

Numerical Growth—The ministry results of the recreation and sports ministry should be measurable in membership, baptisms, and attendance levels as it impacts the other ministry areas of the church. These visible, tangible results are evidence of ministry effectiveness.

Spiritual Transformation/Maturation—Leaders and participants alike should be maturing spiritually. Nonbelievers are transformed as they come to Christ. Christians are matured as they grow to be more like Christ—on and off the court.

Ministry Expansion—New avenues of ministry are found as the Holy Spirit provides new opportunities and brings new people into the ministry. Recreation and sports ministry will always be expanding as new tools become available.

Kingdom Advance—Recreation and sports ministry affords many mission and ministry opportunities. Any sport, league, workshop, class, fellowship, outdoor education activity, continuing education class, or health and wellness event that can be done at a church can be taken on the road and done as a mission or ministry action. Recreation and sports ministry will open many doors and provide many opportunities to reach out as it seeks to advance the kingdom of God. Recreation and Sports Ministry offers an excellent way to "get outside the walls" into the community that can be used to advance the Kingdom of God as it touches and impacts those in the community.

Recreation and sports ministry is a part of the whole, a ministry team strategy that impacts and builds every other ministry strategy in the church. Relationships with all other ministry strategy areas are vital to the longevity and functionality of the ministry. Recreation and sports ministry is neither more important nor less important than any other ministry area or strategy in the church. As all ministry strategies learn to function as a whole, the church will see people won to Christ, people discipled, and people multiplying themselves in ministry across all ministry areas of the church.

Intentional Ministry

People come to Christ as the Holy Spirit works through others—the right people at the right time bringing them to the point of commitment. After the commitment is made, the process of discipleship is started that lasts a lifetime. As a ministry team's strategy, recreation and sports ministry offers the church a non-threatening first touch in people's lives. The following outline of the spiritual pilgrimage is typical for most people.

Most of the time, a person does not come to Christ the first time he or she hears the gospel. A process of the work of the Holy Spirit happens in a person's life over time. Often this process involves a decision point or crisis event. Alan Tippett, an Australian Methodist missionary, in his book *Verdict Theology in Missionary Theory,* describes the process as one of change that includes a period of awareness, a point of realization, a point of encounter, and a period of incorporation. It is illustrated here in stages that include a recreation and sports ministry encounter.[18]

1. **Period of No Awareness of Need for Christ**
   - The participant is unaware of his or her need for salvation
2. **Period of Initial Awareness**
   - The participant has a perceived need. Example: to play softball, or exercise

- The participant joins in a recreation activity to meet perceived needs
- The participant has encounter with believer(s)—teammates, class leader etc.
- The participant becomes aware of real (spirit) need (as over time Christ is shared in word and deed by believers on the team or in a class)
- Hopefully the participant sees gospel lived out in a real world way

3. **Period of Encounter**
   - The participant meets other Christians on the team or in the class
   - The participant continues recreation activity involvement
   - The participant hears the gospel explained and sees it lived out

4. **Period of Decision**
   - Slowly the participant begins to understand his/her need for Christ
   - The class seeks to build/strengthen relationships
   - The participant is introduced to larger church life (invited to small group or worship)
   - The participant may join a small group bible study or start to attend worship
   - The participant may join other recreation or church activities
   - The participant may face crisis or period of questioning past experiences
   - Hopefully the participant turns his/her new Christian friends for answers
   - The participant recognizes the need for change through salvation
   - The participant has the opportunity to receive Christ provided by the class or team

5. **Period of Incorporation**
   - Participant turns to Christ through repentance

- Begins time of spiritual growth (in a discipleship group experience)
- As they mature, the participant takes on roles in recreation ministry according to interest (referee, time keeper, assistant coach, helper in a class)
- After time and becoming spiritually mature, the participant feels prepared to take on larger role in life of the ministry and church

6. **Period of Multiplication**
   - The process has now come full-circle. the participant begins to reach out to others using his/her gifts, talents, and abilities multiplying self in the lives of others through involvement in a ministry team.

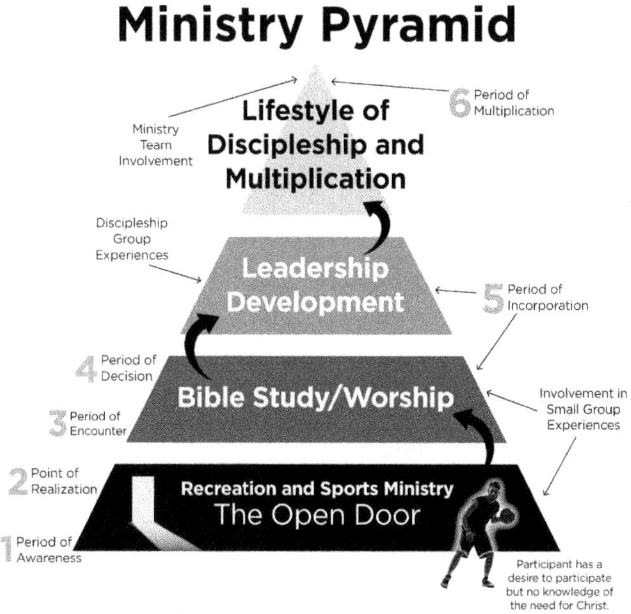

Ministry Pyramid

6 Period of Multiplication

Ministry Team Involvement

Lifestyle of Discipleship and Multiplication

Discipleship Group Experiences

Leadership Development

5 Period of Incorporation

4 Period of Decision

Bible Study/Worship

3 Period of Encounter

Involvement in Small Group Experiences

2 Point of Realization

Recreation and Sports Ministry
The Open Door

1 Period of Awareness

Participant has a desire to participate but no knowledge of the need for Christ.

Figure 1-2: Ministry Pyramid

Recreation and sports ministry offers the church one of the best avenues to impact our leisure oriented culture. To the skateboarder, we will offer skateboarding events. To the hiker, we will offer hiking experiences.

To the fitness minded, we will offer aerobics and nutrition classes. To the basketball player, we will offer opportunities to play the game.

As we attempt to reach these groups, we must be intentional in sharing the gospel at each opportunity. We must be deliberate, with a settled determination and a calculated plan to win people to Christ, using all the tools at our disposal. Otherwise, we become like any other recreation and sports activity supplier. The Christ distinctive must permeate all that we do.

NOTES

1. "The Modern Movement for Better Rural Church Buildings." *Church Administration* 2(October 1927).
2. Kansas Sports Hall of Fame, "Dr. James Naismith." Kansas Sports Hall of Fame, http://www.kshof.org/inductees/naismith.html (accessed September 4, 2002).
3. Mathisen, James A. "'I'm Majoring in SPORT Ministry': Religion and Sport in Christian Colleges," *Books & Culture* (May/June 1998): 24.
4. Ciulla, Joanne B. *The Working Life: The Promise and Betrayal of Modern Work*, as cited in Alice Stein Wellner "The End of Leisure," *American Demographics* (July 1, 2000): 50.
5. Saad, Lydia. "The '40-Hour' Work-Week is Actually Longer—by Seven Hours." Gallup Research. http://www.gallup.com/poll/175286/hour-workweek-actually-longer-seven-hours.aspx (accessed March 15, 2016).
6. "LeisureTrak." *Leisure Trends.* http://www.leisuretrends.com (accessed January 27, 2002).
7. Dahl, Gordon. "Emergence of a Leisure Ethic." *Christian Century* 1 (November 8,1972): 124–27.
8. Ibid.
9. Ibid., 26.
10. Briner, Bob. *Roaring Lambs* (Grand Rapids, MI: Zondervan, 1993), 31.
11. Maston, T. B. *A Handbook for Church Recreation Leaders* (Nashville, TN: The Sunday School Board of the Southern Baptist Convention, 1937), 33.

12. Dahl, Gordon J. *Work, Play and Worship* (Minneapolis, MN: Augsburg Publishing House, 1972): 61–62.

13. Brightbill, Charles K. *The Challenge of Leisure* (Englewood Cliffs, NJ: PrenticeHall, 1960), 4.

14. Carlton, Deppe, and MacLean. *Recreation in American Life* (Belmont: Wadsworth Publishing Company, Inc., 1963), 3–4.

15. Hurd, Amy R. and Denise M. Anderson. *Parks and Recreation Professional Handbook* (Champaign, IL: Human Kinetics Publishers, 2011), 9.

16. Godbey, Geoffrey. *Leisure in Your Life,* 2nd ed. (State College, PA: Venture Publishing, Inc. 1985), 70.

17. Raughton, Alan. "Report on Church Ministry Leadership," *LifeWay Christian Resources,* (2002).

18. Tippett, A. R. *Verdict Theology in Missionary Theory* (Lincoln, IL: Lincoln Christian College Press, 1969), 100–103.

2

Biblical Foundations of Sports Ministry
DEFINING THE PHENOMENON

Rodger Oswald

"Sports Ministry is biblically defensible, and stands on solid theological footing."

CULTURAL/HISTORICAL PERSPECTIVE

The phenomenon of sports ministry as a church tool is sometimes rejected because some may think the Jewish and/or early church cultures—as well as the cultures in which they existed—did not participate in any form of recreation or sports. Actually, that is not the case. While the Jewish culture certainly rejected the recreational and sporting bent of Egyptian, Babylonian, and Assyrian cultures (all having various forms of leisure activities, various celebrations, and sporting competition relating to preparation for war and/or worship of pagan gods), archeological discoveries indicate that some leisure time was devoted to "word games" and "board games." Geoffrey Godbey put it this way: "Of all the links between leisure and religion, the common root of celebration is the most important."[1] These same discoveries included finding children's dolls.

Even in Scripture, play is evident as a part of the Jewish culture as Zechariah (8:5) and Isaiah (11:8–9) make reference to boys and girls playing. The leisure aspect of the "garden experience" speaks to leisure within the context of walking through this peaceful environment with God.

Like the nation of Israel, the early Christian community avoided most overt expressions of sporting competition that were replete in the Roman and Hellenized cultures around them, but even the forerunners to the Olympic Games were fodder for Paul's metaphorical language in explaining the Christian experience (1 Cor. 9:24–27; 2 Tim. 2:5;

4:7). Jesus also taught, without condemnation, about innocent, playful children, that the kingdom of God would be discovered in their innocence and openness.

The reality is that while the Old Testament Jews and the New Testament believers did avoid most sporting activities, play, games, and leisure activities did permeate their cultures, and Scripture does not criticize those activities. Certainly one's motivations, actions, and attitudes within those activities give opportunity for rebuke and/or instruction, but the activities themselves are not condemned.

THEOLOGICAL PERSPECTIVE

This is not intended to be a thorough examination of a theological position to justify recreation and sports ministry; however, it seems prudent at least to offer a theological grid through which we can pass the sports ministry in order to establish a logical position, consistent with Scripture, regarding this cultural phenomenon.

Theology introduces us to the facts that the God of the Bible is a redemptive God (Gen. 3, 7, 12; Luke 19:10). God is also declared to be a relational God (John 1:12; Heb. 4:16) who is gracious and liberating (Rom. 5:8; Eph. 2:8–9; Gal. 2:16).[2] *Anthropology* declares that man is a fallen creature (Rom. 3:10–12) with the consequence that he is separated from a Holy God (Rom. 3:23).[3] *Soteriology's* blessed message is that because God is redemptive and relational, man has the potential to become a child of God (Rom. 6:23; John 1:12; 3:16). With this new identity (relationship), redeemed man now has holy purpose; he has responsibilities that accompany his position (1 Pet. 1:16; 2:9; Acts 1:8). Having been redeemed, man is actively involved in growing in holiness as he becomes a herald of the gospel, a witness of Jesus Christ.[4] *Ecclesiology* speaks to the issue of the church being God's agency for the Age of Grace (also called the Church Age); however, since the word *church (ecclesia)* is defined as "called out ones," the church is not a building but a worldwide body of believers. While these believers are, heaven bound, the earthly call is to congregate to worship, to grow into the likeness of Christ, and to participate in the global mission of making Jesus Christ known.[5] As people examine these four theological positions, they will discover that nowhere does Scripture forbid the use of leisure, recreation, and/or sports. In fact, once one recognizes that a redemptive God has given a commission to make Christ known, the issue for the believer is how to best accomplish that commission. More than ever today's church is demonstrating that redeemed man within the context of a well-organized recreation and sports ministry (usually within a local church) can be an extremely effective tool for communicating Jesus Christ, seeing people come to faith, assimilating them into the local church, and assisting them in their spiritual growth.

BIBLICAL PERSPECTIVE
The Mandate

In attempting to discover the place of sports and recreation in the church, the question must be asked, "Is there a clear mandate that compels the believer?" In other words, is there evidence of an overarching command given by the Lord that applies to all believers? Jesus answered that question in all four Gospel accounts as well as the Book of Acts. In Mark 16:15, Jesus said that the gospel is to be preached to all creation. In Luke 24:47, Jesus said that forgiveness in his name is to be proclaimed to all the nations. In Matthew 28:19, Jesus said that disciples were to be made of all the nations (people groups). In John 17:18, Jesus, as he prayed to his Father, said that he was sending his disciples into the world, just as the Father had sent him. Some feel that Jesus was talking about the Apostles only, but in verse 20 Jesus said, "I pray not only for these [the Apostles], but also for those who believe in Me through their message."

In debate, the preferred speaking position is last since people tend to remember what was spoken last. Perhaps that might give even greater credence to this mandate when one looks at Acts 1:8 and the postresurrection scene when Jesus uttered his last words on earth just before he ascended into heaven: "And you will be My witnesses in Jerusalem, in all Judea and Samaria, and to the ends of the earth."

The mandate is clear: Jesus is to be proclaimed. Jesus is to be preached. Christians are to have a testimony. We are to be witnesses of Jesus Christ into all the world.

The Means

While the command of Jesus is abundantly clear, the question remains, who is supposed to do this? It seems to be clear by the calling of disciples (Matt. 4:19; Mark 1:17) that Jesus meant to impact individuals so that they, in turn, could impact others. The apostle Paul certainly understood and taught this same principle (2 Tim. 2:2).

Often this individual responsibility is referred to as a *call*. While the term *call* is used in a more specific way (particularly as applied to pastors and missionaries, for example), there is a sense in which Jesus says to every believer, "Follow me." This can be referred to as the *general* call of those who say they are Christians (followers of Christ) or disciples (those who follow after, learn from, and apply the things that are learned).

Beyond the general call, Scripture clearly communicates a *personal* call. In 2 Corinthians 5:17–20, the apostle Paul described the "new things" that come into the life of one who is "in Christ" (a Christian). One of those new things, according to verse 18, is to become a minister (servant) of the message of reconciliation—to serve the message that, as God has made up with me, he also is willing to make up with you. In addition to being a servant of the message of God's reconciling love, the one who is in Christ is also called on to be an ambassador of Christ—to represent the policies of our sovereign King in the world. The personal passion of this calling is seen in that we would even beg (plead, implore) people to be reconciled to God.

In addition to the general and the personal calls, there seems to be a *specific* call based on the people God uses throughout Scripture. As Acts describes the birth of the church and that church begins to grow, a variety of people are "called" into service to the gospel message. Not all of these people are spiritual giants, graduates of seminaries, or longtime leaders of the church. Using just one example from Acts 15, Paul and Barnabas separated over the issue of taking John Mark with them on the second missionary journey. It is not clear why Barnabas was so adamant about taking John Mark. While it might be a family connection, a case can be made that Barnabas saw in John Mark some quality that, in spite of previous failure, would make him uniquely serviceable for the sake of the gospel. Certainly the Gospel of Mark gives credence to the confidence Barnabas had in him.

While Barnabas took John Mark with him, Paul chose to take a man named Silas. It would be fair to ask, "Why Silas?" While Scripture doesn't answer this question, some conclusions could be reached. Paul is going to preach to Roman citizens. Who better to take than a Roman citizen? Paul was going as a representative of the Jerusalem Council. Who better to take than a member of that council? Paul was going to preach about a living God. Who better to take than a prophet of God?

Providentially, Silas was a Roman citizen (Acts 16:37), a member of the Jerusalem Council (Acts 15:22), and a prophet (Acts 15:32). But think about this: *did* Paul take Silas because he had the right passport, was a member of the right organization, and would serve as a spokesman for God? While the last is certainly a critical component, the first two seem to be circumstantial reasons. Perhaps Paul took Silas because of a "special call" of God to use the distinctives of his life for the sake of the gospel.

The significance of this can be seen in that each person has unique gifts and talents that make that person valuable in distinct situations. While some may be profitable "for the sake of the gospel" because they sing or play an instrument, others will be profitable because they kick a soccer ball, wield a paint brush, hit a baseball, run swiftly, love the out of doors, or shoot a basketball with accuracy. Could it be that this special call creates a platform whereby the athlete has access to other athletes because of a special skill? Could it be that one's talents create an opportunity to impact the millions who watch, read about, or participate in sports on a recreational level? The bottom line is that while there is a general and a personal call, there is also a special call as people use unique talents or abilities to fulfill the mandate given by the Savior.

Of course, God never intended for the individual to operate independently. By command, by his presence, and by the blending of gifts, God intends for the individual to be a part of a greater whole known as the church. While the Greek word for *church (ecclesia)* refers to people who are "the called-out ones," the fuller expression of this phenomenon is the "local assembly" that Hebrews (10:25) warns us not to for-sake. The birthing of the church in Acts is fleshed out in 1 and 2 Timothy and Titus, and the church that Jesus said he would build (Matt. 16:18) takes shape. As one reads the pastoral Epistles, the ministry of the local church becomes clearer. While some debate the issue of primacy, the local church has three primary functions: first, to pro-vide/create vibrant corporate worship; second, to create an environment and opportunity to grow in faith (often referred to as edification or the process of discipleship); and third, to mobilize to fulfill the Great Commission (often referred to as evangelism).

The Methodology

If the mandate is clear and the means to carry out that mandate is equally clear, the issue, then, is for the church to determine a biblical pattern for carrying out the mandate. At this point it would be wonderful if we could go to Scripture and discover chapter and verse that clearly communicated that X church should employ sports and recreation as a means of fulfilling God-ordained responsibilities. The problem is that chapter and verse cannot be found that condones, charges, or advocates the use of sports and recreation as a part of the church mission. The Bible is equally silent about other issues, yet we find precedence by biblical principles. For example, the Bible is silent regarding watching of television or going to movies, but God's Word contains principles that guide us as to what to watch, how much to watch, and how much to spend to watch.

While the Bible is silent regarding television, it is not silent about the principle of a transformed mind (Rom. 12:2) or the wise use of time (Eph. 5:16). By the same token, biblical principles are germane to the propriety of sports and recreation ministry while carrying out the man-dates of Christ.

The following principles are offered to create an apologetic that endorses, liberates, and compels one to consider where this unique ministry ought to fit into one's life or into the ministry life of the church.

Principle of Divine Diversity

The God of the Bible is a majestic, multifaceted God. He is diverse in his essence; he is a triune God—Father, Son, and Holy Spirit.

He is diverse in his *character*. In the Old Testament, the Jews referred to God based on how they personally experienced him and, therefore, called him Jehovah Jeri, God my Provider; or Jehovah Nissi, God my Banner, the one who goes before me; or El Elyon, Almighty God. In the New Testament, John's Gospel refers to Jesus as "the door," "the resurrection, and the life," "the way, the truth, and the life," and "the good shepherd," all ways of communicating his diverse personhood.

In both the Old and the New Testaments, the godhead is seen as diverse in ministry. To carry out the will and work of God, God works in diverse ways. In the Old Testament, God walked and talked with Adam; to Moses he was a burning bush, and to the nation of Israel he was the Shechinah Glory—a pillar of fire by night and a cloud by day. In the New Testament, Jesus healed some but not all; he preached to multitudes but discipled a few, focusing on twelve. He preached to many, gently rebuked a few, and intentionally provoked others. The Holy Spirit counsels, convicts, teaches, and comforts. The point is that our majestic God works in a variety of ways. He is creative and diverse.

Genesis 1:26–27 says that man has been created in the image of God. Since Scripture reveals that God is not flesh and bone (Luke 24:39), the question arises: in what way are we like God's image? The answer could be that as our God is diverse and creative, his creation is blessed with that same creative bent, some more than others; but all of creation seems to have the capacity to meet and resolve problems, overcome barriers, and deal with the circumstances of life.

God has granted to human beings the ability to deal creatively with the world around them. Of course, that ability is flawed and frail until a person comes into a relationship with God through Jesus Christ. The created needs to learn to be as creative as the Creator.

With that as the premise, it seems logical that people would discover the most creative ways of carrying out the mandate of Jesus. It seems that Christians, within the context of the church (the means), need to discover the most strategic methodology to accomplish that mandate. The creative bent ought to turn people to sports and recreation not because sports and recreation is so important but because it becomes a means to build relationships with the lost. Through those relationships Jesus Christ can be lived out and proclaimed. The questions ought to be asked: Where are the people of our society? Where do they congregate? The answer is in the gymnasiums and on the fields of sports and recreation. In *IN HIS STEPS*, author Charles Sheldon's main character encouraged his church members to ask "What would Jesus do?" the question today should be asked "Where would Jesus be?" Certainly to reach people, he would be on the field, in the stands in the gymnasium…wherever people congregated. Today they congregate on those fields of play and/or competition.

Principle of Human Talents

This principle is not to be confused with spiritual gifts. This principle refers to human gifts and abilities that are God given. In Psalm 139, the psalmist praises God for the fact that he is an omnipresent God, so omnipresent that he was even involved intimately in the psalmist's birth (v. 13). The psalmist declares that God created him as a spiritual being (inward parts is a Hebrew expression for soul or spirit), as a physical being (frame is the Hebrew word for bones), and that God's work was thoughtful and careful (skillfully wrought is the Hebrew expression for carefully made; a literal translation of the word means "to crochet; to create delicate lace"). The implication here is that God has made each person exactly as He willed and that creation is "fearfully and wonderfully made."

If we serve a God of order and not chaos, there is logic and purpose behind his every act, even the granting of physical skills and ability. In Exodus 35–36, Moses was following the command of the Lord and having the tabernacle of the Lord built. Those two chapters reveal that God gave the physical ability to those who were to build a dwelling place for God. God gave the craftsmanship to those who were to design and construct this structure. This is an Old Testament picture of the fact that God dwelt "among" his people (Exodus 25:8). In the New Testament, God dwells "in" his people (Gal. 2:20) in order that they might create the ultimate tabernacle revealed in 1 Peter 2:5 when Peter wrote, "You yourselves [we], as living stones, are being built into a spiritual house for a holy priesthood." As God indwells the believer, we, as living stones, fulfill our role as priests, proclaiming "the praises of the One who called you out of darkness into His marvelous light" (1 Pet. 2:9). In doing so we participate in kingdom building, in creating that ultimate spiritual house.

God has blessed every person with certain physical skills and/or abilities, and each person participates in kingdom building when those skills and abilities are used to declare Jesus Christ. When the soloist sings, or the pastor preaches, or the athlete uses his or her sport as a platform for serving the purposes of God, each is fulfilling God's will as it pertains to his kingdom purposes. To fail to use what God has given us through our physical creation denies the very order and sovereignty of God.

Principle of Liberty

Since this is an attempt to discover the latitude that the church has (individually or corporately) to employ sports and recreation as a ministry tool, the principle of liberty is crucial. If this principle cannot be substantiated, the church ought not consider this type of ministry.

Paul was an advocate of liberty—not license but true liberty in Jesus Christ. He, like Jesus Christ, fought against religiosity or legalism that constrained rather than freed the believer. In fact, in 1 Corinthians 9:1, Paul made his declaration of independence when he said, "Am I not free?" He was not saying he was free to do whatever he wanted or free to do any-thing that was unrighteous. He was indicating that he was free from any sort of legalistic posture or man-made rules if they interfered with the proclamation of the gospel. First Corinthians 9:23 says, "Now I do all this because of the gospel." That was Paul's driving desire. It was so important to him that he was willing to fight convention if it meant a greater audience for the gospel. This proclamation of freedom was so strong that he indicated he was willing to be Jewish (those under the Law) or "pagan" (those without the Law) for the sake of their salvation. Paul was saying that he was willing to be culturally relevant even if it meant adapting to another culture at the expense of his own.

When Paul wanted to reach his Jewish brethren, he went to the synagogue in his yarmulke and robe; but when they were unresponsive, he took off the yarmulke and robe and went to the city gates or town square where the Gentiles (pagans) were. He would adapt culturally for the sake of preaching the gospel. Paul went so far as to be willing to go to a specific location to reach a specific portion of his society (the philosophers on Mars Hill) to preach Jesus Christ. He was even unconventional enough to rent a pagan meeting place for the sake of preaching Christ (Acts 19:9).

If Paul can be that free, is it possible that today's church can be equally free and as culturally relevant? If so, the church must go to today's Mars Hill or Halls of Tyrannus. The church must go to the fields of play or the buildings that house competition and games.

Paul addressed the same issue of freedom in Galatians 5. In verse 1 Paul said, "Christ has liberated us into freedom. Therefore, stand firm and don't submit again to a yoke of slavery." The freedom Paul addressed is the freedom from man-made rules, in this case the rules that would add Jewish ceremony to salvation by grace through faith alone. Today there are those who condemn sports and recreation ministry, not because the Bible condemns it but because man-made rules have determined that it is wrong. Paul's answer would be that he has been freed from the conventions and rules of men and that he yields to a higher set of rules. The first is that he has been set free by grace. In other words Paul wanted to be set free to proclaim Christ without being hindered by arbitrary rules.

The only question the church must ask is whether something violates the clear teaching of Scripture. There is freedom in Christ, freedom to experience the grace of God in salvation as well as sanctification in order to realize freedom in making Christ known. Some conjecture that sports and recreation ought to be one of these freedoms. In fact, if the apostle Paul were alive today, he might be an athletic musician or a musical athlete because those are two universal languages that would give him greatest access to people in order to proclaim Jesus Christ.

Principle of Silence

Often when ministry through sports and recreation is challenged, the argument is that Scripture does not clearly say a church should have this type of ministry. The sentiment that silence precludes the use of sports ministry is actually an argument for sports ministry.

When discussing this issue, one must agree that the Bible does not promote or indicate that a church should have a sports ministry. By the same token, the Bible does not denigrate, deny, nor state that a church should not have a sports ministry. The reality is that the Bible is silent on the issue, but this silence speaks rather loudly when one carefully examines Scripture.

In dealing with the silence issue, the question must be asked, "Who wrote the Bible?" Using Scripture to answer the question, the answer is that God wrote the Bible (2 Tim. 3:16; 2 Pet. 1:21). Yes, writers were involved, but the reality is that they wrote only what the Holy Spirit prompted them to write, and the Holy Spirit only prompted what God spoke. Therefore, when Paul referred to the Christian experience as running in a race, and the writer of Hebrews referred to one's life as a Christian as an endurance race, and when Paul compared Christianity to an athlete, who really wrote that—man or God? The answer is God.

That, then, leads to another question, this one dealing with God's character. Is he holy? The obvious answer is yes; the conclusion, then, is that what God has written is wholly righteous, without sin, totally holy. Therefore, if something were inherently evil or sinful about sports, a holy God would not have used sports or athletes as a metaphor for the Christian experience. While the Bible is silent, the use of sporting metaphors clearly indicates that God has no problem with sports. Otherwise, he would have added a caveat when those comparisons were used in 1 Corinthians, Hebrews, and 2 Timothy.

Other Principles

Without going into detail, numerous other principles could be used. For example, the Principle of Tithing or of Stewardship could be used to go along with the Principle of Human Talents. If God has given gifts to the believer, should the believer not use them to bring glory to God? Should the recipient not carefully tend and use everything entrusted to him by God, even the ability to hit a baseball or shoot a basketball, pro-viding those activities were used to glorify and thank God (Col. 3:17, 23)?

Another powerful principle is the Principle of Preparation. Since the Christian experience includes the process of being conformed to the image of Christ (Rom. 8:29) and this process is not completed until the believer dies (Phil. 1:6), how is it possible to develop the character that James (James 1:2–4), Peter (1 Pet. 1:6–7), and Paul (Rom. 5:3–5) describe? All three seem to indicate that trials (problems) will be a part of this refining process. That process is exacerbated by the fact that we are all engaged in spiritual warfare (Eph. 6:10–20; 1 Pet. 5:8), and, like any soldier, we need to go through boot camp. The fields of sports competition are the training ground in secular things so that the competitor might learn to succeed in spiritual battle.

While the Bible is silent on the specific issue of sports and recreation ministry, it is not silent on the call of the individual and the church to carry out the mandate of making Jesus Christ known in our own back-yard and then to the whole world. It seems prudent to find the most effective way of doing that without compromising any standard of holiness.

Since sports and recreation are merely games, it seems unfair to classify them as sinful or a wrong pursuit for the individual or the church. What would be wrong is if God has given us a culturally strategic means of reaching people with the gospel and we failed to use it because some-one says, "I think it is wrong," or "I think sports is sinful," or "We've never done this before."

Surely the biblical principles discussed (and there are others) grant the individual or the church the latitude to consider this type of ministry. The error would be to fail to implement what God has not condemned on the notion that He has, when that notion is merely man-made.

If the Bible condemns sports or recreation or if the Bible warns against them, the believer and the church should take notice and obey out of respect for God's Word, or as a demonstration of wisdom. However, there is no biblical condemnation, not even a suggestion of condemnation, of sports or recreation. Individuals need to feel freedom to use their athletic gifts, and the church needs to feel freedom to use their athletically gifted, as long as those gifts are used to the Lord, for his glory and for the kingdom's sake.

NOTES

1. Godbey, Geoffrey. *Leisure in Your Life: An Exploration,* 5th ed. (State College, PA: Venture Publishing, 1999), 162.
2. Chafer, Lewis Sperry. *Chafer Systematic Theology,* Vol. 1 (Dallas Seminary/Zondervan, 1947), 129, 244, 257, 313.
3. Chafer, Lewis Sperry. *Chafer Systematic Theology,* Vol. 2 (Dallas Seminary/Zondervan, 1947), 217–23, 360–61.
4. Chafer, Lewis Sperry. *Chafer Systematic Theology,* Vol. 3 (Dallas Seminary/Zondervan, 1947), 55–72, 223–51, 255.
5. Chafer, Lewis Sperry. *Chafer Systematic Theology,* Vol. 4 (Dallas Seminary/Zondervan, 1947), 16, 21, 149–51.

3

Visions and Re-Visions

A HISTORY OF THE MODERN CHURCH RECREATION AND SPORTS MOVEMENT IN THE UNITED STATES

Brad Wesner

"The modern church recreation movement, the roots of church recreation extend to both ancient Israel and ancient Greece."

Today most Americans take recreation for granted in the church setting. From church softball teams to church picnics, the congregation just wouldn't be a church if it weren't for recreation. Believe it or not, though, the American church has not always been so favorable toward recreation.

The modern church recreation and sports movement in the United States has roots extending through the Old Testament, pagan cultures, and church history. In the United States, church recreation developed in three stages—an era of apathy and disgust, an era of acceptance, and an era of promotion.

The first period, the Era of Apathy and Disgust, began with the colonization of New England in 1620 and continued through 1872. Although the church generally frowned upon recreation during this period (if it noticed recreation at all), modern church recreation leaders drew upon unique pieces of philosophy from this period to justify the church's eventual incorporation of recreation.

The Era of Apathy and Disgust closed in 1872 with a dramatic win by anti-recreation leaders. In 1872, the Methodist Episcopal Church passed legislation banning all amusements in general and many by name, including dancing, theatergoing, and horse racing. Other denominations had already passed similar bans. The Presbyterian Church had singled out dancing and theater in an 1843 ban, which it reaffirmed in 1865. The Provincial Council of Baltimore, the voice of the bishops of the Roman Catholic Church, had banned the theater and novels in 1869. The Episcopal Church had targeted "gaming," "amusements involving cruelty to the brute creation," and "theatrical representations" in an 1817 ban. And numerous Southern Baptist congregations had established rules banning dancing. It was the Methodist ban, though, that had the greatest influence. Because of the ban's wording and because of Methodist influence in society, the Methodist ban received attention in other denominations and was so widely disseminated in secular culture that it could not be ignored.[1] Although intended to stop recreation, the ban inspired recreation within the church! Recreation proponents in various denominations organized themselves and set out to establish a philosophy of recreation. After the pendulum, had swung to the extreme right, a new era got under-way, and the church's view of recreation became much more liberal. From 1873 to 1918, from the beginning of the ban to the end of World War I, church recreation moved through an Era of Acceptance.

In 1919, the church took the next step, moving from merely accepting recreation to actively promoting recreation. In fact, both the Methodist Church and the Southern Baptist Convention established recreation offices at the national level and strove to teach local congregations how to best use recreation. Although the church has periodic set-backs—for instance, both the Methodist Church and the Southern Baptists have discontinued their departments of recreation—we continue to live in this era of Church recreation promotion.

PRE-AMERICAN ROOTS OF THE CHURCH RECREATION MOVEMENT

Although Americans may have shaped church recreation and led the modern church recreation movement, the roots of church recreation extend to both ancient Israel and ancient Greece. Leisure in the modern sense did not exist in biblical times, but scriptural writers clearly distinguished between work and rest. Moses stated, "Six days do your work, but on the seventh day do not work, so that your ox and your donkey may rest and the slave born in your household, and the alien as well, may be refreshed" (Exodus 23:12). Moses also set aside a sabbatical year, one in seven, when even the land was unattended, and he declared that after seven Sabbath years, people set aside the fiftieth year as the Year of Jubilee (Lev. 25:4). As part of the Year of Jubilee, the church held special religious feasts. Later, as clergy developed ancient Judaism, they added more days of feast and festivity.

Meanwhile, from the Greeks, clergy learned about building and planning for leisure. The Greeks constructed parks, stadiums, and theaters and supplied these facilities with programs. Greek programs and philosophy greatly influenced the early apostles. Paul of Tarsus compared the Christian life to athletic events (1 Cor. 9:24; Gal. 2:2, 5:7; 2 Tim. 4:7; and Heb. 12:1). He also used Greek dualism to compare the flesh to the spirit regarding the desire for pleasure (2 Tim. 3:1–5).[2]

The apostles and other leaders of the early Christian church established patterns later generations referred to as guideposts. Many Christians, appalled at the pleasure-seeking Romans, reacted by banning recreational activities. Clergy also banned sports, drama, and other recreation because of the activities' close association with pagan religions. For instance, Romans, like their Greek predecessors, often honored a god at a sporting event. In 744, Pope Zacharias pronounced the first Christian church-wide ban on recreation. In time, an "implicit, if not avowed, doctrine of the church" claimed that amusements substituted for prayer and meditation, and, as such, were sinful.[3]

During the Middle Ages, monks and clergy continued to perceive recreation as sinful, claiming such activities took the mind from God and from preparation for the next world. However, for multiple reasons—too many laborers, not enough work, and the belief that people needed time away from work to do good deeds—the powerful medieval Christian church instituted 170 annual holy days, holidays from regular activities. These feasts, such as the Feast of Visitation and the Feast of the Immaculate

Conception, included considerable merrymaking. Jews, too, celebrated special feast days, such as Hanukkah and Passover. In addition to feasts, clergy also promoted recreation in the forms of painting, literature, dance, music, and drama, usually stressing a religious theme.[4]

Also during the Middle Ages, clergy contemplated the concept of recreation. They accepted Augustine's notion that God and rest were one; therefore, if one knew God, one had a permanent state of leisure. They also accepted Augustine's argument that Christians could incorporate much of pagan culture, including its forms of recreation, since something pagan was not necessarily unholy. Thomas Aquinas' view that clerical occupations were superior to other occupations was accepted by clergy, and they divided labor into sacred and secular compartments. Clergy were also influenced by Aquinas' adaptation of Aristotle's belief that the contemplative life supercedes the active life and that leisure in this sense was desirable. In Summa Theologia, Aquinas gave dignity to rest: "Rest is taken in two senses; in one sense, meaning a cessation from work, in the other, the fulfilling of desire." Although both Augustine and Aquinas taught physical pleasure belonged to beasts, not people, both furthered leisure within the church.[5]

Martin Luther, an Augustinian friar who founded both Lutheranism and the Protestant Reformation, combined Augustine's and Aquinas' ideas, arguing that all work, whether contemplative or active, by clergy or by laity, was equal in God's sight. In fact, he deemed all of life as sacred; people could use any wholesome activity, including free-time activities, for God's glory.[6] Luther also challenged the idea of pleasure being sinful. Prior to the Reformation, monks degraded their bodies to glorify their soul; they considered the pleasures that recreation provided for the body as sinful. Luther argued against degrading the body: "God has indeed created body and soul and desires both to be allowed and give recreation but with proper measure and purpose." Luther also spoke out for participation in recreation. In a 1534 letter, he wrote, "To have pleasure in sins is of the devil, but participation in proper and honorable pleasures with good and God-fearing people is pleasing to God." In Table Talk, a book of Luther's discourses assembled in 1848, Luther quipped, "Our loving God wills that we eat, drink, and be merry."[7]

Roman Catholics also spoke in favor of recreation. In 1609, St. Francis De Soles, in *Introduction to the Devout Life,* argued in favor of playing games: "Those games in which the gain serves as a recompense for the dexterity and industry of the body or the mind...are recreations in them-selves good and lawful." In 1695, St. John Baptist De LaSalle, in *The Rules of Christian Manners and Civility,* wrote that holidays had God's blessing and followed the precedent found in the Old Testament: "God, who knows the weakness of our nature, authorizes us to take that rest and refreshment which are necessary to keeping up the strength of mind and body. In the brightest days of the church, the fruitful, though still anointed by pristine fervor, devoted certain days to rest and rejoicing."[8]

The Jewish people also turned their attention to recreation in the Middle Ages and Reformation, particularly to swimming. In the *Sculchanara,* a sixteenth-century compilation of laws governing the life and behavior of Jews, rabbis instructed every father to teach his son to swim. Although opponents of recreation interpret this rule as implying a lifesaving precaution, recreation proponents interpret it as a Jewish push for family fun.[9]

In 1618, England's King James issued an edict, later known as the *Book of Sports,* which made Sunday sports and recreation lawful following Divine Service. Noting that commoners could not enjoy sports on Sunday when they had free time and that they worked all other days, he approved archery, leaping, vaulting, dancing, May games, and other activities. However, he did prohibit bear and bull baiting, considering them too cruel for Sunday. Much of the negative Puritan philosophy regarding recreation stemmed as a rebellion to this document.

ERA OF APATHY AND DISGUST

The American colonists imported a religion that contained a wide range of opinion concerning recreation. Regardless of one's denomination, social life outside the family frequently revolved around church meetings.

Some colonists, though, celebrated religious holidays such as Passover and Christmas with feasts that contained both secular and religious elements.

Most early religious Americans approved of participation in play when done for God's glory and one's individual salvation. However, they believed that play for the sake of play, just like work for the sake of work, was incompatible with the Scriptures. Although they often considered it spiritually dangerous to have a good time, colonists opposed most recreation for patriotic and economic reasons, not religious ones. The colonists were generally comprised of dissonant groups who had struggled to cause reforms in England. Unsuccessful, they had come to the colonies, carrying with them their scorn of their opponents' lifestyles, including their recreational activities. Most imported holidays celebrated English national history, and on the whole the Puritans had little fondness for the motherland. Too, due to harsh climate, little time remained for celebrations. In New England, the civic body, often synonymous with the religious body, legislated against the more secular and/or highbrow activities, jailing citizens who danced around May poles, decorated Christmas trees, danced at weddings, conducted sports events, or gave theatrical performances.[10]

Colonial society recognized the need for archery and similar survival skills, and clergy did little to prohibit these leisure activities. Inadvertently, the church also offered recreation through community projects such as cornhuskings and barn raisings and through service projects such as quilting bees. Although these community gatherings accomplished tasks for the social good, they also provided the occasion for feasts, games, and social recreation.

Around the Revolutionary War, clergy accepted recreation as a part of secular society, first in the South and then in the North. Climate conditions and social factors, not theologies, account for most of the differences between Southern and Northern clergy perceptions of recreation. Temperatures plunged during New England winters, and therefore time Southerners could spend in leisure activities Northerners had to spend shoveling snow. Too, although some genteel citizens settled in the North, the slave-holding aristocracy who had the time, wealth, and taste to patronize the arts generally settled in the South. Northern clergy also maintained tighter control over their flocks than Southern clergy did; whereas a Southern parson might ignore his parishioners' ventures with questionable recreation activities provided it was not habitual, Northern clergy generally had something to say.[11]

As Americans moved west, clergy developed programs to cope with frontier life. In the name of education and community service, they allowed the first professed recreation program, the lecture, into the church in 1818. These lectures became formalized in 1826 when Josiah Holbrook, an American educator, established the first lyceum, a lecture series named after the ancient lyceum, the park near Athens, Greece, where Aristotle lectured in 400 B.C. Holbrook followed this Mulburry, Massachusetts, lecture series with other series in nearby towns, establishing circuits for lecturers. A local lyceum committee, usually closely allied with the church, coordinated the lectures. Often having the only auditorium in town, clergy found themselves hosting the lectures.[12]

Following the Civil War, clergy frequently spoke against the growing amusements, believing that, though scriptural writers did not specifically condemn amusements, amusements remained conducive to immorality. Fearful that the eager rush of society after such diversions as dancing, card playing, theatergoing, and sports would corrupt its members, clergy sought to banish these pastimes by stigmatizing such diversions as so potential for evil that no one could participate in them.

Although the effort to do away with recreation continued long past 1872, the 1872 ban by the Methodist Episcopal Church represents the pinnacle of the success of recreation opponents. At the 1872 quadrennial conference of the Methodist Episcopal Church, the Committee on the State of the Church, chaired by Daniel Curry, framed and secured passage of a bill that amended the *Discipline* chapter on "Imprudent Conduct" to include "dancing, playing at games of chance, attending theaters, horse races, circuses, dancing parties, or patronizing dancing schools, or taking such other amusements as are obviously of misleading or questionable moral tendency."[13]

The legislation, passed 179 to 75 on the twenty-eighth day of the month-long conference, contained several flaws that opponents exploited until successfully repealing the ban in 1924. Although few could argue with Curry's goal to "arrest, if possible, practices which portend so much evil to the Church and to the world," the ban provided the catalyst to focus the church's attention on recreation, the need to think through the philosophy of recreation being in the church, and the occasion to state their case carefully.

As the twentieth century prepared to open, recreation became a hot issue within the American church. Both pro- and anti-recreation leaders of later generations used early American thoughts and deeds as a springboard. For instance, pro-recreation leaders focused on the Puritan goals of a better society, while anti-recreation leaders focused on the Puritan bans of many recreational activities. As the Era of Apathy and Distrust closed, the future of the church's relationship with recreation was at a fork in the road, and its leaders could choose only one of the four prongs: to oppose recreation, to be apathetic toward recreation, to merely accept recreation, or to promote recreation. Which prong they would choose, though, was unclear.

ERA OF ACCEPTANCE

Although the Methodist Episcopal Church's 1872 ban reached the most people and received the most attention, other groups of Methodists, including the General Conference of the Methodist Protestants and the Methodist Episcopal Church—South, as well as other denominations, such as Presbyterians, Catholics, and Baptists, had bans as well. Despite anti-recreation forces having enough votes initially to pass their legislation, pressure to repeal the bans soon came from both internal and external sources.

Supporters of the 1872 Methodist ban answered the mounting cries to repeal it. They argued that God remained the same from year to year, and, if the activities in the 1872 ban were sinful then, they were still sinful in the present time and would remain so in the future. They claimed that specifying recreation activities by name eliminated any doubt in parishioners' minds of the activities' harm. However, even those in favor of keeping a ban soon realized the folly of this argument of specifying sinful amusements, for "the devil is constantly devising new amusements."[14]

Delegates gave the ban more attention each passing general conference. The front page of the *Daily Advocate* called the amusement debate "the hottest issue" of the 1900 General Conference! In 1924, the general conference voted to overturn the ban and return to John Wesley's advice of using one's conscience concerning amusements. With the ban over-turned, the amusement question quickly faded as an issue at the general conference.

The overturning of the ban signaled approval of the growth of recreational programs throughout the denomination. Most of these early pro-grams, though, failed. Due to the stigma of theatergoing and dancing, leaders could not provide high-class recreation such as Shakespearean plays and balls, and therefore church recreation programs were perceived as second-rate by the public. Too, most church recreation leaders had no training, resulting in sloppy productions of material many members already found suspect.

Church recreation leaders of this era made the mistake of focusing too narrowly. The leaders tended to focus on one form of recreation, usually physical, to the exclusion of other forms. Muscular Christianity—sometimes called Muscular Judaism when offered in the synagogue setting—received its name because leaders reconciled a robust physical life with Christian morality and duty. They claimed the church had to focus on both morals and muscles, since the body serves as the temple of the Spirit, and they maintained that physical strength built character and righteousness, making the believer fit for God's work.[15]

For both theological and practical reasons, clergy-led recreation appeared to be a passing fad. However, with the advent of World War I, a need arose for clergy-led recreation, both on the home front and on the war front. Clergy answered the call, and many received valuable training in leading recreation through the Young Men's Christian Association

(YMCA). As rationing forced people to stay in their own community, church-led programs grew popular. Church-led recreation activities were soon accepted as a part of society, and church members began to plan annual recreation activities. For instance, urban congregations often had fairs and bazaars in the fall and strawberry festivals in the spring, while rural congregations had an annual picnic each summer. By the time the war ended, church recreation wasn't only accepted; it was expected!

As the need for recreation grew within the church, the church developed facilities to meet recreational needs. The most famous and widely used architectural design was the Akron Plan, drafted by Lewis Miller and Jacob Snyder in Akron, Ohio, as part of a national experiment approved by the Methodist Episcopal Church. The plan for the Akron Methodist Episcopal Church greatly aided the church recreation movement through its "collapsible walls." One could pull the curtain-like folding walls out to form many rooms, or one could collapse them so that the many rooms became one auditorium. Although Lewis and Snyder intended the individual rooms as classrooms for the Sunday school and the auditorium as a meeting place for all classes to come together to open the Sunday school session, congregations soon realized that the auditorium had gymnasium and fellowship hall possibilities and that the individual classrooms had club room possibilities. The plan received wide use throughout Protestant congregations through the 1910s, until leaders replaced it with architectural plans that provided permanent classrooms, libraries, kitchens, banquet rooms, and gymnasiums.[16]

Although clergy continued to be antagonistic toward much commercial recreation, they approved of most recreation provided by voluntary associations such as the YMCA and public agencies such as park districts. Although the church often tied doctrinal training into its own recreation programs, the church developed a two-way working relationship with these other agencies regarding recreation. In 1912, the Playground Association of America reported that the church either directly created or inspired 40 percent of the playgrounds inaugurated in 1911. By the 1930s, many municipal departments organized church athletic leagues, supplied leadership for parties and picnics, gave program suggestions, and trained the church's recreation leaders. In exchange, public recreation departments often freely used church facilities.[17]

In the Era of Acceptance, leaders established church recreation as one facet of multifaceted church programs, such as a rural congregation's youth program or an institutional church's outreach. The scope of the recreation programs varied, depending on facilities, leaders' skills, and church atmosphere. During this era, programs grew more sophisticated, more elaborate, and in the eyes of some, more bawdy. Although a minority perceived the growth of recreation in the church setting as a fulfilling of their prophecies of the church's decay and of recreation's addictive qualities, the majority saw the dawning "of the day when the devil will no longer monopolize the grand opportunities in recreation that the Church should control."[18]

ERA OF PROMOTION

In the Era of Promotion, leaders sought to guarantee the long-term partnership of religion with recreation. Clergy of this era were unlike the clergy of the past era: To them recreation was not a sideshow, a way to raise money, or bait to attract sinners; it was serious ministry! Congregations no longer perceived their recreation leaders as entertainers or purveyors of amusement but rather as overseers of one of society's most vital cultural responsibilities.

At the turn of the century, leaders had designed most all-church recreation programs to meet bills generated elsewhere in the congregation. Oyster suppers, strawberry festivals, and ice cream suppers paid for themselves and other programs. These recreational activities were "offered more for the sake of filling the church's pockets than for meeting a need of the people," for leaders designed them to get "money out of people who had given all they thought they could" and to get donations from people whom leaders could not normally ask to give, such as members of other denominations.

In the Era of Promotion, though, recreation programs required more money to operate than they generated! Although the money did not go for individual gain by anyone in the congregation, clergy had to meet expenses such as upkeep of the fields and halls, the rental of equipment, the janitor's salary, and the guest leader's fee. The new programs also meant building new physical plants, including office space, art galleries, lecture halls, clubrooms, and gymnasiums.

After the church accepted the philosophy that "recreation and secular activity fall well within the scope of Christian life if they are disciplined in that direction," leaders realized recreation directors would have to be trained and supervised. They turned to a combination of laypeople who could afford to donate the time to supervise activities and professionals who had the expertise to oversee the programs.[19]

As the 1920s began, both secular and religious officials expressed dissatisfaction with society's recreation, claiming that "somebody put a wreck in recreation" and "took the unity out of community." The push for congregations to offer recreational activities came from both outside and inside the church. Externally, the push came from leaders of public recreation. For instance, Howard Braucher, president of the National Recreation Association, said, "Make wider use of recreation in connection with Sunday schools, young people's societies, and other organizations to give a richer life to the members of the churches. Hold institutes for training church membership as volunteers to give recreational leadership in their own homes, in their neighborhoods, and in all organizations where they belong."[20]

Meanwhile, the push also came internally from Protestant, Catholic, and Jewish officials. The Right Reverend Doctor William T. Manning, bishop of New York, Protestant Episcopal Church, said, "The instinct for play is as divinely planted in human nature as the instinct for worship." The Reverend Doctor Harry E. Fosdick, a Baptist, pastor of Riverside Church, New York, stated, "The spirit of play, which is the crown of work and of home life, is also the crown of religion." Norman Richardson, professor of religious education at Northwestern, a Methodist Episcopal school, wrote, "The subject of play has come to be one of the most serious matters which the Church can possibly take into consideration." Dr. Ahba Silver, rabbi at The Temple of Cleveland, Ohio, wrote, "The Church is interested in leisure because it knows that no culture, no civilization, no spiritual religion is possible without leisure, for culture requires leisure."[21]

Denominational leaders began to set forth principles of recreation, including standards of recreation program excellence. As they established principles, they grew bureaucracies at both the local and the national levels to share and enforce the principles. They also produced an explosion of books detailing recreation philosophy and suggesting acceptable recreation activities within the church. As congregations recognized recreation as a viable, necessary ministry, they no longer left recreation to chance. Recreation professionals emerged, seminaries began to offer recreation courses, and denominations provided hands-on workshops.

In 1914, the general conference of the Methodist Episcopal Church—South suggested the need for a denomination-wide church recreation program. Thus, the denomination formed a position on its national General Epworth League Board, the board in charge of over-seeing youth activities, and assigned the position the duties of overseeing a national church recreation program among youth. The League waited until the completion of World War I to hire Elvin Harbin, an ordained Methodist minister who had established a national reputation as a youth leader. Although lectures, camps, potlucks, quilting bees, fairs, and other forms of church recreation existed decades before Harbin's birth, national recreation leaders such as Joseph Lee, Howard Braucher, and Charles Brightbill still regarded Harbin as the founder of church recreation, for he solidified recreation as a legitimate ministry, set standards, and provided the field with a philosophy.[22]

Convinced that most parishioners could not innately perform recreational services but could be taught to be recreation leaders— "Recreation leaders are not born. They are made. They are made by study, hard work, and a deep appreciation of the importance of recreation as a factor in human welfare"—Harbin founded the South Wide Leisure Time

Conference, a recreation laboratory in which participants heard lectures about the philosophy of church recreation and in which they gained hands-on experience in drama, storytelling, crafts, games, and numerous other forms of church recreation. After the Methodist Episcopal Church South merged with the Methodist Episcopal Church and the Methodist Protestant Church to become the Methodist Church, Harbin was named director of Leisure-Recreation Ministries on the newly formed Board of Education, and he promptly established four other regional hands-on training centers.[23]

Church recreation was also introduced as a formal course in colleges, universities, and seminaries. Boston University, which formed the Department of Religious Education in 1918 and the Department of Young People's Work in 1920, offered the first course in church recreation. Lynn Rohrbough wrote the first thesis on church recreation in 1925, a handbook of recreation leadership in the church setting, which he later published as Handy. In 1926, Rohrbough introduced the term church recreation to describe church-centered recreational programs.

Lynn Rohrbough became an ordained Methodist and established the first clearinghouse for church recreation, Church Recreation Service, in 1924. Through his ecumenical co-op, later renamed Cooperative Recreation Service, he also made and sold traditional table board games from around the world. Through his business, Rohrbough sought to train recreation leaders, improve standards of recreation, and publish wholesome recreational materials not available elsewhere. The Methodist Church frequently recommended the books he published, but when Rohrbough turned his attention to songbooks, the Methodist Church increased its own production of materials, which it sold to its own congregations, other denominations, public schools, and recreation agencies.

Methodists weren't the only ones establishing formal church recreation training. T. B. Maston taught the first Baptist seminary course in recreation in 1922 at Southwestern Baptist Theological Seminary in Fort Worth, Texas. Agnes Pylant, his former student, and William Marshall, Wayland College president, then established a church recreation department and a degree program at Wayland College in 1949.

The Southern Baptists, at their national publishing house, established the Church Recreation Department, originally known as Church Recreation Service. Chester Swor, the catalyst, delivered the speech "Our Youth of Today" to the Southern Baptist Convention in 1942, hoping to stimulate interest in recreational activity by suggesting that congregations provide wholesome alternatives to unwholesome activities, particularly for youth.

In January 1943, the Executive Committee of the Sunday School Board approved the creation of Church Recreation Service. However, although the Convention gave approval, the Sunday School Board undertook no implementation. Swor, upset that the Board had not implemented the plan by 1948, addressed the Convention again, bluntly asking that the Sunday School Board establish a Church Recreation Department. The Convention overwhelmingly favored accepting Swor's recommendation. The department began to function in February 1954 with Agnes Pylant as director.[24]

The Church Recreation Department sought to "meet the challenge of leisure through an accelerated program of promotion and leadership training" and then to have congregations do the same in their community. Because of a limited number of personnel, Pylant focused most of the department's energy on writing, believing this would allow the staff to reach the most people. Along with producing *Church Recreation Magazine*, Pylant and her staff wrote numerous books, brochures, and articles. They also offered consultation and hands-on training.[25]

Both the Methodist and the Baptist recreation office peaked, entrenched, and declined. In 1968, the Methodist Church merged with the United Brethren Church, and in 1972 the resulting United Methodist Church eliminated the recreation director by splitting his duties among other departments, notably camping and youth work. The national church recreation departments had worked themselves out of a job; they had so infiltrated recreation into the church setting that church authorities felt the need for a specific office to promote recreation was no longer valid. The Southern Baptist office lasted two decades longer, but eventually it and its groundbreaking periodical *Church Recreation Magazine* also ceased.[26]

Southern Baptists have continued their work in church recreation. In 1964, under Bob Boyd's direction, they began their annual training conference called Rec Lab, which grew into the longest-lasting and largest training experience in the field of recreation and sports ministry. In 1971, Ray Conner became director of the Church Recreation Department until his retirement in 1993. Under his direction the department added staff for all ministry areas of recreation-producing ministry resources and holding conferences for all denominations. Perhaps the best-known area of work under Conner's direction is that of a recreationally oriented youth camp called Centrifuge, which under its first director, Don Mattingly, became an international camp experience for more than sixty thousand teenagers each year. From Centrifuge grew the sports camp Crosspoint and several other mission and sports-related camp experiences for children and teenagers. The Church Recreation Department morphed into LifeWay Recreation and Sports Ministry in 1993. The next department director, Dr. Tommy Yessick led the department to produce the ground and tradition breaking "Adventure Week" curriculum which changed the way VBS is now done around the world. Adventure Week incorporated: themed curriculum, recorded sing-along contemporary music tracks, the use of video, games, snacks, crafts and bible study. This model has been adapted and used by all VBS curriculum providers. The department also was instrumental in helping many parachurch ministries like Upward Unlimited and In His Grip Golf get off the ground helping churches use sports as outreach tools. Southern Baptists were active in the work until 2013. LifeWay Christian Resources (formerly the Sunday School Board) officially ended its promotion of LifeWay Recreation and Sports Ministry as a denominational emphasis in 2014 passing the promotion and training to the conservator-ship of Oklahoma Baptist University which now houses and staffs the program of Recreation and Sports Ministry.

The recreation and sports ministry movement is indebted to Methodists and Southern Baptists as they were the only two major denominations to undertake establishing a national chair/department of recreation. Other denominations expected groups such as the National

Council of Churches to oversee recreation education. The National Council of Churches did get involved in several recreation pro-grams, including camping, drama, and social recreation. It even sponsored some recreation services, such as placing recreation leaders in public parks. However, overall, it sought to train leaders rather than provide services. Leaders of the National Council of Churches perceived the Council as a catalyst, planning ministries that local leaders would eventually control. Unfortunately, they sent mixed signals of their intentions, and many denominations—particularly the Lutherans, Presbyterians, and American Baptists—ceased to expand their recreation programs because they thought the National Council would oversee recreation education.[27]

Church recreation took another blow when two television evangelists, Jimmy Swaggart and James Bakker, succumbed to temptation. Ironically, Jimmy Swaggart, pastor of the Family Worship Center, an Assembly of God church in Baton Rouge, Louisiana, claimed he opposed modern recreation. He even considered Christian aerobics inappropriate, referring to Christian aerobics as modern dance. Although he officially opposed much church recreation being offered in other denominations, Swaggart inadvertently had a great influence on Pentecostals in getting those congregations to accept church recreation.

Swaggart, the cousin of rock star Jerry Lee Lewis, introduced the Assemblies of God to both a new form of music and a new medium. Swaggart followed in the footsteps of early American congregations that had often blended secular tavern songs with new words to create religious hymns, and he introduced a honky-tonk form of gospel music. To spread his music and message, Swaggart turned to radio and television. Although early Assemblies clergy banned the radio and the television, Swaggart recognized their potential for spreading the gospel, and in 1969 he launched a radio program. He also launched a series of albums, selling more than twelve million. His use of the media not only spread the gospel, but also an acceptance of radio, television, and recorded music as acceptable Christian diversions. Swaggart's influence waned in the late 1980s.[28]

James Bakker was another Assemblies of God television evangelist who greatly furthered the church recreation movement and then left his ministry position in disgrace. Bakker took the previously established concept of the Christian campground and combined commercial recreation with religion, opening a "Jesus" theme amusement park, Heritage USA, in Fort Mill, South Carolina, in 1985. The park was designed to compete with Disneyland, Six Flags, and other large theme park chains. A high-tech Passion play emerged as the twenty-three-hundred-acre park's most popular attraction. Other activities for guests included spiritual counseling, weekly baptisms in the hotel swimming pool, typical resort recreations, and the opportunity to watch the Jim and Tammy Faye Bakker broadcasts in person. Heritage USA initially experienced considerable success. In 1987, it attracted more than six million people, trailing only Disneyland and Disney World in attendance. However, Jim Bakker, accused of selling thousand-dollar partnerships that promised lifetime lodging rights at his theme park to far more partners than could be accommodated, turned administration over to Jerry Falwell, a Southern Baptist television evangelist. In 1990, following Hurricane Hugo's destruction and facing bankruptcy, Falwell closed the park. In December 1990, Morris Cerullo, another television evangelist, bought the park with the long-term goal of reopening it as New Heritage USA. Much of the land has since been sold, and, although far from its former glory as a tourist destination, religious broadcasts still happen there.[29]

The church appears to be on the verge of a new era in its relationship with recreation and sports ministry. Budget cuts and internal reorganizations have done away with national recreation offices. Those who led church recreation in the twentieth century are retiring. Many older youth, a group the church has often targeted for leisure services, no longer make time to participate in church active recreation, opting for more passive forms of recreation such as electronic media and streaming video. Previously stable programs such as the crafts classes are declining in popularity, reflecting a lack of interest among parishioners. Church attendance is trending downward, and the church is no longer a leading voice in many communities. Recreation is so ingrained within the church that most Christians are apathetic toward learning more about it, for they cannot picture the church without it. The annual ski trip is so automatic no thought is given as to why a church should be promoting skiing. Other events have been modified to fit the times—the annual chili supper is now a chili-cookoff. Recreation in the church is not going away, but because people do not learn more about recreation, its potential is far from realized.

The Era of Promotion is coming to an end. A new era is about to get underway. As someone interested in leading church recreation, you have a voice in the forming of the new era. You now have an understanding of the past, of how the field got to where it is today. As you now know, the church has often formed a vision for recreation, and then it has recast that vision. You are a part of today's revisioning process. Where will you lead the field?

Church recreation has ties to both religion and secular culture. Religion and culture share a two-sided relationship, for culture influences the approach to religion, and religious attitude influences culture. As Washington Gladden, a Congregationalist and a proponent of church recreation observed, "Religion cannot be kept alive without alliance with social forces; the social forces cannot be kept in healthful operation with-out the aid of religion. Because of the interdependency between the Church and culture, religious groups can not ignore recreation, nor can the Recreation Movement ignore the church."[30]

NOTES

1. *Minutes of the General Assembly of the Presbyterian Church in the United States of America* (New York: Fanshaw, 1843); Crane, J. T. Popular Amusements (Cincinnati, OH: Hitchcock and Waldin, 1869).

2. Kraus, R. *Recreation and Modern Society,* 3rd ed. (Glenview, IL: Scott-Foresman, 1984).

3. Van Dalen, D., E. D. Mitchell, and B. L. Bennett. *A World History of Physical Education* (New York, NY: Prentice-Hall, 1953); Gladden,

W. "Christianity and Popular Movements," Century 29 no. 3 (1885): 384–92.

4. Huizinga, J. *Homo Ludens: A Study of the Play Element in Culture* (Boston, MA: Beacon, 1950); Lee, R. Religion and Leisure in America: A Study in Four Dimensions (New York, NY: Abingdon, 1964).

5. Kelly, J. *Leisure* (Englewood Cliffs, NJ: Prentice-Hall, 1982).

6. Lehman, H. D. *In Praise of Leisure* (Scottsdale, PA: Herald, 1974).

7. Lueker, E., ed. *Lutheran Cyclopedia* (St. Louis, MO: Concordia, 1955); Woods, R. L., ed. T*he World Treasury of Religious Quotations: Diverse Beliefs, Convictions, Comments, Dissents, and Opinions from Ancient and Modern Sources* (New York, NY: Hawtorn, 1966), 738–39.

8. Mencken, H. L. *A Dictionary of Quotations on Historical Principles from Ancient and Modern Sources* (New York, NY: Knopf, 1942), 443, 1011.

9. National Recreation Association, *Proceedings* (New York, NY: National Recreation Association, 1937); Berlatsky, E. "Recreation and the Faiths: A Look at the Jewish Philosophy at Work," *Selected Papers Presented at the Forty-Second National Recreation Congress* (New York, NY: National Recreation Association, 1961): 181–83; Baron, S. W. *A Social and Religious History of the Jews,* Vol. 2, 2nd ed. (New York, NY: Columbia, 1952).

10. Boyd, R. M. "Footprints of Fellowship," *Church Recreation* 4 (February 1964); Bayne, S. "Christian Doctrine of Play," *Proceedings, National Recreation Congress* (New York, NY: National Recreation Association, 1952), 26–31.

11. Eisen, G. "The Concept of Time, Play, and Leisure in Early Protestant Religious Ethic," *Play and Culture* 4 (1991): 223–36; Kraus, *Recreation and Modern Society.*

12. Holbrook, J. "Exchange Lyceum," *Western Christian Advocate* (September 30, 1842): 96.

13. *Journal of the Delegated General Conference of Methodist Episcopal Church* (1872): 379–80; Mains, G. P. "Our Special Legislation

on Amusements: Honest Doubt as to Its Wisdom," *The Methodist Review* (May 1892): 375–89.

14. Mains, G. P. "Special Legislation," 388; Harman, C. W. "Amusement," *Daily Christian Advocate* 14 (1900): 355.

15. Hale, E. E. "Public Amusements and Public Morality," *Christian Examiner* (July 1857): 47–65; Spalding, T. W. *The Premier See: A History of the Archdiocese in Baltimore,* (Baltimore, MD: Johns Hopkins University, 1989): 1789–1989.

16. Egbert, D. and C. Moore, "Religious Expression in American Architecture." In *Religious Perspectives in American Culture*, edited by J. Smith and A. Jamison, 361–42. Princeton, NJ: Princeton, 1961; Lundburn, G., M. Komarovsky, and M. McInerny. *Leisure: A Suburban Study* (New York, NY: Columbia University, 1935); Miller, L. "The Akron Plan," In *Seven Graded Sunday Schools: A Series of Practical Papers,* edited by J. Hurlbut, 11–32. New York: Hunt & Eaton, 1893.

17. Cutting, R. *The Church and Society* (New York, NY: Macmillan, 1912); Vettiner, C. J. *Rural Recreation for America* (Louisville, KY: Rural Recreation for America, 1949); Griggs, J. E. and L. J. Moore, "Men's Ministry." In *Perpetuating Pentecost: A History of the First 75 Years of the Southern Missouri District of the Assemblies of God,* edited by B. Newby, J. E. Griggs, and S. D. Eutsler, 81–85. Springfield, MO: Southern Missouri District Council of the Assemblies of God, 1989); Sapora, A. V. Personal interview (February 3, 1993).

18. Fay, W. "What Attitude Should the Church Take Toward Amusements?" *Homiletic Review* 24 no. 1 (1892): 84–87; Hale, W. B. "Another Year of Church Entertainments," *Forum* (December 1896): 396–405.

19. Eastman, F. "Rural Recreation Through the Church," *Playground* (October 1912): 232–38; Hale, "Another Year," 396–405; Guenther, B. *Commission on Church Architecture of the Lutheran Church— Missouri Synod, Architecture and the Church* (St. Louis, MO: Concordia, 1965), 51.

20. Bowman, C. M. *Guiding Intermediates* (New York, NY: Abingdon-Cokesbury, 1943), 13.

21. Ibid.; Richardson, N. *The Church at Play: A Manual for Directors of Social and Recreational Life,* 2d ed. (New York, NY: Abingdon, 1922), 27.

22. Braden, D. R. *Leisure and Entertainment in America* (Dearborn, MI: Henry Ford Museum and Greenfield Village, 1988); Gulick, L. H. "Play and the Church," *Playground* (1910): 29–30; Mutch, W. "Recreation and the Sunday School." In *The Encyclopedia of Sunday Schools and Religious Education,* vol. 3, edited by J. McFarland and B. Winchester, 864–66. New York, NY: Nelson, 1915; Hipps, R. H. Letter to researcher (September 2, 1992); Brightbill, C. *Man and Leisure: A Philosophy of Recreation* (Englewood Cliffs, NJ: Prentice-Hall, 1961).

23. Harbin, E. O. *The Recreation Leader* (New York, NY: Abingdon-Cokesbury, 1952), 7.

24. Boyd, Robert M. "Recreation and the Faiths: A Look at the Southern Baptist Church Philosophy at Work," *Selected Papers Presented at the Forty-Second National Recreation Congress* (New York, NY: National Recreational Association, 1961), 184–87.

25. Ibid., 198.

26. Hipps, R. H. Telephone interview (December 28, 1992).

27. Ibid.

28. Poloma, M. M. *The Assemblies of God at the Crossroads: Charisma and Institutional Dilemmas* (Knoxville, TN: University of Tennessee, 1989).

29. Woodward, K. L. "A Disneyland for the Devout," *Newsweek* (August 11, 1986): 46–47; Forest, S. A. "You Can't Say Morris Cerullo Has No Faith: Can the Televangelist Cleanse the Soul of Heritage USA?" *Business Week* (December 31, 1990): 59.

30. Gladden, W. *The Church and Modern Life* (Boston, MA: Houghton-Mifflin, 1908).

4

The Recreation and Sports Minister as a Professional

Dale Connally

"Recreation and sports ministers share the core values of the leisure services profession and add a unique perspective."

RECREATION AND SPORTS MINISTRY AS A LEISURE SERVICES PROVIDER

Leisure services is a broad field whose practitioners seek to help clients improve their quality of life through meaningful leisure experiences. Leisure services are typically provided by organizations attached to government entities and both profit and nonprofit corporations in the private sector. Churches and other religious organizations who sponsor recreation and sports ministries are often categorized as a leisure service provider in the nonprofit private sector.[1]

In his study of research and other writings concerning the use of recreation and sports in churches, Ernce concluded that there is no conflict between the church and leisure services when leisure services are provided from a Christian perspective.[2] Both historical and survey research supports the notion that recreation and sports ministries of various denominational churches are a bona fide leisure services provider. In fact, several recreation and sports ministers have also been influential in the secular leisure services professional organizations.[3]

RECREATION AND SPORTS MINISTRY AS A PROFESSION

A body of academic knowledge and technical skills—To understand the unique niche that recreation and sports ministry fills in the leisure services profession, the initial step is to explore the composition of a traditional profession. One element of a profession is a body of academic knowledge and technical skills that is integral to practitioners. Shivers, in *Introduction to Recreational Service,* suggests that recreation and sports professionals need a liberal arts program that includes social sciences, educational theory, and enough culture education to build a theoretical base for more specific course work in leisure services.[4] Kraus and Edginton have identified several key elements of leisure services curricula: recreation history and philosophy, program planning, fiscal and risk management, public relations, and research skills.[5] External agencies including the National Recreation and Park Association (NRPA) and the American Alliance of Health, Physical Education, Recreation and Dance (AAHPERD) are actively involved in identifying key issues to be addressed in academic preparation programs in leisure services.

Academic institutions—Another element of a profession is academic institutions and other organizations to help facilitate the learning of necessary knowledge and skills. Academic programs are offered at the associate, undergraduate, and graduate levels at public and private colleges and universities across the United States. Seminaries also provide course work to prepare ministers for recreation and sports ministry. Numerous other organizations offer training events specifically designed to educate and train recreation and sports ministers. An even larger group of secular professional organizations offers educational conferences highlighting several niche markets within the leisure services field. Appendix 3 lists several secular and religious training events and professional organizations that may be useful for a recreation and sports minister.

Referent authority—An additional element of a profession is referent authority from the public. It is not clear whether the general public views leisure services as a true profession. On one hand, we are living in an age when the clear majority of Americans view their leisure pursuits as essential to their quality of life and are willing to pay for service. Studies have shown that people are aware of and appreciate individual providers of leisure services. However, there is less evidence that people value leisure services as a true profession.[6] Monetary remuneration is often viewed as a barometer of referent authority. Theoretically, the higher the average salary, the more valued the profession. The salaries of leisure services professionals are generally viewed as average, compared to other service occupations. There are other financial indicators beyond salaries that may indicate public perception of leisure services.

The last two decades have brought relative economic prosperity to the United States. However, publicly funded leisure services providers have had to deal with shrinking budgets and rising costs. Such a lack of financial support implies that leisure services may be near the bottom of the public-sector pecking order. A somewhat similar pecking order exists in most churches. Compared to other ministers on a church staff, most recreation and sports ministers face, at best, average salaries and budget appropriations. Moreover, recreation and sports is often the only ministry in a church that is expected to raise its own revenue.

In a study of the ministry as an occupational labor market, the researchers suggest that pastors who minister at larger churches are at the pinnacle of the church job ladder. Few pastors plan to leave the pastorate to pursue other ministry positions. In other words, many of them would view it as a step backward to move from the pastorate to become a recreation and sports minister.[7] The dichotomy of the recreation and sports minister offering relevant programs that are valued by church members and integral to vibrant congregations, yet facing financial challenges, is not unique. Public school teachers, traditionally viewed as among the most honorable professionals, are often relegated to low salaries and woefully inadequate funding for instructional programs.

Ethical practice—The fourth element of a profession is a collective agreement on ethical practice. Ethics are actions based on values. The leisure services profession has several core values: contributing to the quality of life for individuals, advocating for the rights of all people, helping people make wise decisions in leisure, and promoting environmental stewardship.[8] Leisure services professionals seek to help individuals develop intellectually, physically, socially, and spiritually. Leisure

NATIONAL RECREATION AND PARK ASSOCIATION (NRPA)*

The National Recreation and Park Association has provided leadership to the nation in fostering the expansion of recreation and parks. NRPA has stressed the value of recreation, both active and passive, for individual growth and development. Its members are dedicated to the common cause of assuring that people of all ages and abilities have the opportunity to find the most satisfying use of their leisure time and enjoy an improved quality of life.

The Association has consistently affirmed the importance of well informed and professionally trained personnel to improve continually the administration of recreation and park programs. Members of NRPA are encouraged to support the efforts of the Association and profession by supporting state affiliate and national activities and participating in continuing education opportunities, certification, and accreditation.

Membership in NRPA carries with it special responsibilities to the public at large and to the specific communities and agencies in which recreation and park services are offered.

As a member of the National Recreation and Park Association, I accept and agree to abide by this Code of Ethics and pledge myself to:

- Adhere to the highest standards of integrity and honesty in all public and personal activities to inspire public confidence and trust.
- Strive for personal and professional excellence and encourage the professional development of associates and students.
- Strive for the highest standards of professional competence, fairness, impartiality, efficiency, effectiveness, and fiscal responsibility.
- Avoid any interest or activity which conflicts with the performance of job responsibilities.
- Promote the public interest and avoid personal gain or profit from the performance of job duties and responsibilities.
- Support equal employment opportunities.

*Source: http://www.nrpa.org/story.cfm?departmentID=37&story_id=181.

Figure 4-1: Code of Ethics

professionals also focus on leadership and moral character development. These values have led to the National Recreation and Park Association adopting a code of ethics (see Fig. 4-1) for leisure services professionals. Several denominations have developed codes of ethics as a guide for their ministers[9], while others are hesitant to do so considering individual and local church autonomy.

Recreation and sports ministers share the core values of the leisure services profession and add a unique perspective. Recreation and sports ministry does not view programming as an end but rather as a means to foster spiritual growth to believers and nonbelievers. Ministers enter the recreation and sports field out of a sense of calling by God to perform such service. McDuff and Mueller suggest that calling's importance to the ministry field may be unique. They also propose that some sense of calling, not necessarily divine, is a critical factor that separates professional and nonprofessional vocations.[10]

Paternalism—A tenet of the most highly recognized professions is the concept of paternalism. In simple terms, paternalistic behavior occurs when a professional performs an act, either commission or omission, for the advancement of an individual. The act may be performed without the consent of the individual. Lawyers and doctors are frequently trusted to commit acts of paternalism. The leisure services field is extremely hesitant to embrace and practice paternalism. Leisure, by definition, depends on the free will of an individual. Recreation and sports ministers who serve in an environment that values the priesthood of the believer and the free will of the individual are uncomfortable committing acts of paternalism.

Recreation and sports ministry does, however, exhibit one trait essential for paternalism. Paternalistic behaviors occur in situations when a professional has authority over persons who have a need that the market in general will not meet—the unemployed, older adults, and single parent families, for instance.[11] While having no legal connection or obligation, people in these categories who are in need often look to the church as a source of caring support and transformation.

A common set of standards—A final element of a profession is a common set of standards for professionals. Such standards address certification, accreditation, and licensing. Certification is the process of identifying individuals with the needed expertise to function within a profession. NRPA and AAHPERD collaborate to offer the Certified

Park and Recreation Professional (CPRP) certification. Criteria for the certification include certain levels of education, a national examination, and continuing education.[12] The CPRP is highly valued in the public sector but rarely recognized or desired in the private sector, including recreation and sports ministry.

Accreditation refers to the credentialing of individual academic programs or leisure agencies. Most college, university, and seminary programs seek general accreditations such as the Southern Association of Colleges and Schools (SACS) or the Association of Theological Schools (ATS). More specifically, leisure services academic programs and leisure agencies may be accredited through NRPA and AAHPERD. Schools submit evidence in terms of liberal arts program, content of leisure services course work, field experiences, faculty credentials, and workloads. Agencies submit self assessments of programs and personnel. Peer review follows for both academic programs and agencies as outside experts judge whether standards have indeed been met.[13] Agency accreditations are rare in the recreation and sports ministry domain. However, many Christian camps follow a similar procedure to become accredited through the American Camping Association.

Licensing, as it pertains to leisure services, refers to standards set by governmental agencies to oversee areas of professional practice. The common areas addressed by leisure services agencies include, but are not limited to, food preparation and service, transportation, and youth camping. The agency responsible for licenses in each area varies by state but generally involves departments of health, transportation or police, and health or human services, respectively.[14] Licensing is an important element in a risk management plan for recreation and sports ministers. Ministers must work to make sure that their kitchens and food service areas meet standards, that drivers are properly licensed, and that day or resident camps meet state standards.

Given these elements of a traditional profession, is leisure services in fact a profession? Shivers believes leisure services is a quasi-profession that has made progress in the last couple of decades but still has some growth to accomplish. The education that is required is a major weakness. Some entry level positions are still available for individuals with no college education. In addition, many people are in supervisory and upper level management who have little or no formal education in leisure services.[15] This tendency is mirrored in the recreation and sports ministry. Churches do not universally require seminary education, and a specific concentration or degree in leisure services or recreation and sports ministry is rarely required.

As mentioned earlier, accreditation or certification is not universally required in either the secular or sacred leisure or ministry professions. The current CPRP certification addresses knowledge and skills that are somewhat related to the ministry field. The NRPA accreditation process is currently aimed more toward public sector leisure providers than recreation and sports ministry. The development and strengthening of faith based professional organizations that could offer ministry appropriate certifications and accreditation would help recreation and sports ministers pursue a higher level of professionalism.

Due to its link to clergy, recreation and sports ministry is perhaps situated a bit stronger along the professional continuum than other niches within the leisure services profession. The clergy in general has a long history of being viewed by society as a profession. Torkildsen identifies ministers, lawyers, and medical doctors as members of the "original professions."[16] Wesner concludes that during the last century more and more churches recognized recreation and sports ministry as a valid clerical profession.[17]

There is certainly evidence that the leisure service profession may or may not meet the complex criteria for a traditional profession. However, from an individual minister's perspective, one must not view the professionalization of leisure services as a pointless struggle to achieve a static set of criteria necessary for the public to view leisure services as a profession. In other words, one should not forsake meeting people's needs through recreation and sports ministry in a professional manner just because there is not unanimous judgment that the leisure services profession is in fact a profession. Indeed, one must view professionalization as a developmental process. The continuous upgrading of individual ministers' academic preparation, lifelong learning, and professional practice is necessary to strengthen the profession and to be efficient, effective ministers.[18]

BURNOUT AMONG RECREATION AND SPORTS MINISTERS

One of the more popular maladies that may hinder both the efficiency and effectiveness of recreation and sports ministers is burnout. According to pastoralburnout.com 1,500 ministers leave their ministries *each month* due to burnout, conflict, or moral failure. 90% work more than 50 hours a week and clergy in addition to doctors and lawyers, have the most problems with drug abuse, alcoholism, and suicide.[19] Fichter views burnout as feeling overwhelmed with work, coupled with a great deal of emotional stress.[20] Burnout attacks all aspects of a person. Physical symptoms commonly include sleep disorders, chronic fatigue, headaches, and other minor illnesses.

Mental symptoms include withdrawal from work and family, dogmatism, and a general lack of motivation. The burnout victim's emotional experiences entail frustration, anxiety attacks, and a debilitating sense of feeling overwhelmed by work. Without effective coping mechanisms and support systems, the minister suffering from burnout may sink into a situational depression that can greatly diminish the impact of one's job performance.[21]

Several theories seek to explain the causes of burnout. Olsen and Grosch propose that affected ministers often possess a narcissistic personality that craves an inordinate degree of admiring appreciation from congregation members. This craving is often exacerbated by the sense of calling ministers experience. A vicious cycle ensues as a minister senses a divine plan and executes the plan. The congregation showers the minister with accolades, often exaggerated and excessive. Both the minister and the congregation raise their expectations, and the cycle begins again.[22]

Apart from this narcissistic pattern, Olsen and Grosch also believe that the pressures and demands of congregational life in opposition to a minister's family life can lead to burnout. As a minister's family grows in number and maturation, the family's needs for guidance from the minister as parent also grow. Conversely, as the minister feels pressure at home, yet is thriving on the accolades of congregation members, a dichotomy emerges. The minister may be viewed as a hero at church yet as something much less flattering at home.[23]

Grenz theorizes that ministers' burnout may be influenced by spiritual issues. Many ministers have an erroneous view of work and leisure. Traditional ministers mistakenly view leisure as a mere precursor to more productive work. The contemporary minister often sees work as a necessity in order to afford the materialistic leisure common in today's leisure culture. Christians do not work to earn leisure. Instead, they work as a sign of gratitude for the leisure God has provided.[24]

Grenz also states that many Christians have corrupted the relationship between God and man, especially between God and ministers. Some ministers have come to think that God's work cannot be accomplished without them. This is a limiting view of God, often prompting individuals to seek more responsibility than they can effectively fulfill.[25]

Developing a realistic view of one's ministerial responsibilities is one way to prevent burnout. Ministers must also work with congregations to help members support and appreciate the ministers' work appropriately and to form realistic expectations for ministers.[26] Ministers should maintain active hobbies and recreational pursuits, and they should schedule meaningful time with their families.[27]

Ministers can help prevent burnout by examining their individual personalities and problem solving approaches. To avoid burnout one should learn to view change as an opportunity and challenge, not a danger. One should also exert locus of control to help minister responsibly and within one's abilities.[28]

Another successful coping mechanism is to seek God's presence during times of adversity.[29] This would seem like a foregone conclusion for ministers; however, Rodgerson and Piedmont find that ministers sometimes tend to compartmentalize their religious practice as work, often failing to apply religious problem solving approaches.[30] While a vibrant Christian faith does not fully protect one from burnout, a minister should seek God's help to develop and maintain effective ministries. Effective ministries may already be the rule rather than the exception. Fichter reports that only 6 percent of the priests surveyed were candidates for burnout. The overwhelming majority of the respondents are healthy ministers with vibrant ministries.[31]

PROFESSIONAL DEVELOPMENT FOR RECREATION AND SPORTS MINISTERS

Stych identified four types of learners with respect to vibrant lifelong learning for ministers:

Laggards firmly resist innovation. They tend to be creatures of habit, outdated in their skills and approaches to ministry. Occasionally, their archaic approaches may even present safety hazards to participants physically and/or emotionally. They do not value continuing education and usually only participate in learning experiences when mandatory.

Maintainers are slow to accept change. Their involvement with continuing education is sporadic at best. They are suspicious of both nontraditional ministers and nontraditional ministry.

Progressive managers strive to improve professional practice but are drawn to more traditional, proven methods. They value continuing education, especially more traditional offerings. They embrace technology as a ministry tool.

Visionaries seek to improve professional practice. They are willing to pursue nontraditional approaches to lifelong learning and ministry. They are drawn to learn within and beyond their field and are not afraid to take risks.[32]

Seeking formal education is one way for the progressive managers and visionaries better to prepare themselves to use recreation and sports as effective tools for ministry. Formal continuing education may range from taking individual courses to seeking additional undergraduate or graduate degrees. Seminary education is highly valued for some recreation and sports ministers, especially those called to serve in traditional local churches.

Informal continuing education experiences are an alternative to formal academic course work. Traditionally, informal continuing education includes attending seminars and conferences, personal reading, and networking.[33] Ministers should seek informal learning experiences within their denominations, from other denominations, and from secular sources for maximum effectiveness. Learning outside the recreation and sports realm in areas such as technology, science, or vocational pursuits may also enhance one's ministry.[34]

Brown suggests four emerging approaches to informal continuing education that may be implemented by recreation and sports ministers.[35] First is the use of technology and the educational objects technology offers. For example, the Internet is a tremendous tool for locating recreational equipment suppliers and related information. Descriptions of games are also available online. Tremendous amounts of data relating to sports participation and sports ministry are available.

Another emerging approach is a form of networking known as skill exchanges. For instance, one recreation and sports minister might have a background in soccer but lack skills in hunting. She might partner with a fellow minister, offering to hold a soccer clinic at his church. In exchange, he might lead a hunting seminar at her church.

Peer matching is another approach to informal continuing education. An example might be an ecumenical group of recreation and sports ministers from several neighboring communities who meet on a regular basis. The meeting could include social time as well as structured individual ministry case studies shared for group problem solving.

The final approach involves links to educators at large. This could include using academic professionals, from both secular and faith based institutions, as consultants. Such consulting provides valuable educational dialogue. An overloaded minister can often profit from an uninvolved perspective. Consultations also provide professors with real world experiences to keep course work relevant for their students.

Another informal approach to professional development is mentoring.[36] There is much to be gained from partnering seasoned recreation and sports ministers with those just entering the ministry. Such a relationship can often shorten the learning curve for a young professional. Experienced ministers can also become energized from meaningful relationships with enthusiastic, creative young ministers.

The focus of lifelong learning is often related to producing a tangible product because of learning. For example, a recreation and sports minister returning from a conference might be expected to develop new sports leagues or implement new recreational programs. Purdum, on the other hand, stresses the spiritual importance of lifelong learning. Continuing education should go beyond academic study, also providing time for reflection, self assessment, and spiritual renewal. Continuing education should move beyond being a mere professional expectation. Germane lifelong learning helps one to be a good steward, fully utilizing the gifts and talents God has entrusted to his ministers.[37]

Lifelong learning should enhance the ministry potential and professionalism of recreation and sports ministers. Shivers proposes three premises to guide the practice and conduct of responsible leisure services professionals.[38] Each premise will be accompanied by implications for the recreation and sports minister. The first premise is a preoccupation with public welfare. From a study of lifelong learning for Pentecostal ministers, Lavallee states that the primary reason for seeking informal continuing education was a desire to meet the needs of church members.[39] All recreation and sports ministers should remember that ministry's purpose is to meet the needs of the people we serve.

The second premise is a continual search for truth. Ministers are able to discover and share truth. This should be viewed as a tremendous opportunity and responsibility. Historically, the clergy has been well educated and well informed. This must continue to be the case in the rapidly changing Information Age.[40]

The third premise is a dedication to ethical practice. Because of the holistic nature of recreation and sports ministry, individual ministers must continually strive to uphold the highest personal and professional ethics. The central tenets of our ministries should be relevance and excellence.

Recreation and sports ministers must diligently explore the variety of lifelong learning experiences that are available to help them reach their ministry potential. Purdum describes the challenges of reaching one's ministry potential and the role of vocational professionalism. (For more information, see Appendix 3, "Sources for Lifelong Learning and Networking.")

Ministers' days are spent within the bosom of the church, but our ministries are with people whose everyday lives are completely secular.

This is a challenge to our sense of call and the priesthood of all believers. True integrity of vocation is directly linked to a clear-eyed exploration of all the ways in which God might be calling us to live and work.[41]

Through such exploration, recreation and sports ministers will continue to be valuable contributors to both the mission of the church and the goal of advancing the leisure services profession.

NOTES

1. Edginton, Christopher R., et al. *Leisure and Life Satisfaction: Foundational Perspectives,* 3rd ed. (New York, NY: McGraw Hill, 2002), 282–84.

2. Ernce, Keith D. "Church Recreation in the Southern Baptist Convention as a Leisure Consumer, Leisure Provider and Member of the Leisure Services Delivery System" (Ph.D. diss., University of New Mexico, 1987), 132.

3. Wesner, Brad E. "Visions and Revisions: An Exploratory Investigation Sketching the Origins and Growth of the Evolving Relationship Between the Church and Recreation, 1872–1992" (Ph.D. diss., University of Illinois at Urbana-Champaign, 1995), 162–64; Ernce, 132.

4. Shivers, Jay. *Introduction to Recreational Service* (Springfield, IL: C. C. Thomas, 1993), 524.

5. Kraus, Richard. *Recreation and Leisure in Modern Society,* 6th ed. (Sudbury, MA: Jones and Bartlett Publishers, Inc., 2001), 320; Edginton, et al., 372.

6. Kraus, 318.

7. McDuff, Elaine M. and Charles W. Mueller, "The Ministry as an Occupational Labor Market," *Work and Occupations* 27 (2000): 108.

8. Edginton, et al., 373–74.

9. ABC Indiana. "The Covenant and Code of Ethics." http://www. abcindiana.org/Region/Polity/codeethics.html (accessed February 27, 2002); AAPC. "Code of Ethics." http://www.aapc.org/ethics. html (accessed on February 21, 2002; WCG. "Code of Ethics for Elders." http://www.wcg.org/lit/church/ministry/ codeethics.html (accessed February 27, 2002).

10. McDuff and Mueller, 107.

11. McNamee, M. J., H. Sheridan, and J. Buswell, "Paternalism, Professionalism and Public Sector Leisure Provision: The Boundaries of a Leisure Profession," *Leisure Studies* 19 (2000): 200–04.

12. NRPA. "Education and Professional Standards." http://www.nrpa. org/ department.cfm?departmentID=2&publicationID=11&Sub_ DepartmentID=22 (accessed February 27, 2002).

13. NRPA. "What Is Accreditation?" http://www.nrpa.org/story. cfm? storyid=128&departmentID=2&publicationID=11 (accessed February 27, 2002; NRPA. "Agency Accreditation." http://www.nrpa.org/department. cfm?departmentID=2&publicationID=11&Sub_ DepartmentID=233. (accessed February 27, 2002).

14. Kraus, 327.

15. Shivers, 541.

16. Torkildsen, George. Leisure and Recreation Management, 3rd ed. (London: E & FN Spon, 1992), 435.

17. Wesner, 163.

18. Purdum, Elizabeth. "Sanctifying Ministers Through Lifelong Education," *Dialog* 38 (1999): 277.
19. Double Honor Ministries. "Ministerial Burnout Statistics" http://doublehonorministries.com/minister-burnout-statistics/ (accessed March 28, 2016).
20. Fichter, Joseph H. "The Myth of Clergy Burnout," *Sociological Analysis* 45 (1984): 376–77.
21. Watstein, Sarah B. "Burnout: Buzzword or Reality," *ATLA Proceedings* 40 no. 1 (1985): 112.
22. Olsen, David C. and William N. Grosch, "Clergy Burnout: A Self Psychology and Systems Perspective," *Journal of Pastoral Care* 45 (1991): 297–98.
23. Ibid., 301.
24. Grenz, Stanley J. "Burnout: The Cause and the Cure for a Christian Malady," *Currents in Theology and Mission* 26 (1999): 427, 429.
25. Ibid., 430.
26. Olsen and Grosch, 302.
27. Ibid., 303.
28. Harbaugh, Gary L. and Evan Rogers, "Pastoral Burnout: A View from the Seminary," *Journal of Pastoral Care* 38 (1984): 103.
29. Ibid., 104.
30. Rodgerson, Thomas E. and Ralph L. Piedmont, "Assessing the Incremental Validity of the Religious ProblemSolving Scale in the Prediction of Clergy Burnout," *Journal for the Scientific Study of Religion* 37 (1998): 523.
31. Fichter, 379.
32. Stych, Brad E. "Improving Workshop Use with Ministry Professionals," *Christian Education Journal* 15 (1995): 46–47.
33. Edginton, et al., 389.
34. Purdum, 278–80.
35. Brown Jr., George. "Lifelong Learning and Ministry," *Reformed Review* 50 (1997): 163–64.

36. Purdum, 280.
37. Ibid., 277.
38. Shivers, 544–47.
39. Lavalee, Nil N. "A Study of Continuing Learning Among Pentecostal Ministers," *Eastern Journal of Practical Theology* 10 (1996): 31.
40. Davis, Kenneth G. "From Anecdote to Analysis: A Case for Applied Research in Ministry," *Pastoral Psychology* 46 (1997): 104.
41. Purdum, 280.

5

Organization of Recreation and Sports Ministry

John Garner

"Done right, recreation and sports ministry undergirds and complements all other ministries."

Every church uses recreation and sports ministry. Every church. It may not be well organized, but all churches do it. Banquets, parties, fellowships, sports teams, church picnics, drama, camping, and special celebrations are a part of the life of most, if not all, churches. People enjoy and need this fellowship and activity. Churches that seek to meet these needs offer opportunities for social, mental, physical, emotional, and spiritual growth. A well-organized recreation ministry with a balanced program will offer opportunities for growth in all these areas to all ages. Doing this with a vision of reaching, winning, and teaching the lost requires kingdom oriented thinking and planning.

A recreation and sports ministry that reflects kingdom thinking will support and help the church carry out the Great Commission of "going unto all the world." Kingdom planning seeks to minister to all participants, believers and nonbelievers alike, by creatively using the tools of crafts, socials, camping, sports, wellness/fitness, drama, music, and continuing education—anything that can be done in one's leisure time to impact lives with the gospel. As these tools are thought through, planned for, and used wisely, opportunities arise for evangelism, discipleship, fellowship, ministry/service, and worship. This kind of kingdom thinking will result in numerical and spiritual growth along with the expansion of ministry opportunities and missions advance.

Churches that use recreation and sports must do so with the intention of developing relationships with the lost and building the fellowship of the church. As these are done, new church leaders are found and trained, and nonbelievers are reached. Perhaps because there is nothing religious about recreation and sports ministry, to be effective there must be extra caution and a high degree of organization and planning to facilitate effective intentional ministry.

No one can get things accomplished or minister in chaos. The scriptural admonition of 1 Corinthians 14:40 is, "Everything must be done decently and in order." The mechanism that allows everything to run smoothly is organization. Organization provides framework, stability, direction, and accountability. Organization also minimizes conflict, duplication, and wasted effort. In a ministry team environment, a good organization involves:

- *Enlisting*—Finding the right person for each job.
- *Empowerment*—Trusting the people with responsibility and authority to get a job done their way.
- *Nurturing*—Growing people in a job to become more than they thought they could be, thus providing training for larger leadership roles in the future.
- *Developing relationships*—Fostering trust and interdependence among ministry team members.
- *Coaching*—Helping ministry team members be effective.
- *Intentionality*—Making sure that the gospel is presented at every opportunity.

An organized recreation and sports ministry team seeks to allow a wide population of individuals to express their talents, gifts, interests, and abilities in ways that bring personal satisfaction and corporate good. This helps accomplish the work of the church through its members' involvement as outlined in 1 Corinthians 12:12–31. Each part of the body (church) has distinctly different functions. Lived out through well organized, scripturally based, philosophically sound ministry, the outcome of an organized recreation and sports ministry team effort will see many kingdom results.

The organizational structure of recreation and sports ministry of a church must establish and support a "Christ distinctive" in each activity/ministry action. This will set the ministry apart from other recreation efforts by community, private, or other nonprofit entities. Part of this distinctive is creating an atmosphere in which ministry and fellowship are planned for and intentionally happen. Another part of this Christ distinctive is for discipleship to be planned for as personal involvement by members happens. The millennial age group is all about service and community. Personal service and community building opportunities abound in recreation and sports ministry. The organizational structure must provide for member involvement. As evidenced by Oswald earlier, every church member can minister according to his or her giftedness, talents and abilities, or interests. This is the concept of ministry teams.

Scripture guides us as we endeavor to develop a functioning organization that:

- *Seeks every opportunity to reach the lost*—"I have become all things to all people, so that I may by all means save some" (1 Cor. 9:22).
- *Honors God at each event*—"Whatever you do, do everything for God's glory" (1 Cor. 10:31)
- *Relates to the whole person*—"Jesus increased in wisdom and stature, and in favor with God and people" (Luke 2:52)
- *Creates an atmosphere of happiness*—"A cheerful heart is good medicine" (Prov. 17:22)
- *Teaches use of gifts, talents, interests, and abilities*—"Do not neglect the gift that is in you" (1 Tim. 4:14)
- *Develops the fellowship of the church*—"By this all people will know that you are My disciples, if you have love for one another" (John 13:35)[1]

These six principles should guide those planning recreation and sports ministry for all ages in the church.

STEPS TO ORGANIZATION FOR EFFECTIVE RECREATION AND SPORTS MINISTRY

There are nine basic steps to proven success in providing an effective base for recreation and sports ministry. Each step builds on the one before and sets the stage for the one to follow.

1. Establish Church and Staff Support

Recreation and sports ministry must have the support of the pastor, staff, and church in general. This ministry will touch all other ministries and all ages. As the leader of the church, the pastor must understand the concept and support it. No ministry will succeed if the pastor is not behind it. He must see how it can be used as a tool for both discipleship and evangelism. Staff members need to understand how this ministry will support and complement their ministries. There is no room for competition between this ministry and others in the church. Done right, recreation and sports ministry undergirds and complements all other ministries. Recreation and sports ministry funnels prospects to the worship services, to the choirs, to the youth and children's ministry, as well as to the Bible study ministry of the church.

Natural support for "recreation and sports" will be in evidence. Everyone likes to play; however, church members must understand that this will not be activity for activity's sake. They can be involved in recreation and sports ministry as an intentional ministry and can invite their friends with confidence that all who participate will come under the influence of the gospel at some point anytime an event, class, seminar, league, or gathering occurs. Enlisting church member support will take time and continuous training as to why a church would want to get itself organized for recreation and sports ministry.

The leader charged with helping teach recreation and sports ministry principles will need an understanding of how the Great Commission and the five functions of the church—evangelism, discipleship, ministry, fellowship, and worship—are lived out through the small and discipleship groups as outlined in the model and process in Chapter 1 of this book. They will also need to understand how their work will impact the kingdom results of numerical growth, spiritual transformation, ministry expansion, and kingdom advance of the church.

2. Provide Leadership That Has a Vision and Training for Using Recreation and Sports as Ministry Tools

The church must find leadership that has a vision and understanding of how recreation and sports can be used as an intentional ministry tool. This leadership can be a fulltime staff member, a part time staff member, or a volunteer. This person must understand the key role he or she is going to play in teaching the church how to use recreation as a ministry tool. There is nothing religious about recreation and sports ministry. It is neither good nor bad: recreation is morally neutral; sport is morally neutral. The key is what you do with these tools. The leader will need to possess an understanding of and insight into the use of these secular tools in the life of the church. Left on their own, these tools will not lead a church to do ministry. However, as the leader trains the activity leaders to be intentional by providing ministry resources, encouragement, and guidance, these activities can be the instrument opening the door for evangelism and discipleship.

A mistake some churches make is thinking that because the church sponsors an activity it will take on a spiritual dimension. The organization as led by a person called of God to this unique ministry area will constantly have to remind itself why they are doing this ministry, what needs to happen, and how to get where the church wants the ministry to go. For the evangelic church, reaching and discipling people must be primary.

Various sized churches with different staff situations must determine who is responsible at the administrative level for recreation and sports ministry. There may be a natural growth progression as a church grows from one size to the next with differing needs.

For the small church—When the pastor is the only staff member, a gifted and skilled layman may be asked to "direct" and develop the recreation and sports ministry. This volunteer director should have full responsibility for the recreation and sports ministry. He or she should be empowered to call ministry team (committee) meetings, set calendar dates, and work with the pastor in overall coordination of the ministry. Communication with the pastor and the church ministry leadership team is important during formative, implementation, and development stages. Periodic update meetings will keep things compatible with the pastor's and the church's concept of the direction the ministry should take.

When a second staff member is added to the small church model— Recreation supervision and administration usually passes to the new person on staff. The staff member with recreation as one of many responsibilities may choose to continue the "director plan," as the pastor did. He will depend on a ministry team and lead teams to help get the job done. Having multiple staff assignments, the minister will delegate much of the programming and authority for quality ministry in all areas to take place. Many churches with active programs (with a gym, open for programmed hours) work successfully with this arrangement.

*Adding a fulltime recreation and sports minister—*As the church grows numerically and ministry expansion demands that a professionally trained person be added to the staff, the church will seek a fulltime recreation and sports minister. The church will usually begin to plan a comprehensive program and/or a complex drop-in facility. This person's role will be to coordinate a wide-ranging ministry to all ages in all leisure-services areas. He or she still should depend on the recreation and sports ministry leadership team, volunteers, and possibly volunteer and or paid part-time staff for successful ministry and operation of a facility.

In all these situations, the personality of the church and the personality of the minister will determine the design of the ministry team and its effectiveness.[2]

3. Set Up a Ministry Team Structure

The recreation and sports ministry team is made up of people who have an interest in using recreation and sports. This natural interest can be married to the heart of a Christian so that people see how God can use their natural ability as a tool for ministry. Christians want to serve God. Most of us think that unless we preach, lead music, teach a Bible study, or become a missionary we can't serve God. The recreation and sports ministry team allows folks with interests in leisure activities a place to serve God, the church, and the community.

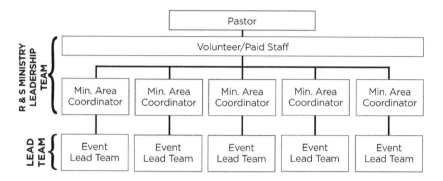

Ministry areas might include arts and crafts, fellowship/social recreation, wellness/fitness, outdoor education, sports, age groups, retreats, community outreach, trips, drama, and music.

Figure 5-1: Ministy Team Structure

Figure 5-1 illustrates how a ministry team might function. The pastor is the exofficio member of each ministry team. In larger churches a staff member may be the liaison between the church staff and the ministry team. Ministry team members function on two levels, one long term and the other short term. The first level is the longer-term level. The team members on this level would serve a two to three-year rotating term. This rotation system assures continuity from year to year. Each ministry team member would have an area of specialization or interest that they would represent on the team. Often these leaders are called coordinators. This level makes up the policymaking and advisory part of the overall team.

All policies directly related to recreation and sports ministry come from this body. If a church has a recreation facility, often this body will give guidance to the facility ministry. However, sometimes a church will have a facility ministry team to give attention to the unique needs that a facility brings. Coordinators give the overall direction to the ministry.

These persons should: (1) be committed Christians, (2) be active church members, (3) have a ministry concept of recreation and sports, (4) understand the inner workings of the church, (5) be dedicated to reaching and growing people for God, and (6) have the time necessary to serve.[3]

Ministry areas might include arts and crafts, fellowship/social recreation, wellness/ fitness, outdoor education, sports, age groups, retreats, community outreach, trips, drama, and music.

The recreation and sports ministry leadership team should be made up of people with diversity of interests. Members should not all be sports oriented. They should represent all membership elements in the church as this ministry team touches every ministry area of the church.

The functions of the recreation and sports ministry leadership team include:

- Advise the staff member associated with recreation and sports ministry.
- Develop and protect the purpose, philosophy, theology, and policies for the recreation and sports used as ministry tools.
- Receive and consolidate calendar dates, leadership enlistment, and budget recommendations from ministry area coordinators.
- Be responsible for long range planning. Serve as a sounding board for new ideas considering the ministry team assignment of the church.
- Focus recreation and/or sports events on evangelism of the unsaved, outreach to prospects, and in-reach to inactive church members.
- Ensure that every aspect of the ministry (1) honors God, (2) is in harmony with the church's purpose/mission statement, and (3) channels people into open and closed groups as appropriate.
- Be vigilant to see that ministry is the purpose of the committee and program's existence.
- Provide a balanced calendar to ensure that the ministry is well rounded, functional, and not dominated by any person or program area.
- Provide a proper atmosphere where intentional ministry can happen.
- Maintain facilities, maximize their use, and project needed improvements.[4]

The ministry team should appoint or elect a chairperson to work with the staff member, coordinate/lead the meetings, and act as a sounding board and advisor to the staff member.

The Lead Team Concept

Lead teams serve for short terms to carry out an activity or event, then are dissolved. Teams are usually made up of persons with interest in particular areas of ministry.

People today usually are hesitant to make long-term commitments to anything. They want to get in, get the job done and move on. That is what the "lead team" concept is all about. When a particular ministry action is planned, the coordinators pull together a short term "lead team" to help plan and implement the event. The lead team is made up of highly motivated members who have an interest in a particular activity area. They come together for a short time to plan and help with the event. After the event is over and evaluated, the lead team then dissolves. The next time that event is to be done, the lead team members may change. Most lead teams function for six to eight weeks. This concept works because people will give short periods of time to something that interests them. No long term commitments are needed, calendars can be scheduled, and other activities planned around the event. Short term commitments are here to stay.

4. **Develop a Biblically Sound Theology of Recreation and Sports Ministry**

For a church to have an organized recreation and sports ministry that is long-lasting effective and supports the mission of the church, the ministry must have a solid foundation in Scripture. While other chapters in this text will go deeper into Scripture and theology, this chapter provides an overview of the basics of what a church will need to know and understand as a rationale for organizing a recreation and sports ministry according to Scripture.

Throughout Scripture God speaks of labor/work and rest or leisure. Where he does not speak directly, he gives principles for living. As the church moves to organize a ministry using recreation and sports, it must teach its members why they are doing this type of ministry.

This is not a onetime event. Because our culture is so leisure-oriented, the natural tendency is to equate recreation with fun and games and not ministry opportunities. Members must be reminded often as to why a church is using recreation and sports, lest they take the natural or secular view and see recreation and sports ministry events as activity for activity's sake.

Five basic understandings mark the beginnings of a biblical worldview of recreation and sports used as ministry tools:

1. God provides meaningful labor (work).
2. God commands the Sabbath or rest.
3. Man has corrupted God's good gifts—work and leisure.
4. Biblical foundations for reaching the culture.
5. Jesus provides the example.

Each of these concepts is based on Scripture in principle or by example for the church to consider.

God provides meaningful labor (work). Some basic Scriptures for this statement include:

"All hard work brings a profit, but mere talk leads only to poverty" (Prov. 14:23).

"That everyone may eat and drink, and find satisfaction in all his toil—this is the gift of God" (Eccles. 3:13).

"The sleep of a laborer is sweet, whether he eats little or much" (Eccles. 5:12).

"The thief must no longer steal. Instead, he must do honest work with his own hands, so that he has something to share with anyone in need" (Eph. 4:28).

"Seek to lead a quiet life, to mind your own business, and to work with your own hands, as we commanded you, so that you may walk properly in the presence of outsiders and not be dependent on anyone" (1 Thess. 4:11–12).

In these passages, we find the principle that work is provided by God as a gift. Work is something that brings meaning and satisfaction to life. In some cases, work provides something to share with others. In other instances, the principle is living a quiet life not dependent on others. Profit is a worthy motive for work, and hard work is said to be sweet. Whatever we do, as North Americans, our work provides for us food, shelter, clothing, transportation, and the means to enjoy our leisure. This aspect of work is one of our primary motivations; our work supports our leisure.

Work has a way of bringing a sense of accomplishment and fulfillment. God in his infinite wisdom has provided work to enrich our lives. The Christian response to work should be one of thankfulness and stewardship as we live out our gifts, talents, interests, and abilities in the workplace. In the workplace Christians meet the world. Christians must live in an attractive and consistent way to attract the unbeliever. This is the reason for stewardship of our labor, "so that you may walk properly in the presence of outsiders" (1 Thess. 4:12).

God commands the Sabbath or rest. Scripture background for this concept is well known:

> "By the seventh day God had finished the work he had been doing; so, on the seventh day he rested from all his work. And God blessed the seventh day and made it holy, because on it he rested from all the work of creating that he had done" (Gen. 2:2–3).

> "For six years sow your fields, and for six years prune your vineyards and gather their crops. But in the seventh year the land is to have a Sabbath of rest, a Sabbath to the LORD. Do not sow your fields or prune your vineyards" (Lev. 25:3–4).

> "Then He told them, 'The Sabbath was made for man, and not man for the Sabbath'" (Mark 2:27).

> "He said to them, 'Come away by yourselves to a remote place and rest a little.' For many people were coming and going, and they did not even have time to eat" (Mark 6:31).

Rest is fundamental to the wellbeing of humankind. We have God's example of his "resting" after creation. Every seventh year, the land was to rest and lay fallow and man was not to work that field for a year. Jesus pointed out that the Sabbath was made for man's good. Jesus also called his disciples to get away to a quiet place and get some rest.

The concept of rest was created and sanctioned by God for man's good. It provides a time to "recreate" our inner being and rejuvenate our bodies. Our fast-paced culture places a premium on leisure pursuits, often to the detriment of much needed rest. Leisure education taught by the church and times of rest provided by the church can help people put this rest principle to work in their lives. A rested person performs better, feels better, and in turn can minister more effectively. We must learn how to lead the church to "come away [with Jesus] to a remote place and rest a little," for God commands the Sabbath.

The dilemma the church faces is how to help Christians understand the need for godly rest in such a fast paced and competitive world. Rest is not only the cessation of activity but can include diversionary activities, anything that gets one out of his or her work routine—reading, biking, hobbies, conversation, trips, lawn work, or going to Bible study or worship. These can bring refreshment and new focus to life, the purpose of rest. Some might call this rest "recreation," and they would be right. This Sabbath rest (restful leisure) recreates the mind, body, and spirit, preparing people to serve God and their fellow man through the meaningful work God has called us to do.

Man, has corrupted God's good gifts—work and leisure. Scripture also supports this understanding:

> "Go to the ant, you sluggard; consider its ways and be wise!…How long will you lie there, you sluggard? When will you get up from your sleep? A little sleep, a little slumber, a little folding of the hands to rest—and poverty will come on you like a bandit and scarcity like an armed man" (Prov. 6:6, 9–11).

> "She who is self-indulgent is dead even while she lives" (1 Tim. 5:6).

> "At the same time, they also learn to be idle, going from house to house;… saying things they shouldn't say" (1 Tim. 5:13).

People find ways to corrupt God's blessings and the good gifts he has provided to us. A person does this by putting his work before God and family or by making the pursuit of leisure the main goal in life. While work is given by God, and it blesses us, people can put work before everything and anyone else. Often people, Christians included, get their sense of worth and self-esteem from what they do at work rather than their relationship with Christ. After meeting, men (more than women) will ask the new acquaintance "What do you do?" thus elevating what a person does over who he or she is. Our work defines us. While it was true that in the recent past boomers were working more hours to be more productive to reap monetary reward. Today, Millennials and younger Gen-Xers, however are bringing a different mindset. They view any longer work hours and more money they may receive as a temporary means to ultimately reach the goal of satisfaction in life—more leisure to enjoy. The adage: "He who dies with most toys wins" is no longer valid. One business writer states "Millennials are concerned with other things. Money is important and they do enjoy making it, however, they long to be part of something bigger than themselves. The workplace doesn't define them to the degree that it did for too many Boomers. Millennials want to lead a balanced life. They want to be happy at home and happy on the job—money is somewhat secondary."[5] The biblical view of work is that God provides us work, so in essence it belongs to him. We are to be stewards of work, not slaves to it. Millennials seem to be seeking a life lived in balance.

So it is with leisure. Leisure is made to be the end rather than the means to an end—that end being restful leisure that prepares us for meaningful work. This new leisure oriented culture has convinced us that having leisure is the main point to life. The pursuit of leisure is not bad. How it is used makes all the difference. Just as the pursuit of finding meaning through work leads to an unbalanced life, the pursuit of leisure as the focus to life results in an unbalanced life also. The corruption of leisure has led us to almost an addiction to leisure itself—not the joy, peace, and fulfillment of the abundant life that Christ talked about in Scripture. Living for pleasure has led many individuals and nations to ruin. While not approaching their look at leisure from a Christian context, Carlson, Deppe, and MacLean state: "Leisure itself is a two-edged sword; it carries no guarantee for Utopian happiness. It may bring opportunity for enjoyment of art, music, and science; for the development of health, strength and satisfaction; or for the acquisition of inner resources that lead to contentment. Conversely, it may bring idleness, boredom, overindulgence, deterioration or corruption....The wise use of the gift of leisure is the challenge of our time."[6] They are right—the wise use of leisure is not only a challenge for our time; it is a challenge of Christian stewardship. Questions to this new Millennial emphasis on leisure are: (1) "Will this millennial shift toward more leisure lead to balance or a further bent toward unfettered demanded leisure? (2) What effect will that have on our culture at large? and (3) How does the church address it?

The Bible lays a foundation for culture. Both the Old Testament and the New Testament have references to sports:

> "This is what the LORD Almighty says: 'Once again men and women of ripe old age will sit in the streets of Jerusalem, each with cane in hand because of his age. The city streets will be filled with boys and girls playing there'" (Zech. 8:4–5).

> "Do you not know that the runners in a stadium all race, but only one receives the prize? Run in such a way that you may win. Now everyone who competes exercises self-control in everything. However, they do it to receive a perishable crown, but we an imperishable one. Therefore I do not run like one who runs aimlessly, or box like one who beats the air. Instead, I discipline my body and bring it under strict control, so that after preaching to others, I myself will not be disqualified" (1 Cor. 9:24–27).

In these passages, we find play and athletics mentioned in the Old Testament and the New Testament. In the Zechariah passage, men and women outside in the street and children playing in the streets carry an image of almost a Mayberry type of harmony and fulfillment. The land is safe, the people are fulfilled, and God is blessing. In the New Testament passage, runners preparing to run a race is one analogy, while boxing is used as another example of Paul taking culturally relevant happenings and using them to teach a spiritual lesson.

Our culture is as varied as the people who make it up. Impacting this culture will take a variety of methods targeting various age and interest groups. The interest in leisure is overwhelming. Senior adults have time and money to spend on leisure pursuits. Middle School and high school students participate in an ever-increasing array of activities. Children's activities are found everywhere, provided by all types of organizations. Sports organizations cannot handle the crowds of children that come to them to play.

The principle for the church is that we must use all the tools at our disposal to influence the culture around us. Paul's example of "speaking the language" as he does in 1 Corinthians 9 shows us the way to capture the imagination of our culture with language they understand.

Jesus provides the example. When Jesus changed the water into wine at the wedding feast, when he attended a banquet in his honor, and at other times, he affirmed fun and fellowship.

> On the third day a wedding took place in Cana of Galilee. Jesus' mother was there, and Jesus and His disciples were invited to the wedding as well. When the wine ran out, Jesus' mother told Him, "They don't have any wine." "What has this concern of yours to do with Me, woman?" Jesus asked. "My hour has not yet come." "Do whatever He tells you," His mother told the servants. Now six stone water jars had been set there for Jewish purification. Each contained twenty or thirty gallons.
>
> "Fill the jars with water," Jesus told them. So they filled them to the brim. Then He said to them, "Now draw some out and take it to the chief servant." And they did. When the chief servant tasted the water (after it had become wine), he did not know where it came from—though the servants who had drawn the water knew. He called the groom and told him, "Everybody sets out the

fine wine first, then, after people have drunk freely, the inferior. But you have kept the fine wine until now" (John 2:1-10).

Then Levi hosted a grand banquet for Him at his house. Now there was a large crowd of tax collectors and others who were guests with them. But the Pharisees and their scribes were complaining to His disciples, "Why do you eat and drink with tax collectors and sinners?" (Luke 5:29–30).

In these passages we find Jesus giving his blessing to parties and banquets. Jesus enjoyed people. He had a message for them, and he went to where they were to deliver the message. The church should follow Jesus' example and go to were the people are—at the ballpark, golf course, lake, football game, Olympics, fishing hole, park, crafts fair, party, stock car races, rodeo, school carnival, and theme parks. Wherever people are, the church needs to be there, taking the presence of Christ. If a church wants to reach families in the summer, where will it find them in the evenings and weekends? At the ballparks, soccer fields, or hockey rink with their children. We must go there!

Jesus was outside the synagogue with the people teaching great spiritual truth using tools and things they understood: sports analogies, agricultural object lessons, a little boy's lunch of fish and bread, and sometimes a miracle, often with people some did not like very much. The principle is plain enough to see: go where the people are and use tools they understand to teach them the love of God, the sacrifice of the Son, and the presence of the Holy Spirit.

Applying biblical concepts is key to good organization for recreation and sports ministry. Understanding these things will keep a focus on ministry and not activity. The Bible is the basis for all ministry. The principles and guidance it gives will keep one focused on the main things: reaching people, discipling believers, and multiplying ministering Christians.

5. Develop a Mission and Vision Statement

A mission statement for the recreation and sports ministry of any church must complement the church's mission statement. Each mission statement will be different for each church based on the church's local culture and church practice.

When developing a mission statement, the ministry team under the direction of the pastor or staff will:

1. Consider the church mission statement.
2. Seek mission statements from other churches.
3. Develop a philosophy of ministry based on Scripture.
4. Seek input from members and staff.
5. Seek to include the concepts of evangelism, worship, discipleship, ministry, and fellowship, which result in numerical growth for the church, spiritual transformation of participants, expanded ministry opportunity, and advancement of the kingdom of God.

A vision statement for recreation and sports ministry might include the following thoughts:

Vision—Recreation and sports ministry seeks to be a Great Commission and Great Commandment ministry that builds the kingdom of God by using recreation and sports as ministry tools. This ministry seeks to "become all things to all people, so that I may by all means save some" (1 Cor. 9:22). We will use these tools to evangelize the lost, disciple believers, minister in Christ's name, facilitate worship, and encourage fellowship.

Mission—Making the name of God and salvation through His son Jesus known using recreation and sports in our community and around the world.

Desired results—In doing this ministry, a church should expect to see visible, tangible results in the areas of numerical growth as people are intentionally evangelized; spiritual growth as Christians are discipled; ministry expansion as Christians use their gifts, talents, and abilities in recreation and sports settings; and kingdom advance as recreation and sports are used to capture the imaginations of a leisure oriented culture outside the walls of the church.

6. Educate the Church

Because there is nothing religious about recreation activities or sporting events, the recreation and sports ministry team must begin to educate the church about what recreation and sports ministry is and what it is not. As earlier stated, this is not a onetime event. Education must be done continuously as new people come into the church. Church members must be reminded why you do this ministry and what the results are expected to be.

One of the jobs of the recreation and sports ministry team will be to seek opportunities to share the story about what is happening in the ministry. This can be done through several means: social media, web sites, newsletters, promotional mailings, reports to the church, flyers, handouts, personal stories about involvement in the ministry, in a recreation and sports ministry blog, when a family or person joins the church or is baptized and other opportunities as they are made available.

Upon election of the ministry team, the team members should be in Bible study classes and at other meetings helping the church understand the recreation and sports ministry vision and expected results. If possible the pastor should preach a sermon on the use of recreation and sports as the church expects to see this ministry done. The story should be told often, pointing out the results in the lives of participants and the growth of the church.

7. Use Surveys to Assess Needs and Opportunities

One of the keys for establishing a well-organized recreation and sports ministry is to find out what the people want in such a ministry. To provide the most comprehensive and well rounded ministry, a series of surveys will help accomplish this.

A recreation and sports ministry survey is a way to get information that will help ensure success. The process involves three types of surveys: property survey, community survey, and membership survey.

The property survey—This survey involves looking at everything on the church property that might be used for recreation and sports ministry activities. The survey will involve looking for inside space suitable for activity and looking at outdoor areas that may host an event.

Survey indoor space. When looking for space inside, look for large open spaces for larger groups, such as a fellowship hall for an all church gathering. For a smaller group, perhaps the dining room is available for crafts classes as water is readily available, or by moving tables and chairs for aerobics ministry classes. Sunday school rooms can be used for continuing education classes, such as computer classes or tutoring.

Look for suitable space for various age groups. Preschool play days could be centered in the preschool Sunday school area, where furniture fits them. A senior adult stretching exercise class could be held in a room on the first floor that has good air exchange. A large Sunday school department might serve well as a game room if storage is available so that the games can be put away on Sunday. Whatever the need, many areas of a church can also be used for recreation events, classes, workshops, or tournaments. Survey all areas inside, and ask, "What could we do in this space?"

Survey outdoor space. Churches usually have a lot of usable outdoor space. Parking lots can be used for many activities: carnivals, bike rodeos, cookouts, basketball, roller hockey, and volleyball. Grassy areas can be used for picnics, ice cream socials, watermelon cuttings, fairs, day camping, adventure games, and VBS recreation.

Safety is an issue when using outdoor areas. Make sure traffic can be blocked if you are using a parking lot. Make sure grassy areas have no broken glass, holes, or any other safety issues. Particular attention should be paid to overhead power lines, ditches, and the grade (slope) of the area.

Outdoor recreation areas need to be adjacent to or have water and rest rooms available. A survey of outdoor areas on your church property will open up new space for recreation and sports ministry.

Community survey—This survey will look at what is available in the community that may be used by the church for recreation and sports ministry activities. Communities have a host of usable sites for recreation and sports ministry activities to take place. A survey of any community will turn up many potential sites. Look for places of business, parks, farms, and other places that could host your group. Bowling alleys could host a church bowling league. local, state, or national parks could be used for day camping, outdoor worship services, cookouts, camp outs, and picnics. Craft shops can often be used to host crafts classes. Shop owners will usually let outside groups hold classes in their shop provided you purchase your materials from them. Schools often let churches use or rent their facilities for basketball or volleyball leagues. City recreation departments often will host church softball leagues. Lakes offer the opportunity for water ski outings or other outdoor activities. Some campgrounds have adventure recreation and ropes courses available for church use. Look for businesses that offer team building apparatus and services.

Membership survey—The most useful survey is the membership survey. From this survey one gains knowledge of what the membership is now doing, would like to do, or could provide leadership for. This survey is made available by both printed and electronic means to the congregation, from middle school through senior adults. The recreation and sports ministry team (committee) will assist in taking the survey. The procedure is as follows:

1. Surveys are made available the congregation online.
2. Online surveys can be periodical or continuous—The point is to gather as much information as possible from as many participants as possible to help the Recreation and Sports Ministry leadership team provide as well rounded offerings for all ages.
3. Survey instruments are numerous: Survey Monkey, Survey Gizmo, Kwik Survey, Zoomerang and many more. Surveys work best if they are integrated into church membership software where interests and leadership skills can be associated with those interested in either participating or providing leadership.
4. Survey Sections and Questions*
   Section Headings:
   Contact Information
   Personal Interest

Arts, Crafts, Hobbies
Fitness/Wellness
Outdoors
Sports
Trips/Social
Education
Willing to Serve (list various places of leadership)

5. If the survey is for a new ministry, a date should be made known when the surveys should be finished. Afterwards, the survey could be either part of the web site or a link sent to new members who would then take the survey.

6. From the information gathered, you will find potential participants and potential leaders and can begin programs.

The job of the recreation and sports ministry leadership team will be to: (1) tally the surveys; (2) decide which activities to start first, as indicated by the most interest found on the survey; (3) check the church calendar to choose the optimum time to begin the chosen activity to avoid conflicts with other ministry areas; (4) to enlist leaders (from indicated interest on survey); (5) to publicize the event; (6) to purchase any needed materials/supplies; (7) to conduct signups; to hold the class, activity, or workshop; (8) evaluate the event; and if successful, (9) schedule the next time you will host that event. If it was not successful, your evaluation will point out weaknesses so that they may be remedied next time.

New surveying should be done every three to five years or as needed. New members should be surveyed as they join a Bible study group or the church. New participants and new leaders will be found. On-going surveys could be offered on the church or sports ministry web site using any one of the many survey tools mentioned above.

Consider these keys to successful startup events:

- Start slowly, and pick the top three to five events/activities.
- Do only what can be done well.
- Publicize effectively.

- Check the calendar, and make sure not to conflict with other church or community events.
- Provide the budget and work within budgeting constraints.
- Find a qualified lead team of interested supporters to help carry out the event.
- Train event leaders to have a ministry mindset. The leadership team has the responsibility to teach those who lead events to use their area of interest as a tool for sharing the gospel. While this may seem elementary, it must be an intentional part of the planning process, or the event will be just an activity and not ministry.
- Do everything with quality.
- Evaluate the process.

8. Work within Existing Calendaring and Budgeting Frameworks

The recreation and sports ministry leadership team will work with the assigned staff member to see that the ministry operates within existing guidelines for calendaring and budgeting. (For sample budget worksheets, see Appendix 13: "Event Cost Projection"; Appendix 14: "Non-Event Cost Projection Worksheet"; Appendix 15: "Total Cost Projection Worksheet"; and Appendix 16: "Recreation and Sports Ministry Budget Accounts.")

9. Provide a Balanced Ministry Calendar for All Ages

Each person who gives leadership to recreation and sports ministry has his or her favorite areas or interests. The tendency of many ministry/program providers is to have an abundance of what they like, leaving out large segments of potential participants. The sports enthusiasts will naturally tend to provide program ministry in sports. The outdoors person will want to provide outdoor experiences because they see potential for activity and ministry there. The leader may not realize that this is happening. A conscientious effort must be made to provide a balanced calendar for all ages—preschoolers to senior adults—in the appropriate programming areas.

Programming is the life-blood to the ministry and key to keeping people involved. It is the reason they want to participate. Done creatively, programming will keep a ministry from becoming stale. Programming comes directly from the survey, meeting the expressed needs of constituents.

Program Planning

- Start with activities that have the most potential participants, according to the survey. The programmer should pick three to five of the most requested events.
- Work within the church calendar and budgeting system.
- Go all out to ensure success, especially if this is a new ministry.
- Promote to build a buzz with creative and imaginative advertising.
- Make the event feel larger than life, something that you would not want to miss.
- Equip to get the best results. Purchase only institutional quality equipment; use visuals to create an atmosphere for socials and provide top quality basketballs for games.
- Train leaders to have an intentional ministry mindset. Recreation and sports events are not religious in nature. Leaders must be trained to use the event, practice, or game for the Gospel's sake. Provide printed helps for leaders.

Programming Formats

- Open play/drop in (church with a facility)
- Clinics: one-day events
- Workshops: one or two-day skill enhancement events
- Classes: several sessions, basic to advanced
- Leagues/tournaments (with facilities or using rented facilities)
- Clubs/affinity groups
- Special events

A helpful tool is a programming grid. Using the grid (see sample in Appendix 17, "The Programmer's Evaluation Cube") the leader gets a quick view of what is being offered in all areas and for all ages. When he or she sees that the programming calendar is overbalanced in one direction or is leaving out one or more populations, the calendar can be adjusted to achieve balance.

10. Evaluate Progress

Any organization goes through stages:

Stage one is conceptualization. In this stage the idea is born and the vision shared with others to see if it is viable.

Stage two is preparation. Getting ready with the right infrastructure is important. With the right foundation in place, the idea can be implemented.

Stage three is evaluation. This stage is often omitted. Organizations that do not evaluate successes and failures are setting themselves up for ineffectiveness if not outright failure. The evaluation process is concerned with the collection of qualitative and quantitative information. The leadership team will evaluate each activity and, at the end of the programming year, evaluate the overall ministry. Areas to be evaluated include:

- *Administration*—Was the administration of the event/year well organized, staffed properly, planned well, and promoted adequately? Did it stay within budget?
- *Leadership/staff*—Was the staff knowledgeable and adequately trained not only in the skill being taught but in intentional ministry? Did we leverage our people resources to the best advantage?
- *The overall program/event*—Did the program/event meet its goals and impact lives? Did the program complement the vision statement of the church and ministry area?
- *Facilities*—Were the facilities adequate, well lighted, and comfortable?
- *The future*—What can we do in the future to enhance this event? Do we keep or drop the event?

Evaluation is the process of making what just happened better the next time around. Talking over and evaluating the five areas above and getting input from participants will give keen insight into the value of an event.

Organizing for recreation and sports ministry is necessary because of the sophistication of our culture and the importance of doing whatever we do with quality. The days of simply rolling out a ball cage into the gym and calling that ministry are long gone. Recreation and sports ministry is a multifaceted and multilayered ministry tool that requires much planning and coordination. Being well organized does not guarantee success. But, not being well organized decreases the chances for success precipitously! Recreation and sports ministries that exhibit professionalism, quality, and grounding in God's Word as foundation stones of their organization will bring honor to Christ and people into the kingdom and greatly increase their success potential.

If we take Scripture seriously, we must heed the Word of God when it says, "Everything must be done decently and in order" (1 Cor. 14:40).

NOTES

1. Adapted from Wendell Newman, *Organizing for Recreation,* edited by John Garner (Nashville: Convention Press, 1986), 8.
2. Ibid., 9–18.
3. Ibid., 12.
4. Ibid., 13.
5. More, Karl. "Millennials Work for Purpose, Not Paycheck," *Forbes Leadership.* http://www.forbes.com/sites/karlmoore/2014/10/02/millennials-work-for-purpose-notpaycheck/#16ebcb365a22 (accessed March 16, 2016).
6. Carlson, Ronald E., Theodore Deppe, and Janet R. MacLean. *Recreation in American Life* (Belmont: Wadsworth Publishing Company, Inc., 1963), 3–4.

6

Recreation and Sports Administration in a Ministry Setting

Dale Adkins

"For the minister, the challenge is balancing both the spiritual and the administrative."

The challenge for the minister of recreation and sports in the twenty-first century is knowing how to manage the human, physical, and fiscal resources necessary to do effective ministry. No longer can ministers merely 'shoot from the hip' to lead a church effectively; they must be able to articulate clearly how the entrusted resources will be organized, used, supervised, and evaluated for ministry. The accountability that is needed and demanded by congregations today—with respect to ministerial leadership—requires that good administrative practices be understood and implemented by today's recreation minister.

It is important to clarify the purpose of administration within the context of recreation and sports ministry. Administration is about people. While the church possesses resources (i.e., facilities, equipment, and finances), the church is people. The church is called to reach people and to multiply them as "fishers of men" as they become committed followers of Christ. The church can exist without a lot of physical assets, but its foundation is Christ. Through him, people respond and are called to serve in a particular area using their gifts, talents, natural abilities, and interests. Administration is ministry.

CHRISTIAN ADMINISTRATION

Much that has been written regarding Christian administration has been written about, for, and by pastors, and it comes from their perspective. Their research and writings are not totally devoid of the needs and issues of other ministers, associates, or directors on a church staff, but these leaders are not as well represented in the literature. This is not surprising since the majority of churches are staffed by one pastor or—as in some cases—a bi-vocational pastor. Being a part of a multi-staff experience is the exception, not the rule, for most pastors and churches.

Robert D. Dale suggests a helpful idea: "In the church and other Christian organizations, administration is growing people, not simply doing things. Administration is vital if a church is to reach its mission."[1] Growing people is also critical to the vibrancy and future of recreation and sports ministry within the local church. It is through growing people that such a ministry can accomplish its unique purpose within a local congregation's overall mission.

According to Caldwell, administration is not only a gift, but it is also people and organization.[2] Those who are called to lead are exercising their gifts in unique areas of ministry. This does not preclude the fact that continuing education is a must for the minister of the twenty-first century. It is through continuing education that a minister's gifts are developed and refined. (Professional development issues for the minister are discussed in Chapter 4.)

The people who the church is seeking to reach, teach, disciple, equip, and empower to do the ministry of the church are at the heart of ministry and administration: "The wise minister learns early on in vocational ministry that we are in the people business and sees the wisdom of getting things done with and through people. Some of these people will be paid to assist in doing church, but most of them will be volunteers in the sense that they are ordinary church members who will be challenged to discover and develop their gifts in ministry."[3]

The church is, after all, an organization, and it requires ministers to understand its unique position with respect to administration. For the minister, the challenge is balancing both the spiritual and the administrative. Recreation ministers must practice their gifts within the local church while balancing this tension.

ADMINISTRATION OF RECREATION
AND SPORTS MINISTRY

Administration of a recreation and sports ministry requires the minister to recognize and embrace the concept that recreation and sports can be ministry. Not all who serve a local congregation in this area will bear the title "minister." In some settings, the designation may be "pastor of" or "director of." Regardless of the title, the person called, empowered, and charged with the recreation and sports ministry is uniquely ministering to the needs of a postmodern culture.

Administration is biblically based and seen as a gift in the New Testament (1 Cor. 12:28), but this does not suggest that everyone who ministers through recreation and sports has or must have the gift of administration. Still, it is clear that God values the ability to orchestrate resources for the life of the church and the accomplishment of its ministry here on earth.

Today the modern church seeks to balance corporate business savvy with the ministry of the church. Some find the integration of business principles into the management of the church bothersome. Others seek to understand the principles and apply business concepts with Christian guidance. Respected business thinkers and authors, such as Ken Blanchard[4] and Peter Drucker,[5] are revered and quoted as the church strives to be more relevant and reach more people in today's world.

PERSONAL ADMINISTRATION

Each minister has strengths and weaknesses. Being able to accurately identify them will help ministers understand how they need to develop in order to manage administrative tasks responsibly and effectively. Professional development and/or other evaluation methods will help determine areas where growth is necessary so that weaknesses can be accommodated and strengths can be accentuated.

The nature of ministry is self-directed. The mission of the church and the mission of recreation and sports ministry give parameters as to what the minister should do. If a staff member holds recreation or sports responsibilities, it will likely be in a multi-staff church. The size of the church, other church staff, and the recreation and sports staff (paid or volunteer) will place demands on recreation and sports ministers to accomplish the many tasks that need attention at any given point in time. While managing time at church is important, the minister must also learn to provide for, protect, and manage his or her time off, taking the time needed to 'practice what they preach' and live a balanced life. Being a good administrator at the church means being refreshed through personal and family times of leisure away from the church.

TIME MANAGEMENT

How recreation and sports ministers utilize time will say a lot about their personal work habits and their ability to juggle responsibilities while staying focused on the tasks at hand. The challenge is seeing even the smallest task as a part of a larger ministry. If ministers see everything as having "a purpose under heaven" (Eccl. 3:1), routine experiences will continue to bring meaning throughout the course of their ministries.

Many ministers use a personal calendar to help manage their schedules. With the advent of personal computers and smart phones, some find that it is quicker and easier to manage their time by logging appointments and daily tasks electronically. A smart phone allows ministers to do multiple things as they travel from place to place, and many prefer to organize their time this way. Several methods and systems of time management are now available—each minister must decide on the method that fits their schedule best.

In larger church settings, support staff—whether a secretary, an administrative assistant, or a corps of volunteers—must be kept apprised of daily schedules. Allowing someone else to help manage time, tasks, and people can provide many benefits, including freeing the minister up to do ministry.

Determining the extent to which other staff can participate in scheduling appointments and meetings is important and will depend on one's sense of security with those on the ministry team. Once this is established, it should also be well communicated.

COMMUNICATION

The nature of the church as an organization denotes the need for communication. The body has many parts, and each part requires attention at some point from the minister. The nurturing and involvement that are necessary in the lives of coaches and leaders by the minister will be more intense and time consuming than others. Again, this is a part of the ministry of administration.

In addition to coaches and activity leaders, the recreation minister has other audiences to nurture and address at any given time. These include peer ministers, other church support staff, governing councils/boards/committees that comprise the church leadership structure, church members at large, and community agencies or organizations that require a relationship with the church through the minister.

Each minister's style of communication will either greatly enhance or greatly detract from their ministry's overall effectiveness. Ensuring that telephone calls, emails, letters, personal notes, and memos clearly reflect the minister's genuine nature is a priority. Ministry happens through these methods of communication, so it behooves the minister to use them wisely and carefully in order to maximize a positive influence on all constituents.

In today's world, the speed of life impacts the church, as well as the way ministry is done and how communication is delivered at all levels and in all settings. The key for recreation ministers is to keep in mind that everything they do must be personal. Remembering why the church exists and how the ministries in it are a part of accomplishing that purpose will guide the minister in making choices that keep every task person-centered. "If a church is to deepen spiritual lives, it has to know its members."[6] When members and their needs are known, communication can be tailored to reach them.

Communication is about sending a message and making sure the message is received. The fact that it takes multiple impressions to get specified information to an audience challenges church staff to use all outlets available. Informing church members about opportunities for growth, ministry, and outreach through recreation and sports requires creativity and making sure the information is presented in a timely, professional manner. The church's message is life-changing and eternal, so how it is communicated is important. In fact, the importance of communication cannot be emphasized enough. A wise minister will strive to use all possible means of communication so that individuals stay informed and updated about ministry as it relates to the church in general and to the pastor and staff in particular. This will help allay 'surprises' and misinformation.

CONFLICT RESOLUTION

Even with the best of intentions, miscommunication can lead to conflict. Some people deal with conflict well, while others avoid it at all costs. The minister of recreation will encounter conflict because the nature of the ministry is personal and directly impacts people's lives.

No organization is devoid of conflict, and this includes the church. Where there are people—there is conflict. Osborne suggests that the three groups in the church in which conflict will happen are: (1) the congregation, (2) the governing boards/councils/committees, and (3) the staff.[7] In recreation and sports ministry, conflicts may occur within program areas, volunteer management, sponsorship of an activity, or other areas. The key to neutralizing conflict is having a strategy to deal directly and openly with it.

Jordan proposes a seven-phase model for managing difficulties. The phases are:

1. Define the objectives.
2. Identify the problem.
3. Analyze and interpret data.
4. Facilitate solutions.
5. Select the best solution.
6. Generate and implement the solution.
7. Evaluate results.[8]

Each phase ultimately moves toward conflict resolution, though resolution does not necessarily mean that the final solution will be satisfactory to all involved.

Jordan's steps toward resolution allow all involved to move toward a sense of reconciliation, which should always be the goal of the church, even in matters of conflict. This approach enables everyone to participate in seeking solutions while having ownership in the process. A systematic plan for dealing with conflicts—which will occur within all three groups at some point—will allow the recreation minister to thoughtfully and carefully approach conflict resolution.

The way ministers of recreation manage professional time, communication, and conflict shapes their personal administration and their leadership. Understanding how time, communication, and conflict influence their ministry will make the difference in the longevity of ministers' impact.

STRATEGIC PLANNING

Strategic planning is not a destination but the process by which an organization gives direction to its work. Focusing on how each ministry interacts with the church allows members and leaders to shape the ministry of the church as it reaches the world for Christ's kingdom. There are four types of planning that any organization—regardless of size—should do. In addition to strategic planning, churches (and the sports ministries within them) should devote time and energy toward comprehensive planning, community planning, and internal systems planning.

Wegner and Jarvi suggest that "the strategic planning process provides a means for developing a shared vision of the organization's future and then determining the best way to make this vision a reality."[9] Recreation and sports ministers have the opportunity within the overall mission of the church to plan strategically for a specific area of ministry.

The life of a recreation and sports ministry directly correlates to the church's mission as a whole. When church members recognize recreation and sports ministry as part of the church's mission to reach people with the Gospel, they will not only commit to the ministry, but will also encourage those outside the church to join them in church-sponsored leisure activities. Strategic planning for every area of ministry, including recreation and sports, is rooted in the overall church mission statement and its strategic plan.

The minister of sports and recreation is critical in developing the strategic planning process for recreation and sports ministry. Making sure that all three groups—the congregation, the governing groups, and staff—are represented in the process is a must. Particularly with recreation and sports ministry, other areas of ministry and interest groups should help define the future of a recreation and sports ministry by contributing thoughts and suggestions.

The resulting road map will help the recreation and sports minister to develop and to make decisions for the ministry. This is an ongoing process—strategic planning is not a onetime event but a continual function of a vibrant and effective ministry.

There are many strategic planning models. The following simple, six-step process incorporates the basic steps that will enable almost any ministry to achieve its goals.

1. **Environmental Scan**

The church must constantly be evaluating its ministries both from within and without. Surveying relevant data and gathering information about competing programs, possible risks, and the program itself is called an environmental scan. An environmental scan is a broad look at how a church recreation and sports ministry provides ministry and service in the context of its community. For instance, if a church is located in a coastal region, winter sports might not be part of the community context. Once an environmental scan has been done, the recreation minister is then able to lead interested groups and leaders in the church to help give movement to the process.

2. Analysis of Ministry Situation

An organized and systematic strategy to gather information is a SWOT analysis. This analysis allows recreation and sports ministers to look at the ministry's Strengths, Weaknesses, ministry Opportunities, and Threats that could hamper or stop the ministry from being effective. This information will help guide the ministry in future decisions based on realistic and honest appraisals from many perspectives. A church may be blessed to have a large playground or sports fields and can offer their use to the community or even manage events because of the expertise of staff or members. Here the *strength* of trained staff and the *opportunity* to provide physical facilities would fit into a SWOT analysis.

3. Vision and Mission Statements

After the information has been gathered from the environmental scan and the SWOT analysis, attention will shift to a vision statement. Scriptural guidance helps at this point: "Where there is no vision, the people perish" (Prov. 29:18). This admonition also applies to recreation and sports ministry. The planning committee needs to answer the question, "Where do we want the ministry to be in the future?" A vision statement can help answer this question and define the preferred future for the recreation and sports ministry. This is not to discredit or fail to acknowledge the Spirit's leadership in committee member selection or work to be done. The whole process involves seeking divine leadership. It is to help the church focus on, and better understand, what good work God wants to do within and through a local congregation and its recreation and sports ministry.

The recreation and sports ministry must clearly define its purpose within the context of the local church. Developing a mission statement is the next step in the process. For most recreation and sports ministries, the mission statement centers on strengthening church fellowship and providing a vehicle for outreach and evangelism. Some churches may also see it as an opportunity to minister to the community. The intent and heart of the ministry would be outreach through relationship, but the expanded mission would be driven by the vision statement and the information collected from the strategic planning process.

4. Goals and Objectives

Once vision and mission statements have been developed out of information gathered from an environmental scan and SWOT analysis, it is time to write out some goals and objectives. Goals and objectives must be developed for both the recreation and sports ministry as a whole as well as for the individual areas/programs that make up the ministry. Rossman and Schlatter present insight on how goals and objectives are interrelated at all levels.[10] This concept of interrelated goals and objectives gives direction to recreation and sports ministry as it relates to strategic planning.

5. Action Plans

Strategic planning allows the development of goals and objectives for many different aspects of the plan. Action plans track the goals and objectives and monitor them in relation to accomplishment, deadlines, and persons responsible. Without this step, the planning process will never reach its full potential. Action plans include the steps needed to accomplish a given task: What is going to be done? Who is responsible for what? When should these tasks be done? Who will purchase/provide/collect/supply any equipment needed? An action plan master list should be kept by the minister who will periodically check with the assigned person(s) to make sure the tasks are completed on time.

6. Evaluation

Once the plan has been carried out, regular evaluation will complete the planning process. It will help identify successes, failures, and decisions that can ensure the future effectiveness of each area of ministry within the overall recreation and sports ministry. This part of the strategic planning process should be done consistently for all programs within the ministry. It will assist in the annual review of the entire recreation and sports ministry. Any adjustments and changes to programs can be based on solid information and feedback from a variety of audiences.

The recreation minister must make this step a priority in order for the planning process to be effective and to move the ministry forward.

It is easy to base the value of a program solely on numbers. Such analysis is the business world's model. But if the church is trying to deepen and influence lives for Christ, then evaluating other types of information will prove necessary—both quantitative and qualitative analyses should be incorporated. Keep in mind that all areas/programs of recreation and sports ministry should be evaluated in order to assist and give direction to the overall strategic planning process. If evaluation is not intentional or regularly planned, then decisions will be made on unreliable and inaccurate information—all in the name of ministry! Do not forget that an important part of evaluation is seeing how the recreation and sports ministry strategic plan complements and fits within the church's overall plan.

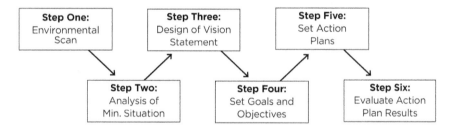

Six Step Strategic Planning Process

Figure 6-1: Six Step Strategic Planning Process

PERSONNEL MANAGEMENT

Once strategic planning is complete, the next area to address is personnel management. The strategic plan will determine the staff needed to execute the actions within the plan. Regardless of whether staff members are paid or volunteer, fulltime or part-time, the recreation minister will be required to work with at least one or more of these personnel categories to carry out the vision and mission of the ministry. Even a single-staff pastor must be able to guide and lead a staff of individuals to minister through recreation and sports.

Managing staff, whether paid or volunteer, requires more similar strategies than different, so the word staff will refer to both paid staff and volunteers unless otherwise noted. Areas to be considered are staff relations, volunteer management, working with committees/councils/boards, and interns.

Staff Relations

Individuals who choose to work with a particular minister want to be involved in a particular area of ministry. They might be motivated by wanting to use their spiritual gifts, skills, and interests from vocational or recreational experience(s), a deep desire to serve God in a unique way, or the charisma of the minister. The bottom line is that they want to be part of a winning team. Whatever the motivation, the minister must mold and shape the ministry team to be effective, while at the same time making sure the experience is satisfying and fulfilling for everyone involved.

Depending on the staff structure within a church, the recreation minister may have several options when it comes to personnel. One approach is to work with a staff minister who oversees personnel for the entire church, with laypeople involved in the process. The second approach is to work directly with a church personnel committee in staff selection; this is particularly for paid staff. A third approach is for the recreation minister to work with a church committee/council/board in staff selection. In a fourth approach, the church empowers the minister to seek staff and to be responsible for hiring and terminating on behalf of the church. The fourth approach may be the least preferred if work-related problems arise with lay leaders and staff members in the future. These conflicts would reflect poorly on the recreation minister.

A recreation minister may have responsibilities of recruiting, interviewing, hiring, training, supervising, evaluating, and terminating. All of these tasks take time and energy. The minister must learn and adhere to procedures unique to the church. Knowing the expectations of the church regarding personnel will help the minister in staff selection and make the process more positive for everyone involved.

Once the right staff are in place, staff development is a critical and ongoing responsibility of the recreation minister. One strategy to ensure success is to meet with staff members individually on a weekly or semiweekly basis. This allows staff to have the minister's undivided attention and enables the minister to monitor projects and areas of responsibility. Staff are able to seek guidance and insight that will assist in their success. A minister's ministry is with his or her staff.

Bjorklund quotes Bobb Biehl's questions for getting better results from staff. Leaders should regularly ask:

1. What decisions do you need from me?
2. What problems are keeping you from reaching your goals?
3. What plans are you making that have not been discussed?
4. What progress have you made?
5. On a scale of one to ten, how are you personally? Why?
6. How can I be praying for you?[11]

In this approach to staff development, the minister empowers staff to move ahead without someone looking over their shoulders. Recreation ministers must feel secure about the ministry team as well as their ability to share the ministry with others. Using this collaborative approach with a person-centered focus helps define the nature of the work to be done within Christian ministry.

Wise recreation and sports ministers will recognize the importance of other church staff to their ministry and realize that recreation and sports ministry supports all other ministries in the church. Tidwell gives some insight on the relationship between the pastor and other staff members:

1. Acknowledge and respect one another's call of God.
2. Let all ministers be called by church action.
3. Extend trust and develop trust with one another.
4. Practice frequent, regular, and accurate communication.
5. Be close enough to one another that staff are confident of closeness, even when physical proximity is not close.[12]

Even though time is spent with staff in one-on-ones and staff meetings, some individuals might not fit the position or the ministry team or are unable to perform. When this occurs, documentation over a period of time is needed to reconcile the matter.

The tedious job of documenting is necessary to build the body of information required to terminate or redirect the staff member to either fill another position within the organization (church) or seek another avenue for ministry/employment. The recreation minister should view this as an opportunity for the growth of both the employee and the minister.

Terminating a staff member is a sensitive issue and can be an emotional experience for the employee as well as the supervisor. Making sure that expectations are clearly articulated at the time of hiring is one key to avoiding this situation altogether. Securing reliable references and using situational interview questions can assist in a positive hiring and placement of staff.

Having staff means committing time, energy, and resources. But it also means sharing the joys and the sorrows of ministry and working together to equip the saints to go out into the world.

Volunteer Management

Working with volunteers is different than working with paid staff. They need a management style that is more like coaching than supervising. A volunteer's motivation is not extrinsic—working for a reward or paycheck. Instead, it is intrinsic—based on gaining personal satisfaction through making a difference for a cause. Volunteers are not forever. Life situations, family life cycles, and changing personal interests and experiences make volunteer management a fluid task. Stewart quotes Peter Drucker: "Volunteers need special handling—they can't be bossed like galley slaves."[13]

Volunteerism in the church is big business. As Stewart indicates, religion, when compared to corporate America, is fairly sizable: "Whatever else it is, religion is big business. America has more clergy than Ford and Chrysler together have employees. If U.S. religion were a company, it would be No. 5 on the Fortune 500, its $50 billion of revenues putting it behind IBM and just ahead of GE. Church land and buildings are worth uncounted billions. And God's business is really far bigger than mammon's numbers suggest: The figures don't include volunteer work, worth a jaw-dropping $75 billion a year."[14]

Volunteers are agents of the church and act on its behalf. Therefore, churches and their ministries are liable for actions taken by volunteers. As a matter of risk management, recruiting and training volunteers must be approached in the same manner that recruiting and training paid staff would be.

Volunteers need a task description. While it is true that many jobs within the church do not demand a formal job description, if volunteers assume major leadership roles within recreation and sports ministry, a formal job description should be developed and approved by leaders within the church. Volunteers want to know who their supervisors are, the expectations for the task at hand, training that is provided, length of commitment, and what, if any, recognition can be expected.

Some volunteer literature suggests that organizations can offer benefits to a volunteer. Benefits can be both tangible and intangible. Intangible benefits for volunteers include using their skills and talents to serve God through a particular ministry or gaining satisfaction from making a difference in the life of a child or teen. Tangible benefits include an annual recognition banquet, money for professional development or training to equip them for a specific ministry, or mileage reimbursement for travel required by the program. Each church and recreation minister should determine the type of benefits the church can provide based on its resources and philosophy. The most important thing a church can offer is a kind "thank you." Hearing, "You did a great job!" is meaningful for most volunteers.

Committees/Boards/Councils

In most churches, governing structures are comprised of volunteers. Depending on the unique organization and approach to governance within a local congregation, most churches use committees—sometimes called ministry teams, boards, or councils, or some combination thereof.

Each of these leadership groups form and re-form as people join and leave throughout the life of the group. Whenever a new person joins a leadership team, the group begins a new history. The recreation minister must constantly be aware of group dynamics and the vitality of the committees, boards, or councils which help oversee this unique ministry within the church.

Many churches use committees in a variety of ways. Some committees are policy-making in nature and oversee particular areas of ministry. In some instances, they function as "working committees" and make business decisions regarding the ministries. The role of the working group varies according to each individual church and how governance is viewed within that church. It also depends on how the mission of the church is carried out and which fundraising and sponsorship practices are considered acceptable.

Just like individual volunteers, committees/boards/councils demand an investment of time, energy, resources, and recognition by the recreation minister. The purpose, task, and mission of the group will dictate how much investment will be required by the minister. The dividends of a smoothly functioning and involved committee are a result of a commitment to committee training and development. Positive results in ministry will be in direct proportion to the value the minister places on the role of committees in the life of the recreation and sports ministry.

Noyce suggests four areas of attention that committees need in order to be effective. Groups need: (1) cohesion, (2) task performance, (3) personal satisfaction, and (4) vision.[15] Committees need to feel connected. This can be done through a variety of ways, depending on how the group does business. An annual retreat might give longtime and just-appointed/elected committee members the opportunity to create a new history as they serve together. Committees need cohesiveness in order to understand the group's task and to feel a sense of accomplishment when it is done. Each member must also gain a sense of satisfaction for their personal commitment to the life of a group—feeling like they are making a difference is a critical factor in people's willingness to continue to serve.

Underneath it all is the committee's ability to understand and articulate its vision. When this happens, all work and decision-making can be filtered by and evaluated according to the vision outlined in the strategic plan. This is yet another way that strategic planning supports the ministry of the church—and specifically the recreation and sports ministry.

Interns

Interns from a college, university, or seminary can also be a great source of leadership and personnel. But, keep in mind that interns are not free labor. In fact, most institutions would likely not place a student intern with a recreation and sports ministry if that perception was given when enlisting the intern.

A minister should seek out an intern because of the intern's commitment to ministry and to the profession. If both the minister and the intern hope to benefit from the relationship, the minister should be prepared to invest time, energy, and resources into the intern. Hiring an intern is a good way to groom a new staff member, and a positive internship may result in pursuing the intern to fill an opening on staff. The most important thing to remember, however, is that an intern is a student learner and not a paid staff member.

Most interns participate for a semester or more, depending on their institution, and many receive some type of academic credit for the experience. The minister should work with the school's intern supervisor when making the arrangements. This may require submitting credentials and professional involvement to qualify the church as a site for an intern placement. The recreation and sports ministry should be able to articulate what kinds of experiences the intern can expect, the support (financial and housing) available, and any other features or benefits of the internship.

Having an intern is a mentoring opportunity for a minister, as interns need time and supervision. One-on-one weekly meetings will help them learn from the recreation and sports minister, and opportunities to fully participate in church staff culture will give them a broad perspective of ministry, helping them understand the daily ministry and work dynamics. Both are important.

BUDGETING

Budgeting can be complex or simple, depending on which process a congregation has adopted. Simply put, a budget reflects the financial commitment of an organization to the things its members deem important and valuable. This statement of intent is a result of planning and visioning and is a public declaration of what will happen if church resources (financial, human, and physical) are available.

The five aspects of budgeting are:

1. Planning
2. Authorization
3. Management
4. Control
5. Evaluation[16]

The church may have different ways of implementing each aspect, but each one is necessary—not only for the budgeting process to be effective but for the recreation and sports ministry to reach its goals as well.

Most churches use either a line-item budget or a ministry-based budget to reflect their commitment to ministry for the upcoming year.[17] Within the broader field of recreation and leisure services, other categories of budgets can include zero-based, revenue, cash flow, and performance.

A line-item budget indicates items for funding without regard for specific program areas or ministries. A ministry-based budget reflects planning and support for the mission and goals set forth by individuals and groups within the recreation and sports ministry. Allocation of resources to specific areas of ministry allows the congregation and governing structures to understand and share the vision for recreation and sports ministry.

Johnson indicates that there are eight steps in the ministry-based process of budgeting:

1. Analyze ministries.
2. Propose ministry actions.
3. Evaluate ministry actions.
4. Prepare the budget.
5. Present the budget.
6. Promote the budget.
7. Report ministry progress.
8. Review and evaluate.[18]

The recreation minister must understand the unique budgeting process within each local church. The process should involve staff and committees that are related to the recreation and sports ministry. This grassroots involvement will give ownership to more individuals and groups so they can promote the budget that supports the recreation and sports ministry.

The recreation and sports minister must learn how to read spreadsheets and make budget forecasts, manage a budget, and, most importantly, work with a budget or finance committee. This committee is usually made up of business people from the church who understand budgeting and budget management. Wise recreation and sports ministers will prepare themselves to think like a business manager when it comes to finances. One of the best ways to do this is to take some basic business classes while in school, at local community college, or online. Understanding what a budget is, how it works, how to manage it, and how to work with the budget or finance committee will improve the relationship between the committee members and the minister, fostering trust and confidence.

RISK MANAGEMENT

The church also has the responsibility to deal with and manage for risk, particularly in the areas of recreation and sports. The litigious society in which the church finds itself today requires a recreation minister who understands risk management.

What is risk management? "Risk management process has three phases: (a) risk identification and assessment, (b) risk response strategies, or what to do about the risks, and (c) management to reduce the frequency and severity of the risks through an operational plan."[19]

Risks within recreation and sports ministry come in many forms. Risks are present not only in activities but also in equipment and facilities, staff that are leading activities, and financial choices that could damage the overall budget and ministry of the church. The astute minister will analyze and evaluate all areas of ministry, making sure that a risk management plan is in place for every aspect of the recreation and sports ministry. Some churches will have a "Risk Management Committee" to assist the minister with this important task.

Liability issues could be damaging to the church's ministries and staff. The minister should thoroughly understand state laws and whether they apply to the church. Documentation is vital for protection and to show prudence on the part of the service provider, which, in this case, would be the church recreation and sports ministry. Common forms used in recreation and sports settings include parental/guardian permission (Appendix 11), participant information (Appendix 9), accident/incident report (Appendix 10), and abuse/neglect report (Appendix 12).

Recreation and sports ministers have the responsibility and the opportunity to influence people as they do ministry. A biblically based understanding of administration as a call to serve others will guide the professional life of the minister. Personal administration through time management, communication, and conflict resolution allows the recreation minister to exhibit specific areas of leadership. Strategic planning, personnel management, risk management, budgeting, and partnerships are tools the recreation minister uses to accomplish ministry. The key for the recreation minister to remember is that administration is done not as a control mechanism, but in order to better reach people with the Gospel and to change lives for the kingdom. Ministry through recreation and sports is people-centered.

NOTES

1. Dale, Robert D. "Managing Christian Churches and Not for Profit Organizations," *Christian Administration Handbook* (Nashville: Broadman & Holman, 1997), 3.
2. Caldwell, William G. "A Theology of Administration," *Southwestern Journal of Theology* 37 (1995).
3. Ibid., 33.
4. Ernsting, Ed. "Turning Vision into Reality: The One Minute Manager Clarifies the Real Issues," *Leadership* 17 (1996).
5. Ernsting, Ed. "Managing to Minister: An Interview with Peter Drucker," *Leadership* 10 (1989).
6. Stewart, Thomas A. "Turning Around the Lord's Business: Marketing and Management Applied to Churches," *Fortune* (September 25, 1989): 117.
7. Osborne, Larry W. "Stopping Conflict Before It Starts," *Leadership* 16 (1995): 53.
8. Jordan, Debra J. *Leadership in Leisure Services: Making a Difference* (State College, PA: Venture Publishing, 2001), 151.
9. Wegner, Dan and Christopher K. Jarvi, "Planning for Strategic Management." In *Management of Park and Recreation Agencies*, edited by Betty van der Smissen, Merry Moiseichik, Vern J. Hartenburg, and Louis F. Twardzik (Ashburn, VA: National Recreation and Park Association, 1999), 104.
10. Rossman, J. Robert and Barbara Elwood Schlatter. *Recreation Programming: Designing Leisure Experiences*, 3rd ed. (Champaign, IL: Sagamore Publishing, 2000), 91–94.
11. Bjorklund, Kurt. "What Your Team Needs from You: Six Questions for Better Staff Development," *Leadership* 20 (1999): 110.
12. Tidwell, Charles A. "The Church Staff as a Ministering Team," *Southwestern Journal of Theology* 29 (1987): 33–34.
13. Stewart, 120.
14. Ibid., 116.

15. Noyce, Gaylord. "How to Keep Committees Focused and Effective," *The Christian Ministry* 26 (January 1995): 19.

16. Holdnak II, Andrew, Edward M. Mahoney, and James R. Garges, "Budgeting," *Management of Park and Recreation Agencies.*

17. Johnson, Bob I. "Planning and Budgeting," *Christian Administration Handbook,* 143–45.

18. Ibid.

19. Kaiser, Ronald and Ken Robinson, "Risk Management," *Management of Park and Recreation Agencies,* 713.

7

Recreation and Sports Ministry

PROGRAMMING PROCESS AND THEORY IN A CHURCH SETTING

Paul Stutz

"A program is the track that guides the participant toward the leisure experience, not the experience itself."

Program planning for ministry must create environments in which people might experience God.

The list of ingredients that comprise successful recreation and sports ministries often reaches to infinity with the vast amount of internal and external forces that affect ministerial outcomes. Geography, competition from within the community for leisure allegiances, and available resources can have a tremendous effect on ministry outcome.

But what ingredient is key? What one thing is common to recreation and sports ministries, regardless of the internal and external forces at work? Answers can be diverse: A leader sold out to God's will? Yes, of course. A charismatic personality that influences people to participate in ministry activities? Perhaps. Someone with a vast knowledge of and experience in leading and coaching in various types of recreation and sports venues? By all means.

The list could go on and on, yet one thing emerges as a common thread. The ability to program, or function as a programmer of activities and facilities, is a paramount consideration for someone fulfilling his or her ministry calling within a recreation and sports ministry. Morlee Maynard suggests that in any recreation or sports ministry, creative programming will be the key to accomplishing its goals.[1] When considering the ministry of recreation and sports to be only a small slice of the total leisure-service delivery system, Rossman and Schlatter address the focus of all recreation and sports professionals, stating that programming is the major function of the profession and is necessary for the existence of leisure-service organizations.[2]

The ability to combine the ingredients of people, environment, and equipment into an event that effects positive change in the lives of those who participate might be considered a gift, and many ministers and leaders in the field of recreation and sports ministries are truly gifted people. On the other hand, it takes additional time and toil for most of us to muster what could be considered a successful recreation and sports event from a ministry perspective. A plan or format is needed to get the most out of ministry energies. The following pages address some areas of concern that assist in ensuring that programming efforts and resource use will result in ministry.

PROGRAMMING FOUNDATIONS

As with other areas of leisure-service delivery, in ministry, the recreation and sports program is the means to an end. Rossman and Schlatter state that the end result of recreation programming should be the leisure experience. Defined, a recreation or sports program is "a designed opportunity for a leisure experience to occur."[3]

A program then is the track that guides the participant toward the leisure experience, not the experience itself. Like an order of worship for a church service, it guides the parishioner toward worship but is not worship in and of itself.

RECREATION AND SPORTS MINISTRY PROGRAMMING MODEL

All too often ministries are developed on the coattails of other successful ventures played out in other congregations or sports ministry environments. What works well in some ministry environments does succeed elsewhere. However, a recreation and sports ministry that produces the most fruit seems to follow a plan, guided by a mission or purpose that becomes a common thread sewing the entire ministry programming process together.

Multiple programming processes have been introduced, each having its own unique element that brings predicted success to the programmer of recreation activities and events.[4] Adapting from the various models, effective ministry can be practiced. The eternal spiritual consequences and God's kingdom purposes are the differences experienced between programming for recreation and sports ministry and programming energies spent in other areas of recreation delivery services.

Program planning might be considered the development of environments in which people might experience leisure, but program planning for ministry must create environments in which people might experience God. An adapted programming model to guide energies and efforts toward ministry being accomplished can be seen in the following steps:

- Assess needs
- Identify ministry objectives
- Design programs for ministry
- Implement ministries
- Evaluate ministries
- Determine disposition of ministries

At each step within the model, intentional ministry efforts need to be assessed before continuing to the next phase. Modifications may need to be made in order to be the most effective steward where resource utilization is concerned. As a process, recreation and sports ministry programming is inherently dynamic. Nothing stands still; the process always moves. Using a plan for ministry, successful recreation and sports programmers are action-oriented and react to the changing needs of people and the ebb and flow of ministry direction.

1. Assess Needs

In ministry environments, leaders often find themselves in anxious times. Events have been planned, publicity has been implemented, and yet people still do not respond to program offerings as leaders expect. Chances are that the target audience for the event was not consulted about their interests and favorite activities. It is easier to plan an event around a target group's preferred activities than to recruit people for an event after the activities have been determined and planned.

Recreation and sports ministry programs should be designed as a response to the church's or organization's assessment of individual and group recreational needs. The attitudes and feelings expressed through a needs assessment should not be taken lightly. People recreate for a variety of reasons, but all reasons point to meeting needs. For this reason, the recreation minister must be mindful of the many physical, emotional, social, psychological, and spiritual needs that are met through recreation participation.[5]

Carpenter and Howe state that "the needs assessment process is vitally important as it sets the tone for the rest of the programming process."[6] It is the element that sets the stage for the development and direction of the ministry plan.

Needs assessments provide the recreation and sports minister two things: First, they generate program possibilities. The data gathered tells the ministry programmer where to begin concerning program offerings as well as which activities and events to avoid because of lack of commitment to participate. Second, needs assessments allow for input from those the ministry desires to reach.[7] The opportunity to discover activities that people want is provided from the most reputable source.

Probably the most widely used needs assessment instrument in recreation and sports ministry venues is the survey. Surveys help the recreation minister feel the heartbeat of people concerning program offerings. Inherent in surveys are also the following advantages:

Surveys can be comprehensive as needs assessment tools.—Depending on time and money, surveys can measure anything from pure demographics to complex items such as feelings and attitudes. Surveys can, and should, be customized. Information gathered to support a recreation and sports ministry in one location will not suffice as a basis for ministry in another church. Tailor-design the instrument to your own target populations— your congregation and your community.

Surveys are versatile.—The survey can be administered orally, in writing, by phone, or through email or webpage attachments.

Surveys are flexible.—The information one seeks can be designed specifically into the instrument without the survey becoming biased. Computers also allow for the acquisition of vast amounts of data.

Surveys are efficient.—It does not take a battalion of people to administer a survey. At most, a recreation and sports ministry team or committee can easily handle the job.8 With the availability of web-based and cloud-based assessment programs, surveying people about their leisure needs becomes an easily accessible tool for the church recreation and sports programmer.

Though it has been established as the standard for determining which recreation and sports ministry programs will best meet needs, the survey is not without deficiencies. Survey weaknesses include:

Surveys are not the ultimate answer in determining programs.—They are a great tool for determination purposes, but other means of assessment should be considered as well.

Simple observation may at times be the most helpful tool for the recreation minister. To all but the strongest Christians, church attendance is simply another leisure choice. Attending church on a Sunday morning lines up with other choices—golfing, camping, or spending a day at the lake. A wise leader in recreation and sports ministries is concerned with where people are and what they are doing when they are absent from church—for spiritual reasons, yes, but also to see if it is possible to harness the passion people have for other leisure pursuits that supersede their worship attendance from time to time and motivate them to be passionate about sharing in a corporate setting.

To put it bluntly, the person who says he can worship God in his bass boat more effectively than in the pew may not just be making excuses. Recreation and sports ministers need to observe these pursuits—not to be condemning, but to be encouraging people to bring this passion for spending time with God into the rest of the body of Christ whenever it gathers.

These ministers need to observe what is happening within recreation and sports trends. Can some of these leisure activities be harnessed for ministry purposes? Can intentional evangelism and spiritual growth be the result of incorporating trendsetting sports and leisure pursuits? The answer to both questions is yes, provided the activities are wholesome and positive.

Surveys can be misunderstood.—Most survey instruments used in recreation and sports ministry settings involve the vague category of asking people whether they are interested in a certain activity. This does provide data from which ministry can be developed but only to a limited degree. Asking people if they are interested in certain activities becomes problematic because everyone is interested in everything to a certain degree. To some, an activity is their life's passion. To others, the same activity is only a passing thought, but still they have a level of interest. The data received from a survey in recreation and sports ministry needs to have what could be called a "field of dreams" concept; that is, if we offer it, will they come? A programmer needs to know a person's actual intentions toward participation in a recreation and sports ministry function.

Some people become exuberant on paper and especially with a mouse! A properly developed survey, whether hard copy or computer generated, will keep people within the bounds of reality as they complete the form. A needs assessment instrument that returns with all activities highly affirmed gives the recreation and sports ministry programmer no better sense of ministry development than instruments that return blank. Here, again, simplicity and tailor-made design help to keep responses within the bounds of realistic program delivery for ministry purposes. Surveys should not include activities and events the ministry cannot deliver. Those activities that are resource prohibitive or do not meet the criteria for ministry purposes need not be included in a survey. Not only does this make good sense, but it keeps people limited to what can be done and keeps the exuberance found in survey completion to a minimum.

2. Identify Ministry Objectives

For decades now, management systems have been driven by schematics and plans that guide their efforts. These plans are based on mission/purpose statements and the development of a related set of goals and objectives that direct organizational efforts toward a mission. Churches and ministries have joined the race to become more efficient in their physical and fiscal expenditures as they attempt to make their efforts significant for the kingdom of God—though some may perceive corporate structure in the church as unscriptural.

Of all managerial entities needing to be guided effectively through goals and objectives, ministries should lead the way. The outcome of ministry is far more important than a product the public simply wants or needs. Ministry deals with the eternal souls of people, not the temporal desires that may be the result of other management-oriented efforts. Without purpose/mission, goals, and objectives to guide the efforts of a recreation and sports ministry, energy is often misdirected or wasted. A purpose statement answers the question: Why does the ministry exist? Goals answer the question: What does the ministry hope to accomplish? Objectives answer the question: What results does the ministry expect to achieve?[10]

A recreation and sports ministry cannot function without a clear statement describing its reason for existence—a mission or purpose statement. The purpose or mission statement for a recreation and sports ministry should be directly related to, and supportive of, the overall mission of the church or governing entity. If the ministry is a stand-alone organization, then its purpose or mission will be the foundation on which all ministry efforts will be placed. A mission statement allows the ministry to focus on awareness of direction, purpose, and a reason for being.[11]

In developing a dynamic purpose or mission statement to guide the efforts of a recreation and sports ministry, the church functions of worship, evangelism, missions, ministry, discipleship, and fellowship would serve well as a basis.[12] Ministry mission should be developed with the idea that a mission accomplished will result in the fulfillment of such functions. Additionally, any activity or event sponsored by the recreation and sports ministry should have the intentional purpose of directly relating to at least one of the above church functions. Without such a target to shoot for in ministry, the delivery of recreation and sports activities will only be activity for activity's sake.

A statement of ministry mission cannot be accurately developed without first considering what Richard Ensman calls strategic strengths and weaknesses. Strategic strengths related to recreation and sports ministry include ministry resources, both tangible and intangible, that allow the ministries to flow with efficiency and effectiveness. Strategic weaknesses involve staff, volunteers, facilities, equipment, or other resource limitations that would hinder or prevent a ministry from producing expected results.[13]

Forming a mission statement is a complex process, and determining which methods to use could cause anxiety within the leadership of a recreation and sports ministry. This is not to say that mission or purpose formulation is all doom and gloom. On the contrary, it should be looked upon as an adventure of determining and 'putting feet' to the will of God through recreation and sports.

A mission or purpose statement for ministry should define three things: audience, value, and uniqueness. First, the mission statement defines the target audience. Who should be affected by the recreation and sports ministry? Why would people come and invest their time and lives in this ministry? Second, the statement should define a value premise. This premise is based not on what the recreation and sports ministry does but in terms of the fundamental value it represents in meeting the ministry needs of the target group. Third, a statement of mission or purpose should delineate what makes the recreation and sports ministry special. To put it all together, what is the ministry's special means for creating value in order to win and sustain the allegiance of the people it is trying to reach?[14]

Albrecht delineates the characteristics of a valid statement of mission or purpose. An effective statement should be:

- *Definitive*—It defines what the person needs, the organizational values available (ministries), and the means to get the two together.
- *Identifying*—It makes the ministry clear.
- *Concise*—A basic statement of mission should easily be written on the back of a business card.
- *Actionable*—It gives the reader some idea of what the statement looks like in action.
- *Memorable*—The statement should be something reachable (within the bounds of faith), yet spectacular![15]

Rossman and Schlatter state that there is a hierarchical structure or arrangement of using goals and objectives that begin with the mission or purpose statement. This statement delimits what the ministry will accomplish and is not measurable. Mission accomplishment, however, is measured through a series of goal and objective statements that are increasingly more specific until an objective is born that is operationally clear, specific, and measurable.[16] V. Kerry Inman agrees that goals are general statements about expected results, yet objectives are concrete statements about measurable results that can be used to determine if the goals were met.[17]

Goals are broad in scope yet enduring in concept. Goals are usually formulated by recreation and sports ministry leadership, perhaps with the assistance of a board of directors or ministry team or committee. The efforts of such groups in the formulation process should include a glimpse at past ministry effectiveness, current ministries, and future ministry hopes and dreams.

Examples of valuable past information for goal construction include successful (and unsuccessful) ministries, budget and resource history, and demographic changes, especially church membership. Types of valuable current information include member involvement in ministry, actions other churches or ministry organizations are doing in the community, and the local image of the church or ministry organization. Data concerning the future includes socioeconomic trends and demographic forecasts.[18]

Goals are broad, enduring statements that express some desired result. They guide a recreation and sports ministry in determining what is important and what achievements are needed to accomplish ministry mission. Neil Dougherty and Diane Bonanno suggest that when writing goals, the statements should:

- Support the mission or purpose statement
- Be acceptable to congregation members or ministry organization members
- Be broad—broad goals are flexible goals that endure with the changing times
- Be clearly stated
- Be written using language that all can understand
- Be within the realm of possibility. Goals in recreation and sports ministry should have a faith element but not be viewed as impossible.[19]

Rossman and Schlatter give excellent insight into proper wording when formulating goals for recreation and sports ministries. Goal and objective statements should include:

- *An infinitive*—Each statement should begin with the infinitive marker to followed by a verb indicative of the action to be taken.
- *A subject*—Each statement should contain a subject that focuses on a finished product and accomplishment.
- *A measurement device*—Each statement should make clear how accomplishing of the goal will be measured and documented—a time frame.

It should be noted, however, that some statements are simply declarations of an agency's (church's or ministry's) intention to accomplish something or to give specific direction.[20] The following are examples of appropriate goals for a recreation and sports ministry:

- To maximize participation in the church recreation center on Friday evenings
- To develop a sports ministry
- To become more evangelistic in our leagues and tournaments

Once goals have been established, the mission achievement focus becomes more specific with the development of objectives that are the operational channels through which goals are achieved. The objective element of achieving recreation and sports ministry mission becomes the track on which the mission train travels. Objectives are the movement of the mission by the people. People become practically involved in ministry through the fulfillment of ministry objectives.

Dale McConkey states that using objectives properly in the church requires active involvement and participation by all members.[21] People orientation continues as Stoner and Freeman contend the "objectives clarify tasks and give people a better understanding of their role in the mission. Objectives also challenge individuals. They give them a sense of purpose and increase motivation."[22] Ministry is like another administrative task: it is most effective when accomplished through people. People want opportunities to share in ministry. Through people, both the mission and the missionary are fulfilled.

When developing objectives, certain characteristics should be considered. Objectives should:

- Be clear and concise
- Be in written form
- Name specific results in key areas
- Be stated for a specific period of time
- Be stated in measurable terms
- Be consistent with the overall mission/purpose
- Be attainable, but with sufficient challenge[23]

Examples of objectives that relate to previously expressed sample goals might read:

Goal:
- To develop a sports ministry.

Objectives:
- To develop a coed basketball league for children ages six to eleven years of age by December 1, 20___, with at least eight teams.
- To provide a soccer clinic for girls thirteen to fifteen years of age by November 1, 20___, with at least fifty girls attending.

To further develop the goal and objective hierarchy, leaders in recreation and sports ministries can tightly focus their energies in order to fulfill ministry purposes for their own unique settings. For the basketball league, additional objectives at the recreation and sports ministry program level could include the following:

- To develop a coed basketball league for children six to ten years of age by December 1, 2004, with at least eight teams.
  Program-focused objectives for the basketball league may include:
- Each player will hear a Gospel presentation.
- Each player will play in every game.
- Each player will be recognized at an awards banquet at the conclusion of the league.
- Each player will have a uniform.

The use of mission/purpose statements, goals, and objectives allows leadership in a recreation and sports ministry to keep their focus on ministry with intentional purposes. The further a purpose or mission is developed through goals and objectives, the more likely that intentional ministry will be kept in focus. These management principles are not solely for corporate systems. There is—and must be—a place in ministry for the development and implementation of a goal-and-objective system that keeps the energies expended through a recreation and sports ministry focused on what is primary: changing the lives of people for the sake of God's kingdom.

3. Design Programs for Ministry

After the formulation of ministry mission, goals, and objectives, decisions need to be made as to how what has already been developed becomes reality. What methods will be used to achieve the mission? What will be the intricacies involved in program development in order to ensure that ministry is the end result? With the vast array of possibilities for using recreation and sports as a ministry tool, decisions must be made on which methods would best suit one's unique, individual ministry setting.

By nature, recreation has a social purpose; that is, it exists for the good of a society. This is why we see parks and recreation services and departments even in the smallest of municipal government systems. These 'societies' determine which recreation and sports events would be beneficial within their boundaries of service. Where ministry is concerned, the church often stands as the society that dictates what is and what is not acceptable for recreation and sports as a ministry tool. When a parachurch ministry organization is responsible, they become the society that dictates what is acceptable for ministry.

Geographical location must also be brought into consideration, for what works as ministry in one locale may not be acceptable in another; the societies are different. Because of the differing external and internal influences affecting the outcomes of a recreation and sports ministry, care needs to be taken in developing those activities that will best deliver ministry as well as be inviting to the intended target population.

Various activity formats are available through which a sports or recreational pursuit may be introduced. Carpenter and Howe consider the recreation activity format as being the most versatile.[24] From a ministry standpoint, their viewpoint is also apropos. Major recreation activity formats consist of:

- Outdoor recreation (camping, hiking, fishing, shooting sports, etc.)
- Sports (team and individual)
- Games (vigorous and passive, physical and mental)
- Fitness
- Arts (drama, music, crafts)

- Social recreation (parties, banquets, receptions, etc.)
- Voluntary service (missions, ministry projects, etc.)
- Special events

An individual activity can also be developed in more than one way in order to meet a variety of needs. For instance, basketball could be formatted as: a league, a clinic, a tournament, or an open facility/gym.

Carpenter and Howe suggest that there are four advantages to developing and using the recreation activity format. First, the formats can be combined. This is especially important when ministry is the objective. A sports awards banquet (social recreation) could be held and the coaches (volunteer service) recognized for their excellent efforts. Also, a trip could be taken (trips and outings) to hold a soccer clinic (sports) for the purpose of evangelism (volunteer service).

Second, the recreation activity format allows for a participant to progress through different skill development levels. In recreation and sports ministries, people's main objective in participating is the development of skills, especially for those outside the congregation or organizational mainline participants. They commit to being involved with skill development in mind, and the spiritual aspects are "extras." Unless participants feel comfortable within the boundaries of the activity skill-wise, they will cease to participate.

Third, the recreation activity format lends itself to an almost limitless array of possibilities programmatically, as long as the offerings are conducive to ministry. It allows for a variety of ministry possibilities and fosters the participant's ability to make choices concerning their recreational pursuits.

A fourth advantage of the recreation activity format is that the activities allow themselves to be analyzed by recreation and sports ministry leaders to determine an activity's effectiveness toward reaching ministry goals.[25] Designing programs that minister sometimes requires recreation and sports ministry leaders to "color outside the lines" in order to be effective.

Rossman and Schlatter address the struggle to be creative with programming while focusing the results of recreation and sports on ministry. Creativity in programming involves the ability to overcome problems by using novel solutions.[26] Innovation is the key. It involves taking a risk to facilitate ministry. This is often discomforting, but new horizons in reaching people for Christ are also rewarding. At the same time, recreation ministers must avoid getting into a rut and staying too long with comfortable programs that have offered some success. The creative abilities are not active for one reason or another. Like any other ministry, sports and recreation programming can get stuck in habitual thinking, using the same solutions to the same problems resulting in the same outcomes. Christ's ministry was definitely "outside the lines." Jesus was so far out of the box that those known for their religious fervor did not recognize or appreciate his message.

In recreation and sports ministry programming, leaders should be limitless in their attitude to do whatever it takes to reach and grow people. To avoid the appearance of a program that lacks substance, recreation ministers design—with great intentions and integrity—their ministry programs. Recreation and sports ministry programs are designed to meet real needs, to change lives for the better, to give people a positive recreation experience, to introduce Christ into people's leisure time, and to succeed.

4. Implement Ministry

In a recreation and sports ministry, activities are delivered to people, through people. Ministry implementation cannot be achieved without people to take the goals and objectives, relate them to the determined activity formats, and deliver a ministry that will make a difference in the lives of those who participate.

As recreation and sports ministry philosophy moves through the programming cycle, more and more people get involved. In the development stage, formats were introduced as a means by which activities are delivered for ministry purposes. In the ministry implementation stage, the activity that was categorized into a format (sports, games, social recreation, etc.) is delivered to a specific group of potential participants for the purpose of intentional ministry.

The plans for ministry are set into motion through people. When programs are implemented, all of the initial surveying, goal and objective development, and organizing prove their worth.[27] Since the potential for involving people is the greatest at the ministry implementation stage, it is imperative that recreation and sports ministry leaders be adept at placing the best people in the right positions to ensure effective ministry. At this juncture of the ministry programming process, leaders must effectively delegate responsibility to qualified people so they can take ownership of the ministry.

In a recreation and sports ministry, administration is defined as the process of planning, organizing, leading, controlling, and evaluating the work of ministry personnel with intentional purposes that include being a steward of human and fiscal resources. Leading, staffing, and controlling are functions of human resource orientation, and without people, these functions have no purpose in the ministry process. This definition of administration, like most, is based on getting things done through people. Which people, however, are best suited for involvement in the implementation of a recreation and sports ministry?

Too often, ministry leadership is simply after someone with a pulse because time has run out and an event must be staffed. But there is a process that can help recreation and sports ministry leaders find the right people for the right ministry tasks. This process is comprised of several elements:

Prayer—The beginning place for staffing a recreation and sports ministry event is at the throne of God. God's hand in the staff selection process is paramount if His will is to be done through the event. Pray for the right people. Pray that God will uncover them for service.

Task analysis—The leaders in a recreation and sports ministry must themselves be knowledgeable about what is involved in completing the various tasks that comprise an activity or event. A question that needs to be asked is, "Do we need someone to occupy a place on the ministry team to complete this task?"

Job description—Yes, even for volunteers! This summary of the duties and responsibilities of the job is paramount if credibility is going to be given to the task. People will feel that their position in ministry is important if there is a written description covering what is expected of them.

Recruitment—The ideal is to have a pool of people who are willing to assist in ministry. Often in ministry circumstances, however, the luxury of choosing people from a pool is nonexistent. To develop a ministry pool, leadership assessments are often a good way to develop a base for involving people in ministry.

Selection—Match the right person to the right ministerial task. In order to do this, leaders must take the time to get to know those from whom they are choosing. Building relationships in ministry should not present a difficulty if leaders are actively ministering within their own circles of influence.[28]

Once the right people have been selected to assist the leaders in recreation and sports ministries, two additional important aspects of staffing must be considered.

First, people need to be properly trained in order to be most effective in ministry circumstances.[29] Handing people job descriptions and pointing them in the right direction is not training. Training involves personal contact with the staff member in order to channel the skills and abilities of the person to the tasks of the job. Training is where ministry team members acquire the necessary tools they need to fulfill the responsibilities of their position.

Second, volunteers need to be properly oriented to their role in the overall recreation and sports ministry scheme.[30] During an orientation session, volunteers should be made to feel that they play a vital role in fulfilling ministry purposes, and this praise must continue throughout the staff member's service. A clear picture of ministry purpose and direction is given as well, along with definitive areas of focus for various roles. Orientation involves making volunteers feel that the ministry cannot be done without their valuable assistance. Orientation answers the questions: Who are the team members in this ministry endeavor? What is the recreation and sports ministry trying to accomplish? What is the volunteer's role in assisting the recreation/sports ministry toward its mission? What impact does the recreation and sports ministry have on the total ministry of the church or organization?

Most recreation and sports ministry events and activities are staffed with volunteers. Although many larger churches and organizations have paid staff, the ministerial load is still carried by volunteers. In some instances, the entire recreation and sports ministry is run by volunteers. Volunteers bring their own needs to the recreation and sports ministry staff.

Gene Pomerance gives helpful insight into why people volunteer. First, some volunteer because they are required to do so. These people may be required to volunteer as part of a missions project. Oftentimes, for example, a recreation and sports ministry has student interns who are volunteering, in a sense, as part of their degree plan. Second, people volunteer for what Pomerance calls inner-directed reasons. These people want to make a difference in their world. They are interested in the opportunity to have a positive impact on society, and in a recreation and sports ministry, they may be the majority as they are 'called' to serve in a ministry environment. Third, some people volunteer for personal growth or self-development reasons. They might be interested in learning a new skill. Some people need experience on a résumé for future employment purposes. Finally, people volunteer for social reasons. They want to meet new people or be around a certain group of people. Like the inner-directed volunteer, social volunteers may be the majority found in recreation and sports ministries.

Because volunteers play such a vital role in recreation and sports ministries, they need to be compensated in some way. Pomerance offers the thought of 'psychic' compensation for volunteers. Psychic compensation is anything other than money that provides a reward for their efforts.[32] In a recreation and sports ministry setting, this may be recognition at a banquet, a certificate of appreciation, or tickets to some sort of amusement or attraction. However, being with God's people or sharing with people outside of one's faith should be the motivation and hallmark of those who volunteer in ministry environments.[31]

Volunteers also need an appraisal process. Appraisal makes them feel that their service to the ministry is as important as that of those who get paid to do it. The appraisal format for volunteers needs to affirm their efforts and assure them that they are not taken for granted by the recreation and sports ministry leaders.

Seasonal Program Implementation

One of the most common ways to implement a recreation and sports ministry program is by a seasonal format. From a pure sports ministry perspective, people are extremely seasonal. They want to play football during football season, basketball during basketball season, and so on. Also, seasons allow for the recreation and sports ministry programmer to use thematic interpretations to promote activities and events. Of special interest to contemporary ministry programmers is the time-deepening format as described by Godbey.[33] Recent research has determined that people will more likely participate in an activity that is complete yet compact in duration. In a recreation ministry that offers an arts and crafts program, for instance, people are more likely to come to a one-time flower-arranging class than to a six-week painting class. The precious element of time becomes a barrier to participation in recreation and sports ministries if activities become too time consuming.

The fast pace of Western culture combined with "time-saving" technological advances have made time a valuable commodity. Geoffrey Godbey states that while people used to speak of passing the time, today people "spend, lose, save, or even make time."[34] To make the most of their time, says Tom Goodale, people do more in less time, different things at the same time, and measure time in smaller, more precise amounts.[35] Factors that stress the time people have to give toward active participation in recreation and sports ministries must be considered by those who implement ministry programs. To become too big of a restraint on people's time will cause the program to become too big of a constraint in the lives of those the ministry is trying to reach.

5. Evaluate Ministries

The evaluation process in recreation and sports ministries, as in other recreation delivery systems, is vital to the fulfillment of ministry mission. Evaluation is necessary to determine if ministry goals and objectives were achieved. To neglect this stage of programming arrangement would be failing to be interested in delivering the best possible recreation and sports ministry offerings. Program evaluation is one of the most important aspects of any leisure-service delivery system.[36]

Ruth Russell agrees about evaluation's importance but adds that it is also one of the least understood and most confusing aspects in program planning.[37] As part of such a delivery system, the recreation and sports ministry is not exempt from such scrutiny. Those involved in ministry ventures are called to rise above the rest when it comes to being effective at what they do. Recreation and sports ministries differ from other agencies delivering the same programs in that ministries are involved with the eternal. The end result is not only a satisfying recreation experience but a closer glimpse of God.

To be most effective at doing this, evaluation of ministry programs is a mandate, not an option. Like most organizations that employ evaluation techniques, recreation and sports ministries also view the need for evaluation from a dual perspective—formative and summative. Formative evaluation monitors the ongoing progress of a program; it is flexible and dynamic. It keeps the ministry on track while the programs are in progress; that is, it forms and improves what is being evaluated while it is being developed. Formative evaluation is process oriented. Summative evaluation makes decisions that "sum up" the overall quality or worth of a program. This type of evaluation is product oriented. It is performed at the conclusion of a program or activity and judges the overall impact that a program had on the intended target audience.[38] Both types of evaluation are necessary if a recreation and sports ministry is to bear the fruit desired by those planning and designing the ministry.

Evaluation of programs in a recreation and sports ministry also needs to consider both the objective and subjective natures of people being involved in an activity based on the intentional ministry purposes. From an objective standpoint, evaluation should provide data concerning the number of participants involved in ministry programs, costs involved in delivering a particular ministry, and stewardship of facilities. Objective evaluation assists recreation and sports ministry leaders in guiding and taking inventory of all resources used to produce a program. The subjective nature of recreation evaluation is especially important in recreation and sports ministry settings. Subjectivity is involved because different programs, or various aspects within the same program, have different meanings to different people. With this in mind, the spiritual dimensions involved in ministry programming must be considered. Some method of determining spiritual effectiveness must be inherent in the evaluation process.

From an overall perspective, evaluation serves many purposes. Knutson offers these as roles fulfilled through evaluation:

- To show others that the program is worthwhile
- To determine whether a program is moving in the right direction
- To determine whether the needs for which the program is designed are being satisfied
- To determine the costs of a program in terms of money and human effort
- To obtain evidence that may demonstrate to others what is already believed to be true regarding the effectiveness of the program
- To support program expansion or reduction
- To assist in comparing different types of programs in terms of their effectiveness[39]

Before an evaluation process can be properly implemented to assist in ministry, Murphy and others suggest that the following questions be considered in order to direct evaluation energies in a manner that will be most productive:

- What will be the purpose of evaluation?
- For whom will the result be intended?

- Who will use the results?
- What resources for conducting the evaluation are available (human, fiscal, and physical)?
- What are the constraints?
- What would hinder the effective implementation of the evaluation process?
- Exactly when would formative and summative evaluation processes begin?
- Are there any deadlines?
- Who will conduct the evaluation?[40]

Concerning the last question, many commercial firms conduct evaluation research from a nonbiased perspective. In the corporate and business world, these services are extremely helpful. In ministry, however, the subjective nature of the spiritual element leans toward those responsible for the ministry also being responsible for the evaluation process.

In a recreation and sports ministry, with the intentional purpose being the common thread that sews the entire programming process together, those involved in the planning and design aspects are most familiar with the ministry's desired outcome. Those outside the ministry circle, though competent to do evaluation research, may not have the ministerial perspective needed to disseminate ministry results.

Evaluation instruments can "run the gamut" when it comes to identifying which method for gathering information is best. Like needs assessments, the recreation and sports ministry should tailor-design an instrument that will give them the information they need to make wise decisions at the conclusion of a program. Also, techniques for formative evaluation must be considered carefully in order for the ministry program to stay on track.

In recreation and sports ministries, evaluation tools that are summative in nature usually attempt to determine two things—one that is objective and one that is subjective. Evaluation of programs of this nature will not be foolproof as respondents are reacting to their perception of how things went. What went well for one respondent might be viewed as disaster by another.

First, an instrument for recreation and sports ministries should discover how people felt about the pragmatics of the program. Participant satisfaction for a particular program is essential if recreation and sports ministry leaders want programs that meet ministry objectives.[41] Examples of relevant information include:

- Was the time of the activity convenient?
- Did the leader communicate adequately?
- Was the activity's duration adequate? Was it too long? Too short?

Open-ended questions are also appropriate in this stage of evaluation. Examples of such questions are:

- If you could change the times, what time would be more convenient for you?
- What additional incentives would make participation more attractive?

In recreation and sports ministries, however, the subjective nature of spiritual change within the lives of participants also needs to be considered somehow. This type of questioning falls into the category of information that Susan Hudson describes as attitudes and beliefs.[41]

Attitudes essentially describe how a person feels about something; however, various influences cause people's attitudes to change.[42] Attitudes are always focused on an object—either physical, social, or abstract. In this case, the abstract is the spiritual element purposefully integrated into recreation program delivery. Attitudes also have a "feeling" component.[43] Of special importance for ministry purposes is a participant's intensity of feelings toward a particular spiritual focus or program element. Questions that allow for discovery in this area include:

- What spiritual growth have you experienced as the result of spending time in this class?

- What spiritual truth have you gained insight toward as a result of your participation in this activity?
- What teachable moments related to spiritual insight were most memorable?

The important thing to remember about evaluation techniques is that information is being collected for three areas of concern to the recreation and sports ministry: Were ministry goals and objectives met? Were the lives of participants changed in a positive spiritual manner? What changes, if any, should be made to the program in order to make it a more effective ministry tool?

6. Determine Disposition of Ministry

In a recreation and sports ministry, or any ministry for that matter, it is difficult to justify and determine the future of various programs. Especially in local church ministry, the status quo often becomes the standard. Those in charge of ministry environments often go to great extremes and are involved in great energy expenditures just to keep up with the latest ministry trends. It becomes easy to simply turn their backs on those programs that are not effective as ministry tools, hoping that they will just go away. But not so.

Robert Rossman reminds the recreation and sports ministry leader that program disposition is also an option. In fact, when recreation and sports are used as ministry, program disposition becomes a matter of stewardship. Rossman and Schlatter state that final disposition of a recreation program should be determined by information gathered during the evaluation process. The three choices are made during the disposition process are:

- Continue the program as is with no changes.
- Continue the program but with modifications.
- Terminate the program.

The disposition of programs must be addressed in what Rossman and Schlatter describe as the 'decline' stage of the recreation program life cycle.

This life cycle includes the stages of program birth (or introduction), program growth, program maturation, program saturation (where the newness wears off, number of participants levels off; in ministry, "tradition" takes over), program decline, and program death.[44]   (See Fig. 7.1.) To avoid unintentional program death, programmers in recreation and sports ministries must make one of the available disposition choices. In ministry environments, the first two alternatives are easy. The termination of a ministry, however, is another issue.

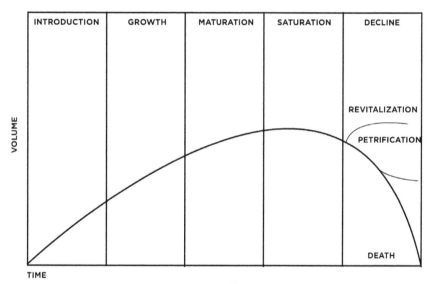

Figure 7-1: Life Cycle

What constitutes ministry termination? When tradition has carried a ministry offering for so long, what characteristics must be evident in order to terminate services? Budgetary issues may or may not allow for certain recreation and sports ministries to continue. It simply costs too much. Recreation trends change. When people become more interested in other leisure outlets and facilities are limited, certain ministries may need to end. The minister thinks the time has come to end the activity. When certain programs are not bearing fruit and resources are limited, certain ministries may need to be terminated.

Ministry termination is often the most difficult of disposition choices because usually something good can be found within any program. A question always worthy of consideration in recreation and sports ministry operations is stewardship: Are we doing the most (providing the best ministries) with what we have (all available resources) to reach and grow people for the kingdom of God? To answer this question, sometimes program termination is not just a vital choice; it is the only choice.

Ministry termination is not the end. It is the making available of resources for the recreation and sports ministry to do something else, to reach new horizons in ministry, to develop and implement new programs with greater kingdom impact. The disposition choices of continuation and continuation with modifications may be easier to administer than program termination, but the same seriousness of intentional mission must be followed. All disposition alternatives are about being the best stewards of the resources God has given. To do anything less would misuse the greatest opportunity—reaching the most people possible in ministry.

The greatest plan for developing recreation and sports ministry programs is invalid without the hand of God being present from the beginning. Often one can get caught up in administration and fail in the duty to minister. Although program planning and implementation is ministry, care must be taken not to get so wrapped up in a system that a minister fails to relate to the everyday needs of people. A delicate balance must be achieved and sustained in order for the recreation and sports minister to be most effective.

On the one hand, there should be a system of operation that guides the ministry toward its fulfillment or mission through the provision of leisure pursuits that have positive physical and spiritual results in the lives of people. On the other hand, the efficiency of such a system should allow the minister freedom to move among the people, becoming personally involved in their lives and growth. A system for planning and providing recreation and sports activities that consumes leadership is of little use in ministry environments.

Full and active recreation and sports ministry facilities are not necessarily the marks of a great ministry, although the more people present, the more ministry opportunities possibly exist. Many programs will run themselves because of recreational trends, the current interests of people, and facilities. What must happen within a ministry context is that offerings that provide the programmer with the most intentional ministry possibilities must be sought.

Today, these activities may not represent the traditional sports and activities that once comprised most ministries. Whatever the activity, there must be a system that guides efforts toward mission accomplishment. Ministry is the mission, and its accomplishment is not only found in great programs but etched into eternity on behalf of those whose lives are touched and grown through participation.

NOTES

1. Maynard, M. H. *We're Here for the Churches: Southern Baptist Entities Working Together* (Nashville, TN: LifeWay Press, 2001), 66.
2. Rossman, J. R. and Barbara Elwood Schlatter, *Recreation Programming: Designing Leisure Experiences,* 6th ed. (Champaign: Sagamore Publishing, 2011), ix.
3. Ibid., 5.
4. Farrell, P. and Herberta Lundgren, Recreation Programming: Theory and Technique, 3rd ed. (State College, PA.: Venture Publishing, Inc., 1991), 25; Rossman, 72; Russell, R. V. *Planning Program in Recreation* (St. Louis, MO: C. V. Mosby, 1982), 25.
5. Corbin, D. H. and Ellen Williams. *Recreation Programming and Leadership,* 4th ed. (Englewood Cliffs: Prentice-Hall, 1987), 59.
6. Carpenter, G. M. and Christine Z. Howe. *Programming Leisure Experiences: A Cyclical Approach* (Englewood Cliffs: Prentice-Hall, 1985), 77.
7. Ibid.

8. Hudson, S. D. *How to Conduct Community Needs Assessment Surveys in Public Parks and Recreation* (Columbus, OH: Publishing Horizons, 1988), 2.

9. Migliore, R. H., Robert Stevens, and Dave Loudon. *Church Ministry Strategic Planning: From Concept to Success* (New York: The Haworth Press, 1994), 9.

10. Inman, V. K. *Planning Church Events with Ease* (Grand Rapids, MI: Zondervan Publishing House, 1988), 31.

11. Holcomb, T. J. *Church Administration from A to Z: Support for Church Growth* (Nashville: Convention Press, 1994), 10.

12. Great Commission Council of the Southern Baptist Convention, *We're Here for the Churches: The Southern Baptist Entities Working Together* (Nashville, TN: LifeWay Christian Resources, 1999), 21–27.

13. Ensman, R. "Preparing the Annual Program Plan," *The Clergy Journal* 69.6 (1993): 46.

14. Albrecht, K. *The Northbound Train: Finding Purpose, Setting the Direction, Shaping the Destiny of Your Organization* (New York, NY: American Management Association, 1994), 153.

15. Ibid., 157.

16. Rossman and Schlatter, 101.

17. Inman, 30.

18. Hunt, S. and Kenneth Brooks. "A Planning Model for Public Recreation Agencies," *Journal of Parks and Recreation Administration* 1.2 (1989), 8.

19. Dougherty, N. and Diane Bonanno. *Management Principles for Sport and Leisure Services* (Minneapolis: Burgess Publishing Company, 1985), 46–47.

20. Rossman and Schlatter, 100.

21. Dale McConkey, MBO for Non-Profit Organizations (New York: American Management Association, 1975), 173.

22. Stoner, J. and R. Edward Freeman. *Management*, 4th ed. (Englewood Cliffs: Prentice Hall, 1989), 253.

23. Migliore, Stevens, and Loudon, 60–61.

24. Carpenter and Howe, 111.

25. Ibid., 111–12.

26. Rossman and Schlatter, 236-237.

27. Ibid., 327-334.

28. Ibid., 335.

29. Ibid., 334.

30. Godby, G. *Leisure In Your Life: An Exploration,* 6th ed., (State College, PA: Venture Publications, 2003.

31. Pomerance, G. "The Care and Feeding of Volunteers," *Parks and Recreation Magazine* (November 1994): 54–55.

32. Ibid., 54.

33. Godbey, G. *Leisure in Your Life: An Exploration,* 3rd ed. (State College, PA: Venture Publishing, 1990), 46.

34. Goodale, T. L. "Is There Enough Time?" in Thomas L. Goodale and Peter Witt, *Recreation and Leisure: Issues in an Era of Change* (State College, PA: Venture Publishing, 1991), 38.

35. Graham, P. J. and Lawrence R. Klar Jr. *Planning and Delivering Leisure Services* (Dubuque, IO: William C. Brown, 1979), 45.

36. Russell, 283.

37. Gay, L. R. and Peter Airasian. *Educational Research: Competencies for Analysis and Application,* 6th ed. (Upper Saddle River, NJ: Merrill, 2000), 8; Farrell and Lundgren, 235; Murphy et al., 365; Theobald, W. F. *Evaluation of Recreation and Parks Programs* (New York, NY: John Wiley & Sons, 1979), 58.

38. Knutson, A. L. "Evaluation for What?" in William F. Theobald, *Proceedings of the Regional Institute on Neurologically Handicapping Conditions in Children in Evaluation of Recreation and Park Programs* (New York: John Wiley & Sons, 1979), 57–58.

39. Murphy et al., 365–66.

40. Ibid., 379.

41. Hudson, 11.

42. Ibid., 14.

43. Rossman and Schlatter, 467.

44. Ibid., 468–71.

8

Recreation and Sports Ministry

AN EVANGELISTIC APPROACH

Greg Linville

"The question for sports and recreation outreach endeavors is this: is it about evangelism or is it about evangelistic disciple making?"

The question for sports and recreation outreach endeavors is: Is it about evangelism or is it about evangelistic disciple-making?

During the 1970s, Francis Schaeffer urged Christians to change their method of evangelizing because Western civilization had entered a post-Christian era. The Western world no longer believed in the existence of God, much less that Jesus Christ was the way to salvation. He predicted ensuing generations would no longer have a working knowledge of Christianity, faith, or the Bible. Consequently, Christians should not expect a friend or family member to pray to receive Christ simply because a follower of Christ asked them to do so. Schaeffer realized and taught that those wishing to be effective in sharing the Gospel of Christ needed to establish long-term relationships with secularized friends, family, and associates and be prepared for a lengthy process of helping these people come to faith in Christ.[1] His words uttered in the 1970s have proved true, and are even more valid in the new millennium.

More profound and disturbing than Schaeffer's prophetic voice however, is what is occurring in the new millennium—a movement that is far more sinister than the benign secularism he envisioned. With increasing acceleration, neo-secularism threatens traditional Christianity with, at best, marginalization, and at worst, hard-core denunciation and even persecution. Amidst these new realities, how is the church to envision and engage in *evangelistic disciple-making*? This chapter addresses the issues surrounding the Great Commission as it is lived out in sport and recreation ministry in these trying times and new reality. Virulent attacks on Christians may be the bad news, but the good news about "The Good News" is that while methodologies must be constantly updated and adapted, Christo-centric theological truths and biblically based philosophical principles for sport and recreation ministries remain the same and provide proven foundations for innovative methodological models!

WHY IS THIS IMPORTANT?

America remains the country with the highest percentage of citizens who self-identify as Christians; however, those who describe themselves as "nones" (ascribing to no religion or faith) is the fastest growing affinity group of people in America. Even more disturbing is that a proven and strategic tool to reach the nones (the sports outreach movement), is in decline.

The sports outreach movement of the mid-20th century was touted as a strategic tool for evangelism, discipleship, and church growth. In addition, most sports outreach ministers and many lead or administrative pastors believed sports outreach to be the most strategic tool the church could employ to accomplish the Great Commission. Yet many church leaders have come to believe it cannot deliver the promised results. These thoughts and concerns are verified by both anecdotal and statistical reports, which tell of local churches laying off sports and rec staff—some even eliminating their entire sports outreach ministries. In addition, due to prevailing cultural shifts, most sport-related parachurch ministries are experiencing increased resistance to their work with university or high school students; sometimes they are even banned from simply walking on a campus. Parachurch ministries that provide direct resources to local congregations have reported as much as a 50% decrease in the number of churches utilizing their services.

Much of this disillusionment and decline can be directly linked to the ineffectiveness of the recreation and sports ministry movement in producing new, growing disciples of Christ. With a few notable exceptions, churches are not experiencing the promised results from their sport and recreation ministries. Perhaps every now and then they celebrate a few baptisms or prayers to receive Christ (praise God for these), but most of these baptisms and prayers do not translate into long-term church participation or membership—all of which paints a dismal picture if the goal is to "go and make disciples." Yet some churches remain open to a more efficient and effective way of doing sport ministry. A new philosophy and new models are needed.

THE GOAL OF THIS CHAPTER

This chapter is designed to shape a new way of thinking about evangelism. It will help local churches—and especially local church sport, recreation, and fitness ministers—envision the changes needed to deconstruct less effective models, based in what is called "evangelism," so that new *evangelistic disciple-making* methodologies can be created. To that end, the contents of the chapter are based on the organizational structure of a *3-Tier Paradigm*. It does so by outlining if, how, and why a sports outreach and recreation ministry meets the *4-Fold Evaluative Process* (strategically relevant and efficiently effective) and is an effective way to expand and enhance God's kingdom as well as provide a successful vehicle for church growth.

THE FLOW OF THIS CHAPTER

The first section of this chapter will briefly introduce the *3-Tier Paradigm* as the biblically based organizational structure from which to envision, plan, and implement an *evangelistic disciple-making* sports and recreation ministry. The second section of the chapter will introduce a few of the primary '-ologies' (theological foundations) for sports and rec ministry which serve as the basis for reconstructing sport and recreation ministries. The third section of the chapter outlines the *Five-B Process* of local church sports outreach for the purpose of acquainting sports ministers and other congregational leaders with the philosophical process on which they can mobilize mission rather than produce program. The fourth section of this chapter will discuss the obstacles encountered by sports, recreation, and fitness ministries whenever they attempt to change the basic methods of their endeavors to "go and make disciples."

THE 3-TIER PARADIGM3
Levels of the 3-Tier Paradigm
- Level #1: The *"why"* of sports ministry—theological truths
- Level #2: The *"when, where and with whom"* of sports ministry—philosophical principles
- Level #3: The *"what and how"* of sports ministry—methodological models

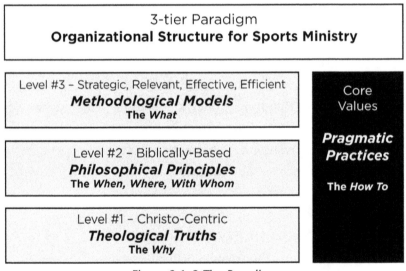

Figure 8-1: 3-Tier Paradigm

The *3-Tier Paradigm* is a biblically based organizational structure designed for local church sports, rec and fitness ministries. It ensures that *what* is done and *how* it is done are based on *why* it is done.

The three levels of the *3-Tier Paradigm* are separate and yet interdependent and inter-related. Each level builds upon and depends upon the others. Each level should be comprehended as being a distinctive body of thoughts and concepts, yet still be perceived as one piece of a unified, whole, and overarching organizational structure from which to envision and build a missional local church sports outreach. The entire paradigm can be best understood after each level is considered separately.

1. Level #1 Theological Truths: Why We Do What We Do

Theological truths provide the foundation for local church sports and recreation outreach, including its parameters and its ethical framework. Theological truths answer the basic question of why ministries do what they do and provide the ethical guidelines for what they do.

The *why* question in Level #1 is primarily answered through the foundational theological tenet of redemption. God is in the business of redeeming humankind to Himself. Jesus said: "I came to seek and save the lost." In addition, Paul writes that Christians are called and empowered to join God in those redemptive activities by being His "ambassadors." Thus the ultimate theological foundation for local church sports outreach ministry is to redeem all men, women, and children by going "into all the world to make disciples." (See Chapter 2 for more on why recreation and sports ministry is done by the church.)

2. Level #2 Philosophical Principles: When, Where, and With Whom We Do Sports Ministry

Theological truths are considered Level #1 because of the necessity of basing local church sports and recreation ministry on Christo-centric ministerial and ethical foundations. This primacy continues in Level #2 philosophical principles but only if such principles are biblically based. Thus, biblically based philosophical principles are differentiated from other philosophies by being theistically-founded as opposed to being based upon humanly conceptualized views or priorities.

When has to do with determining the right time of the year—the month, week, and day—to plan and implement sports outreach activities that best exemplify sensitivity in regards to individual and family schedules, safety, and well-being. *When* also concerns the theological truths of the Sabbath Day and/or the church in terms of participating in traditional congregational worship services. Does the church sponsor sporting events on the Sabbath? This has become an issue for many churches in modern culture.

Where refers to facilities that are both available and functional. This includes ensuring participants' safety and overall well-being, determining if the facilities they own, lease, rent or borrow provide a safe environment, and gauging if the facilities lend themselves to creating a warm and engaging atmosphere conducive to a positive experience. *Where* also takes into consideration such things as easy accessibility for families during the sporting activities and driving time to and from a facility.

With whom is based on the biblical principle of mission (missiology). The Church is commanded to "go and make disciples." Paul outlines this programmatic principle in 1 Corinthians 9: "I became all things to all people." In essence, this passage exhorts Christians to understand that there are differences between various people groups, and each will need to be reached through different methods and models, based on the philosophical principle of "becoming all things to all men" found in 1 Corinthians 9:22. *With whom* also concerns the identification of a local congregation's geographic and demographic positioning. Once a congregation recognizes whom they are to serve and minister to, they will be better able to envision relevant strategies of outreach.

While Level #1 theological truths provide the *why* of local church sports ministry, Level #2 philosophical principles provide the driving force behind *when, where and with whom* churches direct and conduct their sports and recreational outreaches. Level #3 is concerned with the practical application of what is done in recreation/sports ministry.

3. Level #3 Methodological Models: What We Do

Once a church has determined why, where, when and with whom for its sports, recreation and fitness outreach ministries are then able to determine what to do. What a church does is often running of programs. Running programs has fallen into disfavor, and understandably so, but missiologically based programs will never fall out of favor or prove to be ineffective!

The what of sport and rec ministry consists of all the various activities local churches, Christian camps, and sport-related parachurch ministries administrate.

Standards for Judging the Outcome of Sports Ministry Efforts

Briefly stated, the success of any programmatic sports or recreation ministry will be judged by four evaluative standards. Those four standards are:

- Is it strategic?
- Is it relevant?
- Is it effective?
- Is it efficient?

The purpose of recreation and sports ministry is to provide a cross-cultural platform for the sharing the gospel of Jesus Christ. If a sports, rec, or fitness ministry is not successfully making disciples, it is probably because churches and parachurch ministries are producing programs rather than mobilizing missions that are biblically based! So, if a church or ministry is not seeing totally secularized and unchurched nonbelievers enter into a personal relationship with Jesus Christ—as evidenced by becoming intimately involved in the disciple-making endeavors of a local church—it's probably because the ministry is producing programs (i.e., employing faulty methodological models) that are not based in solid biblical foundations (philosophical principles), or because it is based on other faulty theological premises. Knowing why ministry is done is foundational, but knowing how it is done is equally vital.

Foundational Values for Ministry

There is an old saying in sports outreach circles: "Christ is more caught than taught." It is to this end that local church sports outreach ministries need to consider the ethical foundations of what they do. If the overall purpose of sports and recreation outreach is redemption, then envisioning, planning for, and implementing the ministry on solid theological truths is vital. The truth is, participants in a local church sport or recreational activity will not remember the final score of more than a game or two, but they will remember how they were treated and how they felt. Sports ministers cannot guarantee each and every team will win every game. They can, however, create an atmosphere that communicates what the church believes and what it stands for. Regardless of what a local church sports outreach does, how it does what it does should include such core values as: excellence; integrity, consistency, compassion, inclusiveness, honesty, and most of all, love.

So, theological truths mandate why sports and rec ministries exist (to redeem the world to Christ) and also provide a foundation for how (using ethical foundations and core values) local church sports, recreational, and fitness ministries should be done. (For further explanation on ethical foundations of sports ministry see Chapter 8.)

Summary of the 3-Tier Paradigm

As stated before, the purpose of this chapter is to equip local congregations to mobilize, enable, and empower their members for evangelistic disciple-making. Now that we understand the organizational structure, let's look at a few foundational "-ologies" of sport, recreation, and fitness ministries.

UNDERSTANDING THE "-OLOGIES"

In order to more fully comprehend the *3-Tier Paradigm,* one must first become acquainted with what I have termed the "-ologies." -Ologies is short hand for theologies that undergird and inform the *3-Tier Paradigm.* There are many Level #1 theological truth -ologies to be considered in the creation of a comprehensive local church *3-Tier Paradigm* sports ministry, but for the purposes of this chapter, we will concentrate on three of the more foundational ones. All -ologies help establish the why and how sports ministries do what they do.

Ecclesiology—The Theology of the Church

Ecclesiology pertains to the identity and the role of the church.

Who is the Church?

The Christian church is made up of followers of Christ who, for better or worse, have many ministry commitment levels. When these many commitment levels are understood, the relevance of what or who the church is and who is qualified to be a leader in the secularized culture of the twenty-first century comes into sharp focus. Are regular attendees considered members of the local body of believers? If biblical evangelism and discipleship are the focus of sports and recreation ministry, can nonmembers hold positions of leadership, coach, or lead an aerobics or hunter safety class? If so, is a person who lives an alternate lifestyle also eligible to lead? Churches must know, codify, and adhere to their core beliefs, based on scriptural foundations of who the church is and who is qualified for membership and leadership.

When Does the Church Meet?

Sunday sports are another issue affected by cultural shifts and determined by ecclesiology. They raise the question: Is the church restricted to only meeting for traditional worship on Sunday mornings, and how does this impact the use of sports on Sunday?v This idea will be explored in detail later in the chapter.

Where Does the Church Meet?

Another question local church sport ministry raises has to do with where the church meets. Is traditional worship restricted to a sanctuary, or can it occur on a softball field or in a gymnasium? The answer to this is also greatly impacted by ecclesiology.

Summary of Ecclesiology

Local church recreation/sports ministry that is conceptualized through a proper view of ecclesiology will ensure a theologically sound, philosophically coherent, and thus effective, local church sports outreach. These ministries provide a platform for sharing the gospel, winning people to Christ, and discipling them to a deeper relationship with Christ.

Missiology—The Mission of the Church and Sports Ministry Methods

The relevance of missiology to local church sports ministry has to do with questions such as:

- Are Christians to go to reach "the lost?"
- Are Christians to go to all people, countries, and ethnic/cultural groups?
- Are all Christians to go (or only missionaries)?
- Does the reaching of various groups of people require Christians to participate in the culture and activities of those being reached?

There is universal agreement about the answers to the first three questions. They can be summarized in the mantra of the Student Volunteer Movement of the late nineteenth and early twentieth centuries: "All to go and go to all." However, there is considerable controversy over the fourth question, which also relates to the issue of sports on Sunday. For example, some leaders and ministries within the sports outreach movement claim the church must play and even organize sports on Sunday in order to reach those who play sports on the Lord's Day. While the answer to this resides largely in at least two other doctrines—the doctrines of the Sabbath Day and the Lord's Day—a final determination can also be evaluated by another aspect of Level #1 theological truth: logic.

Two points need to be considered on the Sunday sport issue. While the doctrines of the Sabbath and the Lord's Day provide clear theological guidance, as well as boundaries from which philosophical principles can be determined, they leave room for strategic and relevant methodological models. For example, consider the difference between the following two scenarios.

Scenario #1: A Christian baseball player is rightly motivated to reach his unsaved baseball-playing friends. So, he plays baseball with them every Sunday, except perhaps Christmas and Easter. What is the result? His teammates believe baseball is more important than church and one's faith, and thus they feel little motivation to repent and follow Jesus.

Scenario #2: A Christian softball player is also motivated to reach her unsaved friends. However, she attends church each week rather than playing softball with her teammates. One week, the Lord directs her to show up at the ballfield on a Sunday morning to reach out to her friends. When they ask her why she is missing church to be with them, she tells them that the Lord led her to come and communicate how much she, and He, loves them. The result? Her friends know how important church and her faith are to her, and yet realize she loves them so much that she is willing to miss church in order to share God's love with them. It should also be noted she comes to be with them, rather than participate alongside them. More importantly, they understand that repentance means life-change, and becoming a disciple of Christ comes with a cost.

So, it becomes clear, Level #3 methodological models (participating in and sponsoring sports on the Lord's Day) that all ministries must be rooted in solid theological truths and biblically based philosophical principles. A missiological foundation of "all to go and go to all" does not necessarily justify philosophies that go against clear biblical teaching and/or run afoul of sound theological logic. Sports ministers must understand that flawed methodologies often emerge from such faulty philosophies.

The Doctrine of Salvation: Two Views of "Success"

The question arises: are evangelistic endeavors about producing a day's decision or a dedicated disciple? This subtle difference lies in the fact that rather than viewing evangelism and discipleship as a unified continuum, church leaders often perceive them as two separate endeavors—as though the salvation experience is not related to the discipleship process. The proper view is to see both salvation and discipleship as a continual holistic process. They are dependent on each other. This singular effort can be described by the term *"evangelistic disciple-making."*

A Day's Decision or a Dedicated Disciple

To many, evangelism is defined by what could be termed "a day's decision" (or a one-time decision). The end goal of "a day's decision" philosophy of evangelism is for someone to raise a hand, fill out a form, say a prayer, or go forward at a meeting. All subsequent methodologies, therefore, are conceived and implemented so that these "day's decisions" occur. Once they do, there is often little or no follow-up initiated to help the new believer become a true disciple of Christ.

However, most would agree that the end goal of evangelism is making "dedicated disciples." If the end goal is to "go and make disciples," the philosophies and methodologies of a local church sports and recreation outreach ministry will have a significantly different focus. It will intentionally create programs with the long-term goal of producing spiritually mature and multiplying disciples of Jesus. It is because of this that the term evangelistic disciple-making is preferred. This philosophy is best understood using the Five-B Process.

THE FIVE B'S OF SPORTS OUTREACH

The Five B's of sports outreach is a helpful shorthand way to encapsulate the *evangelistic disciple-making* concept and is designed to help leaders of the sports outreach movement conceptualize, implement, and evaluate whether or not they are succeeding in making disciples. Each "B" represents a clear step in the *evangelistic disciple-making* process and a necessary step in the spiritual journey of secularized, unchurched, nonbelievers as they become dedicated disciples of Jesus Christ. The Five B's are the following: 1.) Belonging 2.) Believing 3.) Baptizing 4.) Behaving 5.) Becoming.

BELONGING

Belonging is the term used to articulate the first step in a person's journey toward becoming a dedicated disciple of Jesus Christ. At first, it may seem counter-intuitive or out of order—especially for those committed to a theology that requires belief, baptism, behavior change and/or church membership as prerequisites to joining the church community. A sense of belonging is a primal human desire. Because God created us as social beings, the sense of wanting to belong is strong; belonging fulfils a basic human desire. Rightfully, belonging ushers the unchurched person into a community where the Gospel is "caught more than taught." Thus, belonging leads to—and is often the prerequisite for—belief, baptism, behavior change, and church membership. Belonging to such a Gospel community, is an effective and necessary way in which the Gospel can be observed, fully comprehended, and warmly embraced.

Belonging is a vital first step for many reasons, but before those can be explored, it must be recognized that there are two major obstacles to connecting those far from Christ to a belonging sports community in a local congregation and ultimately, to Christ.

Describing and Defining Two "Dysconnects"

The term dysconnects (misspelling is intentional) reflects the dysfunction and misconnections many Christians and Christian ministries experience as they strive to reach an increasingly secular world.

In an ever-deepening secular culture, local gatherings of the church face an increasingly uphill battle to reach people "far from Christ." While sport, recreation, and fitness ministries offer a strategic and relevant tool for outreach, local congregations must find ways to bridge two substantial gaps that separate the unchurched from becoming involved in congregational life, and ultimately from becoming life-long, dedicated disciples of Jesus Christ.

1. The First Dysconnect—From the Street to the Gym

The first dysconnect is related to connecting people from the community to a local church sports outreach ministry. There are two relevant reasons for this disconnect:

1. The increasing secularization of society in general.
2. The resulting antagonistic attitudes toward Christianity.

Scripture tells us the hearts and minds of many are blinded towards having anything to do with a local church—even participating in a ministry-based church league. Sadly, this dysconnect is becoming more prevalent, even for quality sports offerings.

2. The Second Dysconnect—From the Gym to the Sanctuary

The second dysconnect has beset the church for decades. Both local church sports ministries and sport-related parachurch ministries have struggled to move people from their sports outreach to full participation in the overall activities of a local congregation; thus, their ultimate goal of making dedicated disciples of Jesus Christ goes unfulfilled. This second dysconnect, as well as the first, can be overcome by fully understanding and embracing the importance of the first "B" (belonging). Still, the answer for the parachurch ministry community and the local church community is much simpler to understand in concept than it is to implement in reality.

Overcoming the Two Dysconnects
Overcoming for Sport-Related Parachurch Ministries

For sport-related parachurch ministries, the key to overcoming both dysconnects is an honest assessment of how difficult it would be for the ministry to reorder itself to be fully incorporated—and in full partnership with—local churches. Rather than seeing a parachurch ministry's current program and practices as the ultimate end, such ministries will best serve the kingdom by re-envisioning their goals. This new vision would focus on empowering and enabling local church efforts of making dedicated disciples of Christ who are active members of a local church. This is no small shift, nor is it done without extreme resolve.

Overcoming for the Local Church

For a local church, the difficulty lies in re-envisioning its sports outreach activities to be: a) excellent in all things athletic and, perhaps even more radical, b) to be aligned with the leisure pursuits of the church's members rather than by "what's always been done," or by "what has worked elsewhere."

Both the parachurch ministry world and the local church world should reorder their way of thinking so they can create the most strategically relevant and efficiently effective models for ministry possible.

Reordering the Sports Outreach Community's Methodology to Overcome Dysconnects

The intentional reordering of a methodology is not only vital to the success of a ministry and/or a congregation's evangelistic disciple-making efforts, but also to the expansion and enhancement of the kingdom of Jesus Christ.

Belonging, the first "B," is vital to the overall evangelistic disciple-making success of sports ministries because it is the vehicle by which an unchurched person can be transported along a spiritual journey toward life as a dedicated disciple of Jesus Christ. Two commitments, however, must be adopted first. The local congregation must be committed to providing a vibrant and excellent sporting environment in which the unchurched person encounters a warm and welcoming community. The church must also be committed to building sports outreach activities around the leisure pursuits of the current members of the congregation.

Building an Excellent Sports Environment

The two-fold key to attracting and retaining unchurched people is excellence in the sporting venue and the warm reception of those administrating and participating in the venue. Unchurched people are first attracted by—and feel comfortable with—a church's sports program because they experience a sporting environment they recognize and understand, including high-quality facilities and equipment, which draws them to participate. They remain involved because they are warmly loved and welcomed by current church members who play, coach, and participate alongside them. Such environments are well received by those far from Christ. Little do they know they have begun their spiritual journey by belonging.

Building the Sports Outreach around Church Members' Leisure Pursuits

While excellence in sports outreach is a prerequisite for overcoming the first dysconnect, the key for overcoming the second one is building outreach around the leisure pursuits of the current church members. This enables church members to invite their friends, coworkers, and family members to participate in sports and recreational activities with them. Such missional programming empowers church members to be personally involved in the evangelistic disciple-making process.

A local congregation that creates sport, recreation, and fitness opportunities that mirror the leisure pursuits of its members and community enhances the sense of belonging. Ministries with this sense of belonging will experience the greatest growth and most importantly, will have the greatest impact for the kingdom.

Summarizing Belonging

Belonging is the first step needed to reach secularized, unchurched, nonbelievers for Jesus Christ. By creating a safe and loving community within a sport and recreation environment, local churches enable and empower their members to reach people far from Christ. It is within this community that the unchurched experience the Gospel being lived out and in which they can warmly receive a verbal invitation to receive Jesus Christ as Lord and Savior. Once the Gospel has been lived out (proclaimed) and verbally presented (affirmed), nonbelievers are ready for the second "B": Believing.

BELIEVING

The second step in the Five-B Process is believing. The word believing is used to describe the conversion of a person who, by faith, enters into a personal relationship with Jesus Christ. In the Five-B Process, believing does not predate, nor is it a prerequisite of belonging. Believing is most successfully achieved in and through the belonging of an unchurched person to a local church sports outreach community.

All the realities of believing, including the blessings as well as the "thorns" (see sidebar "Gandhi and the Rose"), are in full view of all. It is what is often described as incarnational ministry, meaning the Gospel is being communicated "in the flesh." What follows are a number of key advantages to the act of believing coming within—and as a result of—belonging to a local church sports and recreation outreach community.

1. The Gospel is Communicated "On the Court"

Followers of Christ live out the Gospel (an act of proclamation) through actually participating in sporting activities. Through sports, Christians model how to overcome obstacles, persevere, strive for athletic excellence, be a consummate teammate, and how to win or lose.

2. The Gospel is Communicated "Off the Court"

It provides opportunities for Christians to befriend and love those far from Christ. The Gospel is communicated as teammates and even co-competitors on opposing teams demonstrate a Christian ethic of love in action (proclamation). Not only how the unchurched are loved—in heartfelt, Christ-like ways—but perhaps more importantly, that the unchurched are loved and cared for by those they hardly know is critical in bringing them to belief.

3. The "Cost" of the Gospel is Communicated

Belonging to a local church sports outreach ministry community leads to believing because it visually and verbally communicates "the cost of discipleship." The unchurched person observes the sacrifices Christian teammates make for their faith. These sacrifices are made visible both on the court, field, or pitch, and off. On the court, disciples of Christ compete in ways that are often out of sync with current culture. This includes refusing to cheat, take unfair advantage of, or physically harm co-competitors (opponents)—even if it means jeopardizing a chance to win a game. In addition, Christians model the relentless pursuit of excellence in their sporting activities, including being the consummate "hustle guy" or "take one for the team gal."

Off the court, followers of Christ can be seen making priorities of their families, vocation or career, and the Lord's Day church participation. Living out the Gospel proclaims the Gospel, which is further affirmed during post-game devotionals when insights into beliefs, commitments, and involvements are shared verbally.x Christians who verbalize how the Bible influences their thinking and how it provides both direction for their lives and strength for enduring life's many struggles communicate a rationale for their faith that is relevant and poignant. It communicates the Gospel in real-life color—warts and all. All of these elements work together for the Gospel to be perceived over a period of time, allowing for a deep comprehension of the blessings and costs of becoming a disciple of Christ.

GANDHI AND THE ROSE

Anna Nixon served as a missionary to India for decades and related a fascinating story involving an encounter between Gandhi and Christian missionaries who were trying to "evangelize" Gandhi at a social gathering. At one point in the discussion, Gandhi stood up, walked across the yard, plucked a rose, and brought it back to the group. While holding the rose up he said…

"You Christian missionaries work so hard. Learn a lesson from the rose. If you had the beauty of this rose…"

And while then passing the rose under the nose of each person he continued…

"And had the aroma of this rose…"

At which time he then placed a petal of the rose in the hand of each missionary. "And had the soft, pleasing feel of these luxuriant petals, people would traverse the garden…"

And now having their full attention, he pricked his finger on the rose's thorn to draw blood and concluded with:

"And even put up with its thorns, just to get next to you!"

4. The Gospel Process is Experienced

The belonging/believing starting point of the Five-B Process is affirmed by, and complementary with, the process missiologists have identified as being necessary for spiritual change to occur. Dr. Allan Tippett, a long-time professor and missiologist, identified four distinct periods (phases) that new converts to Christianity traverse on their spiritual journey: awareness, decision, incorporation, and maturity.

Period of Awareness

For Tippett, awareness was the process whereby the unregenerate (non-Christian) person moved from having no awareness of the Gospel to an initial awareness of the Gospel, thus beginning the journey to a full awareness of the Gospel and all its implications for life change.

Period of Decision

When full awareness of the Gospel and its implications have been reached, people realize a decision must be made. These people are now fully aware and can either choose to make a decision for Christ or turn their backs on Christ. A decision to receive Christ as Lord and Savior ushers people into the third period of the process.

Period of Incorporation

According to Tippett, it is imperative at this point for new converts to begin incorporating their newfound faith into an everyday Christian life. This leads to becoming a dedicated disciple of Jesus Christ.

Period of Maturity

For Tippett, a sincere incorporation of the Christian faith into one's life eventually leads to the fourth and last stage—full maturity.

It is easy to coordinate Tippett's four periods with the Five-B Process of the evangelistic disciple-making concept. The period of awareness coincides with the first "B"—belonging—or what some may describe as pre-evangelism. Tippett's second period—decision—easily fits within the second, and possibly third, "B" of believing and baptism, or what is commonly called evangelism. Tippett's third and fourth periods can then be aligned with the last two or three "B's," or what is often referred to as discipleship. His incorporation and maturity flow easily with baptizing, behaving, and becoming a dedicated disciple of Jesus Christ. *(Editor's Note: An adaptation and application of Tippet's process is found in Chapter 1).*

5. The Gospel is Accelerated

Belonging to a local church sports outreach ministry community has a natural accelerator effect for *evangelistic disciple-making.* The power of observing others who are experiencing life-change through the Gospel cannot be minimized. Hearing the testimonies of teammates professing initial faith in Christ and watching their spiritual growth over the course of time is incredibly inspirational and motivational—convicting even the most reluctant and reticent nonbelievers. All of these experiences accelerate the Gospel taking root in the lives of unbelievers and are great inspirations to believers observing the power of the Gospel as well.

> **ENVISIONING STRATEGIC & RELEVANT OUTREACH EXAMPLE "A"**
>
> If a congregation is located in a suburban residential area made up of young families or in an urban housing development populated by many latchkey kids, a relevant Level #2 "with whom" strategy would be to employ a Level #3 methodological model of youth sports.

A Conduit to the Broader Church

The belonging/believing starting point of the Five-B Process provides natural conduits from the outreach ministry to the broader church. These conduits are experienced in four basic ways:

Conduit #1—Relationships with Church Members

The primary conduit is relationship. For the unchurched person, this can be either a deepening of the relationship they had with the church member who invited them to join the league or activity and/or the development of relationships with new friends who are also members of the church. (See "You and Who" sidebar.)

Conduit #2—Relationships with Church Pastors and Staff

Another relationship conduit that sports outreach provides is between participants and the pastor, pastoral staff, and other church members. Sports outreach ministry leaders understand the strategic relevance of engaging other church staff and leaders in regular sports outreach participation. The most significant results happen when church staff members coach, compete, or otherwise take part as a participant, but if ability, interest, age, or gender precludes such participation, wise pastoral staff will still welcome the opportunity to periodically stop by for a visit or lead a sports devotional for one of the leagues.

ENVISIONING STRATEGIC & RELEVANT OUTREACH EXAMPLE "B"

If a local church is situated in an industrial or civic location with corporate offices and other work places for blue and white collar employees and executives, the relevant Level #2 missiological strategy to provide fitness opportunities and facilities, and/or health services, for the pre- and post-work or lunch-break crowd would prove to be Level #3 methodological model (what is done) that is both an effective outreach and an efficient utilization of resources.

Conduit #3—Involvement with Church Programs and Services

A third way that sports outreach ministry functions as a conduit for connecting unchurched participants with the local church is through making them aware of other services, programs, and activities the church offers. This could include distributing hard-copy brochures and flyers, verbal announcements and invitations presented by church staff and leaders, or social media networking. The most strategic approach is for various church departments to collaborate on integrated or dove-tailed ministries. These might include the sports and children's ministries cooperating on summer day camps and/or having the children's ministers prepare and deliver devotionals for children's leagues, culminating with an invitation to a special children's day at the church. Similar collaborative approaches can be envisioned for the sports and recreation ministry to work with the youth, men's, women's, young adult, and senior ministries of the church.

Conduit #4—Comfort with Church Facilities

This point is often taken for granted, or never even realized, but it should not be overlooked as it is profoundly helpful in connecting sports participants to the broader church. When the unchurched are comfortable on the church's campus it makes taking the next steps toward participating in other church activities much easier.

Coming to faith in Christ through a local church sports outreach community provides a natural process for moving the new believer through their spiritual journey toward becoming a disciple of Jesus Christ. In fact, a lot of discipleship occurs on a regular basis within the sports ministry community, particularly in areas like self-control and perseverance. Stated more strongly—the sports ministry of a local church is one of, if not the, best places for such character-based discipleship lessons to be learned.

BAPTIZING

The third step of the Five-B Process is baptizing.

Baptism Is Vital to Becoming an Obedient Disciple of Jesus Christ

Baptism is an important "first step" of obedience to Christ. The new believer will want to be baptized because Christ was baptized and because

Christ commanded that we should baptize believers. Obedience is a sign of true conversion. Sports ministries should encourage baptism as an act of obedience.

A LEAGUE WITH A HUNDRED REFS?

The sports minister of a local church was asked why his church's adult basketball leagues had no paid referees. His response? "We are called to make disciples of Christ, and by requiring our men to officiate themselves, we enable them to develop their personal character based on the concept of 'what would Jesus do?'" He went on to share that many of his men reported they found it easy to be a Christian in a worship service or Bible study, but extremely hard when faced with calling a foul on themselves during a basketball game—especially when it meant the difference between winning and losing.

Sports ministry in the local church provides an excellent laboratory for disciple-making.

The Relevance of Baptism to Evangelistic Disciple-Making

The relevance of baptism to evangelistic disciple-making within the Five-B Process has to do with how it impacts unchurched people coming to faith in Christ and helping them to become life-long, dedicated disciples of Jesus Christ. In addition, it shows how a local church sports outreach can encourage people in navigating their faith journey. There are three main reasons why baptism is vital to establishing disciples of Jesus Christ.

- *It Solidifies the Decision.* Baptism helps solidify the decision of new believers to become followers of Christ.
- *It Serves as an Inspiration.* Making a public declaration of a private decision through baptism serves as an inspiration to all who were prayerfully and lovingly engaged in aiding the newly baptized believer on their spiritual journey.
- *It is a Line in the Sand.* The public baptism of a new believer forever "draws a line in the sand." Whereas, looking back, people can sometimes become confused as to whether or not they ever made a decision for Christ, memories of going through baptismal classes,

the baptism itself, and gazing at a baptismal certificate with a specific date and signature of the officiating pastor all ensure that it was real.

It is important for all local church sports and recreation ministries to encourage baptism as a part of their evangelistic disciple-making efforts and process. An important consideration for sport-related parachurch-ministries is to have their athletes or coaches who come to Christ be baptized in a local church—preferably the church the parachurch sports ministry leader is an active member of.

> ## YOU AND WHO
>
> One principle for outreach that many churches have found to be successful has been termed the "You and Who" Rule. The rule is implemented in the following way: For all church-sponsored leagues, no church member (You) can participate without bringing a non-church member (Who).

BEHAVING

The fourth step of the Five B's is behaving. Behaving indicates radical life change from a secular, self-centered individual to a Christo-centric member of the church. It assumes a person who has come to faith in Christ has been baptized and has embarked on a lifelong journey of becoming a dedicated disciple of Jesus Christ.

Behaving as a Christian requires, and is built upon, three complementary areas:

- The empowerment of the indwelling Holy Spirit
- The humble submitting of a new disciple's will to Jesus Christ
- An intentional discipleship plan in a church sports ministry or discipleship process administrated by the church at large

Sports and recreation ministry becomes a laboratory in learning and practicing these bold new behaviors.

BECOMING

The fifth step of the Five B's is becoming. Becoming is a perfect descriptor because it communicates not only that evangelistic disciple-making is a process, but also that dedicated disciples of Jesus Christ never fully arrive—they are constantly progressing. More importantly, however, becoming effectively communicates the true essence of the *evangelistic disciple-making* process of the Five B's. Being committed to making dedicated, lifelong disciples of Jesus Christ, as opposed to simply seeing someone make a one-day decision about becoming a Christian, is significantly different.

THE RELEVANCE OF THE FIVE-B PROCESS FOR THE SPORTS OUTREACH MOVEMENT

There may be no other concept more relevant to the sports outreach movement than the Five-B Process. On this Level #2 philosophical principle hang all subsequent Level #3 methodological models. More importantly, all activities, outreaches, and endeavors are built upon the philosophy of ministry. And of course, all Level #2 philosophical principles are informed and shaped by their Level #1 theological truths.

If a church or ministry's Level #1 theological perspective of salvation is to "get someone saved," (a day's decision), then its Five-B approach is, at best, reduced to only two B's—belonging and believing. With this theological mindset, there is no need for the last three B's. If, however, a ministry's theology of salvation includes making disciples (lifelong, dedicated disciples), then each of the Five B's is of vital importance.

So, the question for sports and recreation outreach endeavors is this: Is this outreach about evangelism or is it about evangelistic disciple-making? Is the job of a local church sports outreach ministry completed upon a person's profession of faith, or is that profession of faith a welcomed and celebrated first step on a journey toward becoming a dedicated disciple of Jesus Christ? How sports outreach leaders answer this question will decide the future of the movement—and to a large degree, will impact the future of the church.

NOTES

For further discussion and reading on the 3-Tier Paradigm, the 4-Fold Evaluative Process, Evangelistic Discipleship, as well as other issues and terms described in this chapter, visit www.csrm.org/blog.

1. Tippett's process of change can be more fully studied in the following references: a) an article by Dr. Eiko Takamizama in the Torch Trinity Journal – "Religious Commitment Theory: A Model for Japanese Christians"; and b) a chapter entitled: "The Cultural Anthropology of Conversion." in the "Handbook of Religious Conversion," Editors Newton Malony and Samuel Southard (Birmingham, Alabama: Religious Education Press, 1992), 192-208.

9

Ethics of Competition in a Church Setting

Greg Linville

"When you are the best, people will listen, and your biblical worldview will get heard."

SPORTSMANSHIP, GAMESMANSHIP, OR CHRISTMANSHIP

Church leagues are often known for unruliness and out-of-control competitiveness. Some programs have even been shut down because a few "Christian athletes" let their competitive spirit get out of hand.

The 1980s saw Nike skyrocket as a major supplier of sporting goods in America. The company chose its name well—it comes from the mythological Greek goddess of victory, called Nike, and means "conqueror." All athletes desire to be conquerors. Even though wearing a pair of shoes advertised by professional athletes won't ensure you'll play like a professional, amateur athletes feel more confident when wearing quality shoes and uniforms.

The truth is, Americans want to win, and many adhere to the late Vince Lombardi's famous motto: "Winning isn't everything; it is the only thing." Athletes, coaches, and all those who follow professional athletic teams love to be associated with winners. The problem is that there are always more losers than winners, and even the best athletes fail. What began for many athletes as a joy can end up being a source of frustration and bitterness. So, questions arise. Is it possible to enjoy sports and competition? Can churches administrate leagues and games in which Christ can be glorified and the Gospel lived out? Do athletics have any redeeming value for the individual and the church? Thankfully the answer to these is a resounding, "Absolutely!" Not only can churches have teams that enjoy competing, but they can use competition for evangelism, discipleship, and building Christian character. It is possible to gain not only a victory, but also to experience overwhelming victory as we allow God to use our sports abilities.

SPORTSMANSHIP AND GAMESMANSHIP

Before we can understand where we need to go, we need to understand where we have been and where we are.

Modern day philosophic foundations for competition ethics stem from the concept of sportsmanship. As one contemplates modern-day sports, it is imperative to heed the advice of Dr. Arnold Beisser: "In sports, unless more than the surface is explored, men become slaves, instead of exercising free will."[1] Sportsmanship needs to be reviewed "below the surface," particularly in light of what happens in sports arenas around the world.

Sportsmanship is an admirable goal; however, it is seldom adhered to in athletics. Good sportsmanship is often overruled by a desire or a demand to win—and it is seldom rewarded. Accepting the prevailing views on winning at face value enslaves many to the ethic of "win at all costs." Winning is exalted as the ultimate accomplishment. To subdue and conquer an opponent is the pinnacle of sports success. Conversely, losers are considered worth nothing. They are totally useless, inept, and are taunted and trampled by opponents.

Defining the terms

The following definitions are important to understand any further discussion of competitive ethics.

The word *ship* means "to send, bear, or transport." When used in the English language as a suffix, it denotes "the bearing of a condition, character, office, or skill." The word *man* is the generic word used to describe the human race. Therefore, *man-ship* has the connotation of humankind bearing certain conditions, characteristics, offices, or skills. When *sports* is added to *man-ship*, it becomes *sportsmanship*, the definitive word to describe the characteristics, skills, and ethics that sports people bear upon themselves as they compete.

But the definition of sportsmanship continues to evolve depending on who defines it. Generally it represents acceptable ethics and morals—such as having fun, playing fair, using skills, maximizing abilities, and being a gracious winner or loser—that are all positive traits to exhibit within a church context.

These ethics, however, are determined by the popular opinion of a society, which has no permanent mooring.

Morality changes according to culture, country, religion, or popular opinion. Sportsmanship has no final authority. It fluctuates with places, times, players, and coaches. But one thing does not change—the desire to win. Thus, the final authority or ethic of sports is to win, and the ethic of sports is not determined by a philosophical standard but by a pragmatic one. Although sportsmanship espouses such ideals as fairness and fun, only winners are rewarded.

Therefore, out of sportsmanship a new ethic evolves—gamesmanship. Gamesmanship maintains that the highest ethic of sports is to win. Fun is no longer the foundation of competitive ethics—winning is.

Because gamesmanship has replaced sportsmanship as the basis for determining competitive ethics in secular as well as church sports, athletes have received mixed messages about their attitudes and actions. Often, what's communicated by parents, coaches, and athletic administrators, even in church leagues, is to win, regardless of the cost or means. In fact, it is common for players to observe contradictions between what they are told and what they see. Athletes are told to have fun, be coachable, and respect authority—then they observe coaches, school administrators, and booster club members yelling obscenities at umpires, referees, or opposing teams. Their coach says, "All that matters is to give your best effort," yet the coach only plays the best athletes on the team. The verbal message is to have fun, but the nonverbal message is that adults are only concerned about winning.

Athletes are also confused about what is really fair. One coach accuses another of cheating while also being guilty of cheating. Coaches believe their actions are justifiable because they do not consider those actions to be cheating. They believe they are only "bending the rules" to benefit their own players or program. In essence, they base their morality on humanistic pragmatism, doing whatever it takes to win and communicating by their actions that winning is more important than any standard of morality. These coaches believe they are concerned about their players—but in reality, their only priority is to win.

One of the saddest accounts of what the pressure to win can do to a man is found in the autobiography of Coach Taylor Locke. Locke served as head basketball coach at four major universities. He began to cheat in earnest after losing repeatedly to other universities who had, in his opinion, won because they had cheated. In his book *Caught in the Net,* he relates his experience while coaching at Clemson University.

> "At Clemson I lost touch with my values. Stuff was just lying there. Money came easy and so did the women. There were alumni wives who were quite open about their personal need for affection ... I had never been a part of anything like this before. After I married Nancy and all through my years at West Point and Miami, I wouldn't even consider looking at another woman. It was the way I was brought up.
>
> But, my values changed almost overnight at Clemson. The pressures from losing in my first two or three years made me an easy target, I guess. I was drinking too much Scotch, popping too many pills. Life was moving too fast for this small town guy to handle. My values slipped and slipped and slipped, and the people who got hurt were my family. We had some family problems ... but those problems could be attributed to basketball, not booze, pills, and women.
>
> I was ... married to my job ... Everybody says there is God, your family, and your job. I loved my job first ... If I can offer one bit of advice to a young coach today ... it is that the individual must be willing to accept the unwritten code which already exists ... Just go out and get the job done. If it is recruiting, then go out and recruit. Play the game by the same rules of the street. It is like

in sales or anything else—somewhere down the line you are going to have to give out green stamps. You are going to have to cheat somewhere down the line, but do it and don't talk about it. Take it from someone who cheated and got caught."[2]

Coach Locke admits that he lost his moral compass, but that is not the saddest part of his story. The saddest part is not that his family suffered or that his mental or physical health failed as a direct result of his conscious decisions to cheat and turn his back on what he knew to be right. Even after being caught, fired, and ridiculed, causing everyone great agony, the saddest part is he still does not admit that cheating, lying, and breaking the rules are wrong.

This is the epitome of "gamesmanship." The attitudes and actions of gamesmanship are hardly congruent with the essence of sportsmanship and yet are a direct result of the faulty philosophical premise upon which sportsmanship is based. Some coaches and athletes believe it is acceptable to lose not only your soul, but also your marriage, health, and integrity just to win a few more games. This belief system, based upon humanistic relativism, is not a new one:

"The emphasis upon winning and the absence of a body of established amateur traditions permitted large outlays of money for football, the open recruitment of player talent, fierce training schedules, and clear cases of premeditated brutality. The eligibility problem, professionalism, deaths and serious injuries from football, and a lack of gentlemanly behavior, and the issue of whether to make football even more financially rewarding and respectable all contributed to a virtual state of anarchy among the nation's colleges. Consequently, football became the subject of a vigorous nationwide debate which eventually involved college presidents, faculties, the press, and even the president of the United States ... The spirit of American youth, as of the American man, is to, "get there" by fair means or foul, and the lack of moral scruple which pervades the struggles of the business world meets with temptations equally irresistible in the miniature contest of the football field."[3]

This quote is not from the latest edition of the *New York Times* or *Chicago Tribune*. It was written in 1890. The problem is not a new one. The pressures to win at all costs have been negatively affecting those involved with athletics for years. These problems occur because of the aforementioned fluctuation of morals and values, which even in a church setting have their root in the philosophy of humanistic relativism. The major tenet of relativism is that there is no ultimate or final authority and, therefore, everything is relative. People are free to establish their own morality and do whatever they wish. They decide for themselves what is moral and right. The effect this has on sports and athletes is easily observed.

Since only winners are rewarded, some, but by no means all, athletes believe it is allowable to cheat if cheating helps them win. Moralistic platitudes are forgotten. Victory is the priority. And the result of this relativism is ethical chaos. Teams, leagues, and institutions able to exert the influence of power, money, prestige, or favors increase their chances of winning and decrease their chances of being penalized for cheating even if they get caught. Those who cannot—or will not—cheat or exert unprincipled influences sometimes compete at a great disadvantage. The best athlete or team doesn't always win. Sadly, those with the lowest set of morals are too often the victors.

Tragically, as a result of this cheating, the essence of competition is compromised and victory becomes a hollow shell, lacking meaning. Competitors who cheat to win cheat themselves, because in the end their victory is meaningless.

What began innocently enough as a code of ethics to rule unscrupulous competition among athletes has too often degenerated into immorality. Sportsmanship often devolves into gamesmanship.

For Christian athletes and churches desiring to compete in sports with the proper code of ethics, neither sportsmanship nor gamesmanship is totally satisfying. Total fulfillment and satisfaction can only be found in "Christmanship." Christmanship encourages athletes to live out the characteristics, attitudes, and skills that emulate Christ and conform to his image in the arena of competition.

Christmanship embodies the best of sportsmanship (fun, fairness, being a good loser, etc.) and the best of gamesmanship (giving one's best effort within the rules to win), but it transcends and surpasses them both. It challenges the Christian athlete to compete as Christ would compete. For most athletes, however, this concept of Christmanship may be nothing more than a nebulous idea.

Since there are no known accounts of Jesus competing in leagues or competitions of his day, we must look at different Scriptures that reveal the foundations and parameters from which this ethic can be constructed. Christmanship will prescribe specific actions and attitudes, enabling athletes to experience a total fulfillment and satisfaction in their competitions. Their actions will not be based on relativistic morals that change with the winds, nor will they find their root in the quagmire of pragmatism, but rather their actions will be rooted in the authority of God's will as revealed through his Scriptures. Only through these scriptural concepts and principles will athletes experience overwhelming victory.

REMOLDING OUR MINDS

Before exploring the specific actions and attitudes required for a Christian ethic of competition, an attitude adjustment must take place. The apostle Paul mandates in Romans 12:2 to "be transformed by the renewing of our minds." Jesus Christ must be allowed to remold our minds, and this is never more applicable than in the realm of competition. Athletes must put aside all previously held beliefs concerning sports and allow God to begin afresh with their minds. Most athletes have been coached and have competed according to the ethics that are prevalent in our relativistic society. As previously explained, these ethics are rooted in a pragmatism of winning at all costs.

Prayer and thoughtful contemplation are necessary before considering the following seven areas. At first glance, these actions and attitudes may not fit into a previously held belief. But upon further contemplation, even the most fiercely competitive of athletes will understand that true fulfillment comes only by allowing Jesus Christ to shape their thinking.

The seven areas are teammates, coaches, officials, opponents, competition, winning and losing, and success.

Teammates

At first, athletes might not believe they have a problem with teammates. Commitment to their team is assumed. However, a closer look at why athletes compete often reveals self-centered motivations that have very little to do with concern for their team.

Athletes are rarely bold enough to admit they compete not for the team's sake, but rather for their own glory or personal gratification. Many athletes do not play for a team, school, or club solely for the benefit of that group. They play for their own glory and for their own particular satisfaction, fulfillment, thrill, and excitement. This is a subtle yet profound distinction. If an individual is participating for his or her own gratification and is unwilling to submit to the team's needs, problems arise. Athletes must clarify their own motivations for competing by asking themselves the following questions:

- Why do I feel bad when I make a mistake? Is it because it reflects poorly on me (embarrassment) or because it hurts the team?
- When I'm caught stealing in baseball, miss a shot in basketball or soccer, bowl out in cricket, or miss a tackle in football, is my first thought of how I hurt the team's chances to win or about my own batting average or shooting percentage?
- Do I willingly sacrifice personal gain to enhance the team's chance to succeed?
- When I don't play to my fullest potential (don't run out a pop fly on the baseball field or give all I have to score a try on the rugby pitch) or don't come to a game properly rested and prepared, do I consider that I have let my teammates down?
- Why do I feel excited and good after having play a great game even if the team lost?

Athletes would do well to understand the relevance of Philippians 2:3–4: "Do nothing out of rivalry or conceit, but in humility consider others as more important than yourselves. Everyone should look out not only for his own interests, but also for the interests of others." The apostle Paul indicates that we must "live together in harmony, live together in love."

As important as this biblical principle is, it must be balanced by another concept described in John's Gospel. Athletes should be concerned about teammates and the team's best interest, and they should never feel guilty about their own enjoyment and enthusiasm for competing. In John 10:10, the apostle communicates that Christ came so we might have a fulfilled life. Therefore, we can be assured God rejoices when we compete to our fullest ability and thoroughly enjoy our participation in sports. After all, Christ is the one who created us and knows us in the most intimate sense possible. As a loving Father, he is happy when we experience exhilaration while competing.

The early Greek athletes probably understood this concept better than present-day competitors do. They believed the gods had created them with certain abilities and gave them opportunities to use their gifts. They viewed their competition as an act of worship. In the movie *Chariots of Fire*, Eric Liddell gives one of the most incredible articulations of this in Hollywood history when he describes how he feels about running and how it relates to his call to the mission field. "I believe God made me for a purpose—for China. But he also made me fast, and when I run, I feel his pleasure. To give it up would be to hold him in contempt. To win is to honor him."

Therefore, Christian athletes and church-based sports ministries should promote the joy of competing. They should know that their competition pleases Christ, but they must always keep personal gains, goals, and preferences in balance with the goals and needs of their team and teammates. Some ways to do this are by maintaining a close walk with Christ, participating in an accountability group, and looking to godly mentors who understand the pressures of competition.

Coaches

Players often resent their coaches. They even resent the coaches' demands for hustle, conditioning, and discipline. Many athletes do not understand what discipline really is—they believe that discipline is punishment. Discipline, however, is not necessarily what athletes deserve when they do something wrong.

A dictionary definition of *discipline* is "training to act in accordance with rules or actions." Discipline more clearly suggests the idea of training than it does of punishment. It refers to the constraints that it takes to train athletes in appropriate ways of conducting themselves. Wise athletes will submit themselves fully to knowledgeable coaches who care enough about their athletes to push them to excellence. Athletes should never resent rigorous training or discipline designed to push them to excel. Discipline coming from a caring, educated, and wise coach will be a positive force propelling athletes forward into their greatest potential. This potential will only be reached, however, if the athletes willingly submit and fully apply themselves to it.

It is appropriate for athletes to want, and for churches to try to provide, the best coaching available. Rather than blindly enrolling in the local church league and/or school athletic program, athletes should research the satisfaction levels and successes of the teams and leagues they are considering joining. Questions that should be asked of a league, school, or coach are:

- What is the statement of purpose for your league, school, and/or coach?
- What is your philosophy of competition and coaching?
- What policies do you have about team membership and/or cutting players?
- What added expenses and/or fees are there to participate?
- Are the coaches in the leagues trained in the psychological, emotional, and physiological aspects of coaching?
- What is the philosophy of playing time?
- What is the methodology of teaching styles?

There are times when athletes have no choice regarding who their coach is and will have to play for a coach who is intolerable for one reason or another. If this happens, Christian athletes have a unique opportunity to show evidence of their faith. Of course, Christian players should never obey a coach's demands to cheat or purposely injure an opposing player, but for the most part, they should go beyond what their coach requires in terms of conscientious training and effort. Regardless of how a coach treats players, those players must always demonstrate respect for their coach. Moreover, in relating to a coach, Christian players must keep the goal of emulating Christ as their top priority. Christ will be glorified if church leaders and coaches help athletes keep their priorities straight and seek Christmanship as opposed to personal gain.

Officials

The third area in which church leaders and athletes must remold their minds is the way they view and interact with sports officials. Nowhere in athletics is there more verbal abuse or more frustration vented than from athletes and coaches to referees and umpires. Everyone knows at least one horror story of a Christian athlete or team losing their Christian witness by behaving inappropriately toward an official. Officials, athletes, and church teams must learn to get along as partners in competition.

Athletes must understand that officials are facilitators of competition, not enemies. Officials include league directors and commissioners, referees, umpires, scorekeepers, tournament directors, and others. An official's role is to facilitate leagues, games, competitions, and tournaments, and they are needed to ensure that competitions proceed in the fairest way possible. This is particularly important in a church ministry setting, as officials keep the Christian distinctive central to the competition. Athletes must understand that without officials, there would be no games and no competitions.

Not only should officials be regarded as facilitators, but Christian competitors must also view them as people created in the image of God. Since God created these people—and since Christ died for them—it is imperative that Christian athletes go out of their way to love them. Moreover, Christian athletes must explore how they can enhance officials' ability to do their jobs.

This attitude is diametrically opposed to the mindset of many people who are involved in athletics today. Most competitors operate under the "win at all costs" concept concerning officials. They believe they are entitled to "work officials" to gain an advantage over an opponent. Most athletes have been trained to "work an official." Coaches and trainers have taught their athletes how to gain an unfair advantage by using what they consider "techniques" to get an official to call things their way. Because of this, coaches of most athletes believe they have the right to yell, scream, threaten, intimidate, or even physically abuse an official in order to get a call changed or an event run to one's benefit.

But rather than "work" an official, Christians are called to "live at peace with everyone" (Rom. 12:18). Christian athletes who operate under the Christmanship concept must relate the command of Romans to their interactions with officials. Romans 12 mandates that even if players are persecuted by officials, their response must be to bless them and to strive to live at peace with them. The apostle Paul did not ask us to get along with others as long as the other persons are willing—he said we are to live at peace with them as much as it depends upon us. Christian athletes cannot assume responsibility for an official's actions toward them. They can only be responsible for their own actions toward the official.

A typical interaction with officials often proceeds like this: Coaches or players start badgering officials in subtle ways. If they perceive that the official is not listening to their complaints, then their intensity, volume, and/or profanity increases. If their verbal attacks are regular and consistent, the official usually tunes them out. Or worse—the official is distracted from calling the game. The coach then feels he must become even more demonstrative. Coaches may even intimidate or physically assault an official. Sometimes these actions get immediate results, but the results are always short-term gains. The long-term result is a lost relationship and most likely an official who may spite a coach or athlete who has previously intimidated him. Then the cycle begins again. To experience overwhelming victory, athletes must seek to understand and appreciate officials.

Caz McCaslin, founder and president of Upward Unlimited, has developed the Circle of Praise and the Circle of Criticism to illustrate this idea. In the Circle of Praise, the coach sets the standard for players and spectators. If the coach speaks kindly to the officials, encouraging them and calling attention to good calls, then the team and the spectators will do likewise. The coach's positive actions and positive comments elicit positive actions and reactions from players and spectators alike. The opposite is true for the Circle of Criticism. As a coach talks negatively to officials, finding fault with calls or verbalizing his displeasure, players and spectators alike will take on the negative tones of the coach. These escalate until an "us-against-them" attitude is fostered, creating dissension and tension between coaches, players, and spectators, all directed toward the officials. Thus, a vicious Circle of Criticism is born, bringing dishonor to the cause of Christ and limiting, if not destroying, the opportunity for an effective Christian witness.

Players in youth leagues, junior and senior high school, college, and even professional leagues must realize that they should rarely, if ever, have any confrontations with game officials. This is not their job or role. Confrontations should be left up to coaches and athletic directors. Most coaches and athletic directors have avenues available to them through which they can air their grievances. It is imperative that they go through their given systems to address unfair practices. Athletes should either remain silent in their interactions with officials or seek ways to encourage them.

Opponents

Many amateur church league athletes know the frustration of rushing from work, jumping into their car, and speeding down the highway while simultaneously putting on a uniform and eating a fast-food burger and fries. They arrive at a dusty softball field or a sweat-smelling gymnasium only to find that their opponent did not show up. What was excited anticipation is now nothing more than frustration because there is no one to play. This illustration shows that opponents are important, and athletes need to consider how they view their opponents.

Actually, the word *opponent* is an inappropriate term to describe the players on the other team. *Opponent* conveys the idea that competitors have enemies. There are no enemies when it comes to sports, only other competitors. Athletes must realize the people with whom they compete should be seen as "co-competitors." Without them, there would be no game or competition. Co-competitors must be viewed as people created by God and for whom Christ came and died. They must be treated with the utmost dignity and respect. They must never be cheated, purposely injured, intimidated, discouraged, or forced to compete in a manner that is damaging to them or that hinders any opportunity to bear a good witness. Winning by anything other than one's own ability is not fulfilling. If athletes must cheat or harm their co-competitors to win, the win is not due to their superior skills or team. Rather, it is due to that athlete's lower moral standards. Jesus admonishes us to be the light that drives out darkness and the salt that brings flavor. Cheating to win extinguishes the light and contaminates the salt, hindering the cause of Christ.

Co-competitors must also be encouraged to excel. Not only should they be treated fairly and given an equal opportunity to win, but they also must be encouraged to compete to their fullest. A scene in the movie Chariots of Fire exemplifies this concept. Sprinter Eric Liddell, known as the "Flying Scot," was just about to run the four-hundred-meter race in the Olympics when he was given a note by Jackson Schultz, an opponent on the American team. It read: "It says in the old book, 'He that honors me I will honor.'" The movie does not quite portray reality—the note was actually written by the British team's trainer and signed by the entire British team. The movie director used Schultz, however, to personify all the notes and words of encouragement Liddell did receive from his opponents. Though he suffered much ridicule from others for refusing to participate in a race on Sunday (which he believed would be breaking the commandment to keep the Sabbath holy), Liddell was one of the most respected athletes of his generation and was greatly uplifted by all the encouragement he received from his co-competitors.

Initially, the idea of encouraging one's opponent sounds ludicrous until church leaders, athletes, and coaches examine their premise for competing. If winning is the only goal, then, of course, athletes can do anything to win—including cheating, injuring, intimidating, and discouraging their opponents. If the goal, however, is to compete against the best and to measure oneself against that competition, as well as to win, then true competitors want their co-competitors to push them to their fullest potential. Furthermore, for those who are believers in Christ, the goal of every action is to conform to the image of Christ—Christmanship. In the ethic of Christmanship, cheating, maiming, intimidating, and even discouraging is not appropriate; and winning is only important when it is the measuring device used by both competitors.

Beyond attempts to encourage co-competitors, athletes must also strive to compete at their fullest potentials, regardless of the score. If they do not, they are making a statement that their co-competitors are not worthy of their best efforts. Furthermore, a lack of effort does not challenge a co-competitor to improve. A true competitor never insults a co-competitor by not giving them his or her best effort. There is a difference, however, between competing with full intensity and humiliating an opponent. Ideally, once athletes have an understanding of the full implication of competing in the image of Christ, they will place less emphasis on the score and outcome and more emphasis on their own efforts. But there can still be times when the score differential is so huge that a co-competitor feels humiliated. At times like this, Christian athletes have to ask what Christ would do.

Bob Briner, in *Roaring Lambs*, put the purpose of competition this way:

> Many well-known stars as well as movers and shakers in sports make their commitment to Christ very public. Such Hall of Fame caliber names as Tom Landry and Roger Staubach in football, Julius Irving in basketball, Orel Hershiser and radio announcer Ernie Harwell in baseball, and Stan Smith in

tennis are only a representative few who openly and avidly proclaim Christ. Chapter...It is clear that the call to be salt calls for both competence and commitment—we must be at our best in order to win the kind of hearing Christ deserves.Chapter...Our responsibility is to do our best and to leave the results with Him in the knowledge that the ultimate victory is ours through Christ.[4]

The purpose of competing is to worship God with and through our athletic abilities. We see in Briner's quote that the purpose of training to be the best is to gain a platform. Our culture holds winners up on a pedestal. Once there, they have an opportunity to speak, and people of all ages and all walks of life will listen. Christian athletes must strive to be the best at what they do in order to gain a voice in the world. Competition can thus be considered the fulfillment of one's duty to God—because when you are the best, people will listen, and your biblical worldview will have a platform.

So, we compete to glorify God, be the best we can be, hone our skills, and win the game, never to harm or humiliate an opponent (intentionally or through striving for excellence).

Competition

Although some of the issues surrounding one's co-competitors are complex, they are always best dealt with by asking the question, "What would Christ do in this situation, and how would he compete?"

The issues become clearer when athletes contemplate the meaning of competition itself. Competition is a measuring stick. Just as I want my car's oil to be measured by an accurate stick, I, as a competitor, want to measure myself against proper and accurate competition.

There are people who believe competition is harmful, wrong, and even repugnant to God—they would dispose of all competition if they could. However, just because some believe competition is innately evil does not mean it really is. Is it possible for competition to be acceptable within a Christian worldview or in a church ministry context? The answer is clear. Not only is competition compatible with the Christian worldview, but it is also part of God's design for the world. Competition is part of the universe that God created.

In God's natural revelation to us we see that nature is full of competition. Trees stretch to the sky, competing for sunlight; roots extend deep into the ground, competing for the moisture and nutrients they need to survive. Church leaders should understand that competition is an amoral force. In and of itself, it is neither good nor bad. Competition may bring out the best or the worst in those who compete, but we cannot blame competition itself if athletes fail morally or emotionally.

How athletes choose to respond to competition determines whether it is positive or negative. God uses competition to help mold athletes into the men and women he desires them to be. Any attempt to remove competition from our lives will only hamper our spiritual development, not improve it.

Therefore, competition needs to be redefined. The word *competition* comes from the Latin verb that means "to seek together." Rainer Martens in his book *Joy and Sadness in Children's Sports* has described competition as, "activities directed toward attaining a standard or goal in which a person's or group's performance is evaluated relative to selected other individuals or groups."[5] Competition assumes cooperation. It demands that co-competitors challenge one another to excel. Challenging one another to excel is a different concept than competing *against* someone. When competitors view competition in its proper sense, they can minimize the negatives associated with it and maximize the opportunities for competition to become a truly cooperative effort, helping to develop them into the people they need to become. So, in the classic sense of the word, competitors do not compete *against* one another.

A closer look at the word *against* is now necessary. The word *against* has as its root word, *again*, which means "once more, additionally, or furthermore." From this connotation, the following definitions of the word *against* are derived: "close beside or in front of; in anticipation of; or as contrasted with." Therefore, playing *against* someone in this sense assumes that something is done once more—or again—and in contrast. Competitors contrast their skills *against* other competitors. Thus, competition becomes a gauge or a measuring stick that competitors use to judge themselves. One does not compete *against* an enemy but rather competes *against* a standard. This standard can be embodied in another individual or team but may also be embodied in oneself, a clock, or a challenge.

Winning and Losing

Athletes who want to gain a proper perspective on winning, losing, and competition should ask themselves the following questions:

- Is it fulfilling to win by forfeit?
- Is it fulfilling to win every competition by large margins?
- Is it fulfilling to win a game only by cheating, taking performance-enhancing drugs, or by any other unfair action?
- Is it fulfilling to have my team win a game without my participation?

Hopefully, athletes will recognize that winning by forfeit or by having far superior talent is unfulfilling. It is also unfulfilling to achieve victory by cheating, because cheating does not accurately gauge an athlete's abilities—only their morals. Moreover, athletes are rarely satisfied if they do not play in a game, even if their team wins. When players become so wrapped up in winning and losing, they never enjoy the thrill of simply competing or of meeting the challenge of competing against a standard. It is sad to see so many athletes missing out on the true excitement of competition because they are so focused on winning.

Winning is important, but only when it is a result of one's dedicated and determined effort. Winning is never as important as competing. Trophies pale in comparison to the memory of the game in which the trophy was won. Only when competitors "remold their minds" can they experience fulfillment. This understanding of competition provides a foundation from which to talk about true success.

Children just want to participate; they want to play the game. As they get older, participation often gets overshadowed by winning. But just playing a sport—just participating—will always be a primary motivator for people of all ages. This concept of participation has great implications for the church, because as we provide avenues of participation, we open the doors of the church to the nonbelieving world.

Success

Success is not the gift, but rather what one does with the gift (Matt. 25:14–30). All gifts are of equal value, but all uses are not. The gift of music is just as important as the gift of parenting. The gift of drama is just as important as the gift of athletic prowess. All gifts are necessary to human life, and all gifts are important. The question is, "How can athletes use their gifts?"

Success is not only being number one but also being a consistent winner. The professional basketball team the Los Angeles Clippers finished the 1987 season with a record of 12 and 70. Does this losing record make them unsuccessful? The team consisted of a dozen or so of the top 250 basketball players in the world. They were highly successful athletes. Their team may not have been successful as a unit, but that did not mean as individuals they were not successful. They were not number one, but they could still be considered successful if they adhered to the true spirit of the word competition and cooperatively pushed the teams they played to greater heights. We must always be careful in establishing criteria for success. Christmanship rejoices with the team or individual that finishes first but never maintains that athletes can only be successful by being number one.

Success is not money, prestige, trophies, or any other earthly treasure. For Christian athletes, success is one thing only: maximizing their gifts to the fullest by competing in the image of Jesus Christ. This is significant because this concept of success actually acknowledges the validity and worth of athletics and recreation. Athletes understand that competition is a force capable of molding them into the image of Christ in a way that frees them to realize they can worship God in and through their competing. Then they learn lessons from competing. Competition has tremendous worth when athletes conform themselves to Christ while competing. If athletes can be judged by God as successful by simply using the gifts he gave them, then sports cannot be condemned as being less important than any other endeavor.

Some may argue that sports in and of themselves have no redemptive value, but by that criteria, what does? The world of finance? Teaching? Medicine? The only endeavor that could possibly claim for itself any eternal significance would be some sort of religious activity. But following that reasoning to its logical conclusion would result in everyone becoming full-time religious workers. And that is totally illogical, because the world could not survive without doctors, farmers, and teachers. Athletes and church leaders who use athletics for the Gospel's sake must realize that their efforts are meaningful. They must be set free to use their gifts fully alongside other believers who are using their gifts. But they must not use this idea of success as an excuse for losing consistently. Success is conforming to the image of Christ in whatever he has given us the ability to do (Phil. 3:7–14).

This view of success is difficult to accept by those who have long believed that winning is everything. However, for the Christian competitor, it will bring fulfillment like nothing else can. Churches wanting to impact culture will realize the value of sport and competition as reaching and teaching tools. As these tools are properly used and administered by church leaders, they will be used by God to touch the hearts and minds of those who want to play sports.

In order for athletes to have their minds remolded, one essential question must be answered: Have you said "yes" to Jesus Christ? Do you have a personal relationship with him?

He cannot remold your mind unless you give it to him. You will not experience an overwhelming victory unless you decide to compete Christ's way. Are you frustrated by your athletic experiences? Has the fun disappeared? Is your life lacking peace and fulfillment? Please consider giving your life, including your sporting life, to Christ. It is as simple as praying: "Dear Jesus, please forgive me for trying to live my life on my own. I want you to come into my life. I want a personal relationship with you. Please give me your guidance. Amen." That's all there is to it. If you prayed that prayer, you now have a new coach. His name is Jesus, and he is overjoyed to be in right relationship to you.

Christian athletes must emulate Jesus Christ in everything they do, including the way they compete. They must step out of the humanistic ethic of sportsmanship and the pragmatic ethic of gamesmanship and follow the principles of Christmanship. The practical aspects of Christmanship are attained by competing in the image of Jesus Christ. These precepts include interacting with teammates, coaches, co-competitors, and officials as Christ would interact. These precepts also demand that players not miss the exhilaration of competing by being caught up in winning and losing a game. Athletes must compete with an infectious zeal. They must also have a proper view of success and seek to give their ultimate effort to using and maximizing their gifts. Christian athletes must compete in the image of Christ and allow their experiences in competition to further mold them into the image of Christ. In the words of Brother Lawrence, competitors must "practice the presence of Christ" in everything they do, including their competition!

ETHICS AND RESPONDING TO VALUE-SHATTERING CULTURAL CHANGES

Christmanship provides a solid foundation for dealing with ethical dilemmas related to sports and competition, but there is an entirely different world of ethics and morality that local church sports and recreation ministers must consider. These have less to do with sports and everything to do with encountering people who are increasingly secular. Our culture is becoming ever more antagonistic to Christianity, and athletes from that culture may want to participate in sports ministry programming. Additionally, the scope of Biblical illiteracy has reached historic highs, which means that the uninitiated will likely not understand, much less agree with, a Christian worldview. The tide of societal change and sexual revolution is rising, threatening all but the most securely rooted, biblically grounded church that seeks to exist in accordance and agreement with God's Word. Local church sports and recreation ministers should be informed and prepared to minister in a changing moral landscape. *(Editor's Note: The intent of this book is not to give any legal or policy advice but only to make the recreation and sports minister aware of the issues they may face as they lead the local church in ministry that impacts postmodern culture. Always seek the counsel of the pastor, deacons/elders, denominational leadership and competent legal counsel when dealing with potentially explosive cultural issues.)*

FINAL ADMONITIONS AND ENCOURAGEMENTS

The Church is called to lead, not follow. The Church that remains biblically rooted will no doubt lead, and the world is greatly in need of highly ethical leadership.

Sports and recreation ministers should remember their call to lead, not being unduly swayed by the shifting winds of cultural change. They should be steadfast in organizing and operating their local church's sports and recreation ministry, led by the Holy Spirit in accordance with God's Word in a truly "Jesus Ethic." Eternity for billions of people rests in the balance.

NOTES

1. Shirley, Bill. "Mad About Sports," *The Plain Dealer* (January 18, 1987): G–3. Quoting from Beisser, Arnold R. Madness in *Sports* (Bowie, MD: Charles Press, 1977).

2. Locke, T. *Caught in the Net* (West Point, NY: Leisure Press, 1982), 139, 172, 174.

3. Rader, B. *American Sports* (Englewood Cliffs, NJ: Prentice-Hall, 1983), 134–35.

4. Briner, B. *Roaring Lambs* (Grand Rapids, MI: Zondervan Publishing House, 1993), 44, 46.

5. Martens, R. *Joy and Sadness in Children's Sports* (Champaign, IL: Human Kinetics Press, 1978).

10

Introduction to Recreation and Sports Ministry for All Ages

Judi Jackson

"A well-planned, well-promoted, and well-executed program to all ages offers opportunity to impact the lives of many."

As we consider recreation throughout a lifetime, we need to explore the interests, abilities, and developmental issues typically associated with the different ages and stages of life. What we want to understand are the norms, or the standards, so we may plan recreation programs to suit the age group with which we are working.

Life is separated by stages into general age divisions. Infancy is regarded as the period of childhood between birth and eighteen months (those who are, for the most part, pre-speech). Early childhood (referring to toddlers and preschoolers) generally includes those from eighteen months to five years of age. The category of middle childhood spans the years between five and twelve. The youth, or adolescent, years cover those from thirteen to eighteen (but can be lowered to age ten and raised to age twenty, depending on individual development). Young adults include anyone from age twenty to approximately thirty-five to thirty-nine years old. Median adulthood typically begins at age forty and continues through age sixty. Finally, senior adults are grouped together as anyone sixty years of age and older.

EXPLORING INFANTS AND PRESCHOOLERS

One misconception regarding infants and preschoolers is that there is a particular age at which specific motor skills should be mastered and, if they are not, the child is considered developmentally delayed. On the contrary, the concept of maturation allows for age variation in the unfolding of a child's potential. Granted, the variation is usually subtle in the first year, but no parent should be alarmed, for example, if their child is not walking by ten months of age. On the contrary, a more normal progression involves a child learning to walk after the one year mark and sometimes even closer to two years.[1]

Considering recreational options for newborns is a new phenomenon and focuses on providing infants the appropriate opportunity to progress in a natural, unforced manner. Natural instincts as well as imitation and gentle stimulation guide the development of both gross and fine motor skills. An infant is limited in the amount of motor activity in which he can engage, but his senses are active. When a cylindrical toy or rattle is placed in a baby's palm, the general response is for the fingers to attempt to wrap around the object. A simple game of pat-a-cake helps teach an infant the basics of coordination and relationship with others. Reading a book aloud, even to the youngest of infants, stimulates the child's sense of hearing and may even help to develop the sense of sight as colored pictures are shown throughout the storytelling process. Through these types of trial and error motor activities, infants experiment with their bodies and begin to master the skills necessary for the next developmental levels. Parents and other childcare providers should see their main responsibility as providing a safe environment in which infants can move freely and are protected.[2]

The Playorena program, designed by Michael and Susan Astor in Marion County, California, was structured to take toddlers step-by-step through the stages of early motor development while educating parents in the process. Parental awareness of the sequential and individually differing nature of the developmental process is crucial in reducing the negative effects that result from unrealistic expectations. "Young children have a strong innate need for all different kinds of movement and motion. We know that a parent's confidence in their child, and in their own parenting skills, provides the basis for the child's own self confidence."[3]

In the last twenty-five years, another toddler-oriented program, Gymboree, has used the Play with a Purpose philosophy to emphasize the importance of play, movement, and exploration in the early years. This has led to a lifestyle concept that respects and encourages the natural activity necessary for health, growth, and learning in kids. For example, children need opportunities to experience and practice balance, whether lifting up a tiny head as a six-month-old or sitting erect when sliding as an eighteen-month-old. They also need to grow in body awareness, knowing body parts and how to use them in movement, as well as encounter a variety of visual sensations, sounds, and touch experiences. All of this is done as the parent plays alongside the child, helping to build the foundation for social skills, cognitive development, physical ability, and self-esteem. So whether done in a structured play group environment or one-on-one in the home, this parent-child interaction becomes a valuable foundation for future stages of play and recreation.[4]

The key to playing games with babies is remembering to keep it simple. With so many infant toys and programs available, it may be hard to believe that the parent or caregiver is the child's favorite toy. In their excellent work, Becoming the Parent You Want to Be, Davis and Keyser offered suggestions on how parents can facilitate constructive time for and with their infants:

Give babies plenty of "floor time." While putting babies on the floor is contrary to many of our previous customs, it is one of the best ways to support both physical skills and the development of a baby's sense of competence. Babies who spend time on open, clean, safe, flat surfaces, free of infant seats or other restrictive carriers, have the opportunity to learn about their bodies in space. They get to learn what positions they can get themselves into and out of. They develop the muscles they need for the next developmental challenge. Babies who are playing on the floor are strengthening all of the muscles they will later need to roll over, sit up, and crawl. Babies who are crawling on their own are exercising the muscles they will later need for walking. Limiting the amount of time babies spend in car seats, infant carriers, swings, chairs, and other restrictive containers allows babies to have lots of chances to develop their muscles, skills, and body awareness during "floor time."

Get down on the floor with your baby. In spending floor time with your baby, you can watch and see what your baby does, where she looks,

At 2 years begins to	At 3 years begins to	At 4 years begins to	At 5 years begins to
Walk	Jump and hop on one foot	Run, jump and climb with close supervision	Gain good body control
Run	Climb stairs by alternating feet on each stair	Dress self using buttons, zippers, laces and so on	Throw and catch ball, climb, jump, skip with good coordination
Actively explore environment	Dress and undress self somewhat	Use more sophisticated eating utensils such as knives to cut meat or spread butter	Coordinate movements to music
Sit in a chair without support	Walk a reasonably straight path on floor	Walk balance beam with ease	Put on snowpants, boots, and tie shoes
Climb stairs with help (two feet on each stair)	Walk on balance beam	Walk down stairs alone	Skip
Build block towers	Ride a tricycle	Bounch and catch ball	Jump rope, walk in a straight line
Feed self with fork and spoon	Stand on one foot for a long time	Push/pull wagon	Ride a two-wheel bike
Stand on balance beam	Catch large balls	Cut, following lines	Roller-skate
Throw ball	Hop	Copy figure X	Fold paper
Catch	Gallop	Print first name	Reproduce alphabet and numbers
Jump	Kick ball		Trace
Push and pull	Hit ball		
Hang on bar	Paste		
Slide	String beads, cut paper with scissors, copy figures O and +		

Figure 10-1: Physical Characteristics of the Child Age 2 to 5

how she moves. You can see the world from her perspective. You could sing with her or just talk with her. Just being on her level allows her to communicate with you using all the subtleties of her nonverbal, as well as verbal, communication.

Support your infant's achievements. All parents want to do the best job they can to support their baby's growth. Rather than buying lots of expensive equipment, what babies really need is their parents' attention, observation, and responsiveness. In the first year of life, babies are learning trust. They are figuring out that the world is a place where they will get their needs met, where they can make things happen, and where they can explore safely. Our job is not to "teach" them these things as much as it is to get to know them, to enjoy them, to provide safe and interesting learning spaces, to learn their unique communication systems, and to be responsive to them.[5]

Once children enter the world of crawling, and later walking, new realms of possibilities open up to them. Mobility is now independent of someone else's whim to move them from here to there. Instead, the child is free to explore—within reason—his environment, whether that be a small travel playpen or a wide open backyard. In either situation, supervision and attention continue to be warranted because of the age and relative immaturity of the child. But the key now is that the child can test his level of independence. Lefrançois described the process of learning to walk as the child's "most significant motor achievement, with extremely important social and cognitive implications.Chapter...Self-locomotion facilitates the process of becoming familiar with the world."[6]

Because healthy toddlers are notoriously busy creatures, it is imperative for parents and caregivers to plan proactively, rather than react in a panic. While it would be easier to plop a child into a playpen or stroller to keep him from wandering away, it is really best for a freewheeling toddler to use his body as much as possible. As he walks, runs, jumps, and climbs, he is strengthening important muscles as well as developing a healthy sense of independence.

Using movement games such as Mother, May I?, Red Light Green Light, and Hokey Pokey is a wonderful way to help a young child be active while, at the same time, focusing on specific skills such as stopping and starting on command and learning her body parts. Even purpose-filled quiet times can be useful in training a child in the value of relaxing and unwinding with a favorite song tape or a colorful picture book. (See Fig. 101 for a summary of some physical and motor achievements of early childhood.)

In addition to developing motor skills, most children are growing in their use of language to express feelings, needs, and preferences. Before now, parents and caregivers had to learn the unique dialect of babies. They had to differentiate between the cry of the tired, the cry of the hungry, and even the cry of the lonely. But when words are introduced, a child—even with single syllable grunts—can relate much more of his deeper concerns. He wants to play with *that* toy; he needs *this* shoe tied; he asks for something to eat *now*. This rapid development of verbal skills can be nurtured in a number of play settings as simple directions are given, repetitive rhymes are chanted, and engaging songs are sung. Even reading to the youngster can contribute to this task in a young child's life, offering a wide variety of sounds and words to help grow his vocabulary and ability to communicate.

One writer went so far as to suggest that reading books to a child—whether infant, toddler, or preschooler—is as vital to his development as a healthy diet and a good night's sleep.[7] Orr cited a recommendation from the American Academy of Pediatrics that during well-baby visits pediatricians should prescribe reading activities in an effort to stimulate brain and language development as well as begin to develop literacy skills.[8]

In addition to reading to a child to fuel her imagination, it is also important to provide her with plenty of unstructured time to play. "Play is activity that has no long-range goal, although it might have intermediate objectives (to hop from here to there, to make a sand hill, to fly a kite, to pour a cup of pretend tea). Play is what children, and grownups, do for the fun of it. But that play has no ultimate purpose does not mean it is unimportant and useless. In fact, it is extremely important for all aspects of the child's development: social, physical, and intellectual."[9]

Today's children—even preschoolers—are busy doing lots of good and important things. However, more and more children are preoccupied with electronic media. Much like TV was used as a convenient babysitter, it is not uncommon to see young children occupying their time with media on a smartphone, tablet, laptop, or desktop. Parents often think it is "cute" to see their children picking up and learning how to use electronic devices to play games. While the jury is still out on the value of media involvement at a young age, the church should encourage social interaction, vigorous and physical activity, and plenty of unstructured playtime. Ballet lessons, T-ball team practices, and even children's choir at church are admirable activities in which to involve a child, but care must be taken to give this same child time to physically play. Yes, there is an element of play in each of the above activities, but the required structure forces the child to fit a mold rather than allowing her creative juices to take over and find the fun for herself. Countless studies reveal the danger of too much television viewing and media use in regard to their effect on a children's creative development. But more and more studies are being conducted to determine whether the push for overactive, overstrained children is taking its toll on their ability to participate in freelance play.

EXPLORING MIDDLE CHILDHOOD

The need for unstructured play continues into a child's middle childhood years (ages five through twelve), but unfortunately the addition of a demanding school schedule and a myriad of extracurricular activities cuts into this need greatly. One child psychologist warns parents and professionals to remember that play is a child's way of learning and, through free play, a child learns to function within his peer group, make rules, test the limits of acceptable behavior, and role play future occupations.[10]

Just because research can prove the importance of unstructured free time for children does not ensure that children will always know what to do with the time. They are used to someone else planning their time, and when free time is allotted, they sometimes whine that there is nothing to do. Pellegrini points out that this transition from busy to bored may be "a blessing in disguise. Downtime challenges a child to focus on the present and find something constructive to do. Resist turning this into TV or computer time. These activities do not require any imaginative thinking and do little to help your child's development. When programmed stimulation shuts down, a child's mind opens up."[11]

One key developmental issue of children this age is the need to set and attain personal goals.[12] While some of this will be accomplished through academic pursuits, much of it will be addressed as each child explores his interest in particular hobbies and/or tests his ability in different activities like sports or music. Cooper expresses concern that children are not being allowed to develop at their own pace but, instead, are expected to achieve a certain level of ability at certain ages despite physical, cognitive, or social diversity. "Various studies have confirmed what many coaches and parents have known all along: some children are simply slower than others to develop basic physical skills like catching or hitting balls, or executing movements that require agility. In a few instances, the boys and girls who learn these skills earlier, say at ages 4 to 5, may have a natural ability that others lack. In many cases, though, certain children merely grow and develop faster than the rest, or their parents do more to train them at a young age. The others can still catch up—if they are just given a chance."[13] Cooper calls this the Rule of Rhythm and stresses that the child's personal developmental pace should dictate appropriate recreational challenges, not predetermined age-graded programs.

While recreation for children in this middle developmental stage should not be limited to competitive sports, it is during this time that much team-oriented activity is introduced. Children are given the opportunity to play in Biddy Basketball, Dixie Youth Softball, and an abundance of other kid-oriented leagues. One church-centered program designed for children in the first through sixth grades is exploding around the country. Upward Sports, founded in 1986 by Caz McCaslin in Spartanburg, South Carolina, focuses on developing the self-esteem of each participant while teaching respect for authority, sportsmanship, character, and basketball skills. In addition, because of the involvement of countless volunteers and supportive parents, the evangelistic potential of this ministry is far reaching.

One reason Upward Sports and similar programs are so successful is that they are designed to address a child's basic needs and seek to help him successfully work through the encounter. Hartzell identified several specific needs of children ages five through twelve:[14]

Children need love and acceptance. In the competitiveness of today's athletic climate, a sports program that is designed to allow every child to play equal amounts of time is an anomaly. But no matter how unusual it is, this type of program is vital in responding to a child's need for love and acceptance. Instead of being penalized for not running the fastest or shooting the best, the novice can play hard and develop his abilities alongside others who are hoping to do the same. There is nothing like a "great catch," "good defense," or even a simple pat on the back to get a child pumped for his next opportunity to play. In this atmosphere of unconditional love and acceptance, replete with verbal and nonverbal strokes of affirmation, a child can grow in his ability to play a particular sport or realize that this sport is not really something he enjoys.

Children need strong moral development. While children have a lot of good innate qualities, they also have a lot of questionable influences. In a society that thrives on personal rights rather than universal truths, being intentional about teaching biblically based morality is a must. Children must learn to respect authority, and what better place to do this than on a basketball court with the assumed fairness of trained referees and established rules? Children also must be taught to play by these established rules or suffer the consequences. Penalty kicks are awarded in soccer when a player on the opposing team breaks a rule. In football, penalty flags are thrown, resulting in lost yardage, while baseball players may be subjected to automatic outs due to stealing bases before the appropriate time or batting out of turn. An emphasis on the positive outcomes of respecting authority, playing by the rules, and other issues pertinent to the life lessons of sports can ensure a child's exposure to the right type of influence on his moral development.

Children need to develop motor skills. Just because a child has learned to walk and run doesn't mean he is through developing motor skills. Some children will lean toward a natural propensity to run faster and jump higher but, in a general sense, even these motor skills can be learned and improved. Children need direction to progress at developmentally appropriate levels. My ten-year-old has participated in loosely organized basketball programs in the past few years. She has attempted to dribble the ball, pass to teammates, and even throw a shot toward the goal occasionally. But it was not until her current physical education teacher took the time this year to demonstrate and drill the girls on the proper mechanics that she began to enjoy the sport. While her age may play a vital part in her ability to understand and play the game better, the intentionality of this teacher's instructional strategy factors in heavily for future success.

Children need to learn cooperation. What name has been most prominent in professional basketball in the past? Michael Jordan, of course. But even a player as successful as Michael Jordan cannot do what he has done without a team to play with him. Children need to know that while each individual effort is important, teamwork accomplishes the most.

When only five years old, Sarah was introduced to the public library by her wise paternal grandmother. This same wise grandmother allowed Sarah to check out approximately twenty books to keep her occupied over an extended visit. But even twenty kiddie books can add up in weight, so Grandma Peggy suggested that she and Sarah work together to carry the books to the car. "Let's cooperate" soon became the catchphrase for sharing the load, whether books, groceries, or other weighty items around the house.

Children need to develop their decision-making skills. Experience has taught me that people—even children—like to have choices. Vanilla or chocolate? Paper or plastic? Friday or Saturday? Basketball or soccer? Choir or drama? The list is virtually endless of the choices children can be given as they develop their ability to make decisions and then live with the results. To be able to practice making choices in the safety of childhood builds a strong foundation for the future when decisions can have bigger and longer-lasting consequences.

The women's ministry committee at "First Church" hosts a mother-daughter tea that involves first through sixth grade girls, their mothers, and their guests. The first tea was planned entirely by the committee members, several of whom had daughters in the target age group. Even though the event was well-attended and well-liked, the committee members took a different approach the following year and asked the fifth and sixth graders what they would do differently if they were planning the tea. The most significant suggestion was that they wanted to be involved in the program: they wanted to do a skit, sing a song, or play an instrument. Basically, they wanted to have a sense of ownership in the event.

As children are acquainted with the benefits of love and acceptance, strong moral development, improved motor skills, cooperation, and even decision-making opportunities in recreational settings, they will progress toward the socialization goals that are so important to this time of their lives. Middle childhood is not necessarily the period to specialize in a particular sport or hobby; instead, it should be a laboratory of wide-open opportunity during which individuals are exposed to diverse recreational pursuits, ranging from physical activities (games, sports, and dance), outdoor and nature pursuits, creative pastimes (arts and crafts, music, and drama), individual hobbies and club associations, and many other forms of play.[15] While Kraus acknowledges that these opportunities will differ according to socioeconomic status, physical condition, educational level, and even previous recreational experience, he stresses the value of presenting a variety of encounters, noting that what is learned in childhood is not for childhood alone. Instead, Kraus emphasizes that childhood experiences prepare a person for adolescence which, in turn, prepares a person for the different stages of adulthood. He calls this the "continuous developmental process."[16]

Also factoring into this continuous developmental process are the issues related to gender differentiation. At the beginning of the middle childhood span, children are not as gender exclusive as they tend to be toward the junior high school years. Granted, gender typing has been present throughout their lives as others—particularly adults—have reacted to them in terms of their sex (i.e., dressing girls in pink; giving boys trucks to play with). However, most six year olds seem to be more concerned with who can run the fastest rather than which of the seventh grade boys is the best athlete. As children age, they compare themselves more readily with children of the same sex and age and not with the whole grade in general.

Another gender-related issue deals with which activities are most appropriate for which sex. While the majority of politically correct people may lean toward girls being allowed to play boys' sports (and vice versa), practically speaking, it is usually better in competitive activities to allow the girls to compete against girls and the boys to compete against boys. The physical differences are not as evident in the early grade school years, but as both sexes move closer to the start of puberty, it is not unusual for a twelve-year-old girl to tower over her male counterpart in height. But neither is it unusual for the same age boy to outrun, out-jump, and out-throw his female counterpart.[17] While this discrepancy may send some preteen girls to the couch to watch television or even noncompetitive boys to the world of video games, discerning parents and other caring adults need to step in at this point so that "the growing minds and bodies of these preteens [don't] miss out on the physical activity they so desperately need in this phase of development, thus setting them up for a lifetime of inactivity."[18]

Because physical inactivity has been acknowledged by the American Heart Association (AHA) as one of the main risk factors in developing coronary artery disease, much emphasis has been placed on encouraging children to get out and play. While some might eagerly apply this principle to sedentary adults, the AHA recommends that children age five and older participate in a total of thirty minutes of enjoyable, moderate intensity activities on most days of the week and a minimum of thirty minutes of vigorous physical activity at least three to four days each week to achieve cardiovascular (heart and lung) fitness. If a thirty-minute block of time is not possible in the child's busy schedule, then two fifteen-minute sessions or even three ten-minute sessions spread throughout a day also will reap positive results. In addition to the physical benefits such as weight control, reduced blood pressure, increased HDL ("good") cholesterol, and lowering the risk of diabetes and some kinds of cancer, an active child should also see an improvement in her psychological wellbeing, including more self-confidence and higher self-esteem.[19]

One clinical dietician, who heads a weight reduction program at Children's Hospital in New Orleans, Louisiana, points out that it is not the threat of disease that will motivate a child to eat better or get more active. "What tends to work is telling them that they'll have nicer skin and better muscle tone, that they'll have more fun shopping because they'll fit in a smaller size."[20] Schumacher cited the example of a twelve year old who recently had lost eighteen pounds on the way to his thirty-five pound weight loss goal. His success thus far has resulted in being teased less for his larger size as well as an ability to participate in a variety of sports. "It used to be just baseball," he said. "Now I play football, soccer, and basketball. I feel much lighter. I'm quicker."[21]

EXPLORING ADOLESCENCE

The challenge of involving adolescents in recreational pursuits is greatly influenced by what has been the norm in their lives up to this point. If they have been active children, they will more than likely transition into active teenagers. If they have been inactive (occupying leisure with sedentary activity such as video games, social media/texting, or streaming video, etc.), it will take motivations such as those just discussed to get them to buy into the benefits of a physically active lifestyle. Either way, it is crucial for the church to be prepared to offer recreational options to those in the thirteen to eighteen age range. The Carnegie Council on Adolescent Development pointed out that "the nation cannot afford to raise another generation of young adolescents without the supervision, guidance, and preparation for life that caring adults and strong organizations once provided in communities."[22] Reasons for the church to answer this imperative, as summarized from *Successful Biblical Youth Work,* include the following:[23]

Recreation satisfies a normal need in teenagers. Their bodies demand that they have movement, activity, and life. Christian leaders would do better to spend less time prohibiting youth from participating in certain activities by, instead, providing positive alternatives to the all too popular options offered by secular society. The apostle Paul understood that it is not enough to tell young believers what they *can't* do; we need to instruct them in the things that they *can* and *should* do (Eph. 4:25ff). True recreation involves more than entertainment; it includes participation.

A *Frontline* news show broke the shocking story of a large number of teenagers—even as young as junior high—in Rockdale County, Georgia, involved in sexual promiscuity. As the story line developed, one of the more disturbing sidebars was the adolescents' explanation that they were involved in this sexual activity because "there was nothing for them to do."[24] In a wrap-up article on this tragic situation, Blum suggested that young people be given opportunities, with adult supervision, for active recreation so that they can have fun and enjoy themselves. It is not a matter of locking them away; it is about offering them "good, clean fun."

Recreation builds values in the teenager. Young people are taught some kind of values almost everywhere they go. In school, teachers instruct through value-based education. In Bible study, many leaders break down the Scripture through a value-oriented approach. However, in recreational opportunities, values are more than taught; they are challenged. Does a young person believe it is appropriate to respect authority? Then watch his struggle when a referee makes a call that goes against him or his team. Does a young person believe that rules are a consistent way to ensure fair play? Then watch his reaction to elbows in his face during a particularly tight basketball game. In the heat of competition, values are not just taught to adolescents; they are built into their personality and decision-making process. A wise coach or recreation minister will be intentional in his use of value development in the lives of the teenagers with whom he has been entrusted.

Recreation builds strong personalities. According to Towns, "personality is the sum total of all of our personal attributes—mental, emotional, social, spiritual, and psychological. It is the total impression or effect that we make upon others—or simply 'you.'"[25] Recreation can reveal personality strengths like loyalty and cooperation during a teambuilding activity. But it can also reveal weaknesses like disrespect and a bitter spirit after a disappointing loss. The positive aspect is that personality can be cultivated and developed.

The recreational leader who models good habits and strong personality will be a positive influence on those with whom she comes in contact. Something as simple as starting practice on time speaks volumes to teenagers about respecting their time. And something as crucial as being fair and honest shows them how they can treat their teammates in a like manner.

Recreation relieves the pressures of life for the teenager. Youth need a safety valve through which to relieve the pressures of their lives. Recreation, when designed for "recreation" rather than "wreckcreation," allows a young person to blow off some of the steam of a hard day at school, a tough relationship situation, or even conflict with a parent. It does not make the problem go away, but it does give the teenager a healthy outlet for some of the associated stress—and hopefully a significant adult contact to help him work through the process. Because egocentrism is a natural construct of the adolescent thought process, young people need to be challenged to see beyond the imaginary audience that they perceive is always judging them into a world of personal acceptance and growth.

Recreation trains teenagers in creativity. "Entertainment alone cannot satisfy and bring out the best from youth. Young people learn creativity as they express themselves."[26] Motion Potion is a fun game in which a group of teenagers can get to know one another better by going around the circle, telling his or her name, and then demonstrating an action that can be associated with him or her. For example, Aaron, a baseball enthusiast, would tell his name and then position his body in a batting stance, maybe even pantomiming a homerun swing. Then everyone would say his name in unison and do the same. Each person in the group follows this pattern until everyone has created a motion that will help people remember one another better. By giving young people opportunities to work through solutions as individuals and/or as groups, a focused recreation leader is better preparing these teenagers for a productive and meaningful future.

Recreation provides a sense of belonging for the teenager. It is not news: teenagers want and need to belong. Having friends is important to them. They want to feel included so much that if they do not feel this way, they may never be able to tune into what is being said about the importance of spiritual growth. In the security of a sense of community, many young people can finally open their ears and their hearts to the Gospel message. This may take place on a sports team, during a summer camp, or even at a weekly recreation event. The key ingredient is a recreation facilitator who understands the value of teenagers working together and feeling that their contribution to the big picture really matters.

Recreation gives teenagers an opportunity to meet the opposite sex. Again, this is no news flash: teenagers are curious—maybe it is more accurate to say, very interested—about the opposite sex. And because of this curiosity and interest, most will search out ways to be together. While the church does not need to get into the matchmaking business, leaders can be proactive in offering wholesome activities that allow young people to be together in healthy ways. Towns pulled no punches when he pointed out that "the sex drive is strong and, if steadily pushed, it generates more emotion and tension than can be safely handled." His suggestion was to use recreation to sublimate and redirect sex drives into socially acceptable expression. For example, he noted that, in the recreational setting, "the bashful youth can meet, be on the same team, and share with the opposite sex. Those who are overly motivated can be sublimated and held in check."[27] When one boy heard the statistic that teenage guys think of sex every seventeen seconds, he corrected the presenter and said, "Not when I'm playing basketball." Then let's keep them playing basketball!

Recreation attracts and holds young people. Some people complain that it is a shallow church that uses recreation to attract teenagers to their building and programs. Perhaps these same people have forgotten what it took to attract them to a personal relationship with Jesus Christ in the first place. Most Christians will testify of a "hook" that grabbed their interest in some way at some point in time.

John Garner tells of a smart minister who visited his family after they moved to a new town and told them of the church's pool tables, Ping Pong™ tables, and basketball courts. John was hooked. He did not become a Christian because of the church's recreation facility, but he was initially attracted because of what they had to offer. If a church can develop a reputation for having a quality recreation program or a fun youth group, they will not be able to keep people away. Remember that one characteristic of adolescence is that young people do little in moderation. They like too much of a good thing or, unfortunately, too much of a bad thing. So, if they like something that your church is offering, they will come, and there's a good chance that they will bring their friends.

Recreation is not a cure-all for the inevitable challenges of the youth years. Recreation does not ensure perfect, problem-free kids. But it does guarantee a step in the right direction because it advances the concept of total wellness. Youth are spiritual, social, mental, emotional, and physical beings, and recreation done right helps to advance all of these dimensions in the life of a young person. As Black pointed out, "Youth ministry is more than fun and games. However, youth ministry without fun and games is like eating cold pizza and a month-old soda. The basic ingredients are there, but the warmth and fizz are gone. Too little recreation in youth ministry leads to a lack of spark and vitality."[28]

EXPLORING YOUNG ADULTS

The transition to adulthood is as varied as the people who have to accomplish it. While many include an educational experience (college or vocational-technical training) in the transitional period, others jump right into full-time employment or even military training. Whatever path is chosen for the journey, the common denominator for Millennials and those between the ages of 30 and 40 is a change in focus from growing up to settling down. "Success in this stage of adulthood requires an understanding of new rules and standards, flexibility to adjust and change, and the ability to develop new personal styles and self-concepts."[29]

Accompanying this array of maturity issues is the decision—whether conscious or subconscious—of whether to pursue a lifestyle of wellness.

The busyness of this life period tends to crowd out the importance of a healthy diet or active lifestyle because, for many, the focus is on the present, and right now most everything seems to be in working order. However, a flashing neon sign should be placed in the front yard of every twenty- and thirty-something who forgets that health choices made in these years have a tremendous effect on how well these same folks will age and how long they can maintain a high quality of life.

Because early adulthood is potentially the peak of one's physical development in terms of speed, strength, coordination, and endurance, it is also usually considered a period of high achievement for professional athletes as well as other recreationally oriented individuals. But it does not take an Olympics-style training program for someone to reap significant benefits from an ongoing effort to be active. The American College of Sports Medicine recommends a minimum of three or four thirty-minute periods of moderate intensity exercise a week (or ten- to fifteen-minute sessions that accumulate to thirty to forty minutes per day) to reap cardio-respiratory benefits as well as help in the area of muscular endurance and even increased flexibility. Lifestyle activities may be a promising alternative to organized exercise, but further research is necessary to examine specific forms that can be helpful. The basic premise is that it is necessary to increase daily activity, whether through intentional or incidental exercise, in order to enhance energy production and expenditure.[30]

When asked what types of needs tend to dominate the lives of young adults, one group of Christian graduate students specifically addressed the importance of social contact as it relates to the need to belong. This bumps up against this generation's history as latchkey children who grew up with a strong sense of independence and self-sufficiency. However, this need fits closely with Erikson's psychosocial development construct for this age group: that they achieve a sense of personal identity and self-worth by successfully negotiating their relationships, whether with friends, parents, employers, or potential mates.

Recreational outlets allow young adults relatively safe environments through which to express creativity and productivity in an effort to grow in their ability to cooperate and work together. For example, a hearty game of Catch Phrase® will challenge one's ability to think quickly, work as a team, and laugh at both one's successes and failures. It is not meant to destroy a player's self-esteem; instead, it is a game best played in the context of friends and family to encourage personal growth and not individual domination.

Also important to this group of Christian young adults is the need to fill their lives with pursuits full of purpose and meaning. While the spectrum of ages and life directions included in the description of young adults is wide and diverse, there is still concern in most of them that what they invest their time and interests in really matters. Some may interpret this purposefulness as "tunnel vision," and yet in the big picture, this mindset allows the young adult to pour him or herself into activities, jobs, and relationships as an investment toward the future.

Caz McCaslin, mentioned earlier in this chapter, had served at First Baptist Church of Spartanburg, South Carolina, for ten years. In his early thirties, he was running a successful recreation ministry and could even boast of a children's basketball league that had kids on a waiting list after only three days of registration. But he did not want a waiting list; he wanted a program that could accommodate as many children as wanted to play ball at the church. A wise mentor encouraged him to take his league design and write it as a sports program that could be marketed to churches all over the country. Several years and many churches later, the Upward Basketball program continues to minister to countless children around the country. McCaslin's interest in basketball combined with a passion for outreach translated to a powerful and effective sports ministry.

EXPLORING MIDDLE-AGED ADULTS

As individuals inch toward their forties, a number of curious things begin to occur both mentally and physically. For starters, the phrase "middle-aged" gets thrown their way more and more. While seemingly a statement of ridicule, the practicality of the phrase indicates that these persons have reached a life marker where, should they live to today's normal life expectancy of seventy-five years, then they are already more than halfway there.

Another interesting aspect of entering the middle adult years is the physical change that seems to creep up almost overnight. Although, from scientific research, we know that the slowdown of one's metabolism and the speedup of one's weight gain is usually a gradual process (and not necessarily inevitable), that is not how it feels at the onset of the decade birthdays like forty, fifty, and sixty. With the looming threat of osteoporosis, adult onset diabetes, high blood pressure, and a host of other lifestyle illnesses, the middle adult faces a daily challenge of how she will beat the odds and maintain (or improve to) a certain level of health so that she can age gracefully.

Beverly entered her forties with two teenage children and a busy husband. She was an elementary school teacher, working primarily because her family needed the extra income as they anticipated college and other financial obligations. She enjoyed her fourth grade students but felt trapped, at times, by the restrictions of a daily school schedule. She wanted to exercise regularly, but finding the time was hard. She loved needlework and scrapbooking, but who had time for hobbies anymore? Moreover, there were her church commitments that already kept her away from home two or three nights a week.

It was not until her husband accepted a new job opportunity in a different state that Beverly saw significant changes in her hectic schedule. As one child finished college and the other began, she felt the freedom to stop teaching and begin pursuing other interests. One of those interests was long-distance running. Beverly recently celebrated her fiftieth birthday and, in the last several years, has run at least five half marathons (13.1 miles each). For folks who have been running all of their adult lives, this may not seem like a big deal, but for Beverly—and other middle adults like her—this represents a huge milestone that says chronological age does not have to be the determining factor for physical decline. It is a matter of what you do with the time and body you've been given.

Couey and Yessick stress the value of Christians taking care of their bodies—inside and out—so that they can serve God longer and better. "God created for every individual a uniquely different and highly complicated body in which to live during his or her limited existence. He expects us to care for His temple (our bodies) from our first to our last breath. He expects us to protect and feed our bodies properly and exercise regularly. Christians must grow not only spiritually, mentally, socially, and emotionally, but also physically."[31] Cooper addresses the fact that this stewardship of care is not limited to those under forty; instead, he boldly states:

> It's evident to me from the more than one hundred thousand people we have tested on treadmills at the Aerobics Center in Dallas that it's not necessary for a significant decline in endurance or aerobic capacity to occur after age forty. Chapter…I'm not saying that every older person can become a world-class athlete. But I am saying that there's a good chance that, with serious training, your performance as a middle-aged athlete can approach that of your earlier years. For that matter, even if you weren't in good shape in your teens or twenties, you can still get into great shape today. Many of my patients have reached their highest levels of lifetime fitness well after forty years of age.[32]

In addition to the mental and physical demands of middle adulthood, there is also the challenge of leaving behind the illusions of youth and focusing on a fuller, more balanced life. I love the saying, "It's never too late to change what you want to be when you grow up." In one's youth, the search for significance tends to focus on that "one thing" (one career, one person, one you fill in the blank) that will make you happy. As one matures, the understanding of this broadens so that, after settling the issue of eternal salvation found only in a relationship with Jesus Christ, each individual begins to see that it takes more than "one thing" to define fulfillment in life. Satisfaction is seen as multidimensional, achieved through involvement with family, work, church, friends, and so on. In addition, these dimensions are in a constant state of flux. Children grow up. Job descriptions change. Friends move away. Church needs vary. And so we grow, change, move, and vary with them, hopefully moving closer to becoming all that we were created to be.

Leisure pursuits during this life stage are as varied as the people partaking in them. More important than a grocery list of what middle age adults like to do—such as learning new skills, volunteering, enjoying nature, engaging in exercise and social interaction, and so on—is the understanding that commitment to leisure activities is closely associated with personal happiness.[33]

Remember Beverly? With each finish line she crosses comes a satisfaction that she has stretched herself beyond limitations of earlier years and proven that she is still capable of growth and improvement. She is not denying the long-instilled work ethic that requires she be a productive person; instead, she is learning the benefits of a balanced life and spreading that happiness to her family, her friends, and even her church commitments.

EXPLORING SENIOR ADULTS

This pursuit of productivity and happiness is not sequestered to one's early and middle adult years. On the contrary, as the Baby Boomers (those born between 1946 and 1964) are approaching or are in senior adulthood, there is no longer a sense of succumbing to the inevitability of old age. Instead, we see the field of gerontology exploding with research and scientific study in an attempt to capitalize on the experience as well as the potential of those who are sixty years old and above.

Because of the likelihood of lengthened longevity, descriptors of senior adults are also being subdivided to define the various stages of these advanced years. This becomes increasingly important as not all senior adults fall in line with the old school paradigm that "to be old is to be sick and, after a certain age, to be sick is to be old."[34] More and more, Satchel Paige's famous age-related quotes come into play: "How old would you be if you didn't know how old you are?" and "Age is a question of mind over matter; if you don't mind, it don't matter."[35]

Health status, physical mobility, and mental acuity factor strongly into the definition distinctives. Neugarten used the terms "young old," "middle old," and "old old" to differentiate between those over age sixty.[36] Garner prefers to use their activity choices, dividing the age span into "the challengers," "the goers and doers," and "the stay-at-homers." Challengers are those who will take a challenge, try new things, and desire to experience new places, friends, foods, and so forth. Goers and doers like day trips, in-town mission projects, and ongoing recreation opportunities at church or a community center. But the stay-at-homers are just that: those who prefer to do life from the comfort of their living room or their own backyard. They do not want to be ignored, but they are not the ones that most senior adult recreation programs have traditionally placed their focus.

But no matter where senior adults fall on the descriptive spectrum, all are dealing with changes in physical health and ability. But even the gradual decreases can be unexpected, as seen in this classic gerontological story of how difficult it is to know what constitutes normal aging:

An elderly square dancer went to his doctor because of pain in his left knee. It was causing him so much discomfort that it was keeping him from his favorite weekly dance group. The doctor smiled at the very old man and went into a long discourse on the process of aging. He explained that cells break down, muscles lose elasticity, resistance to movement in the connective tissues around joints and muscles increases, and joints become tender because of changes in the synovial fluid and weakened cartilage; "You see," he added, "it's all part of normal aging." "But, doctor," exclaimed the patient, "my right knee is as old as my left knee, and it doesn't hurt at all."[37]

OLDER ADULTS TODAY ARE ACTIVE

They do not have a rocking chair mentality. They have more energy and longer life expectancies than previous generations. Older adults today want to use their considerable experience to contribute to something worthwhile and be a part of something meaningful. Their lifestyle is a continuation of what they were involved with earlier in life—traveling, giving, spending, seeking new experiences, and being concerned with their quality of life. In short, the older adult population in America is just now coming into its own. At the North American Congress on the Church and the Age Wave, several factors emerged as trends on the horizon:

1. Ageism in the church will diminish. This form of discrimination will see a decline.
2. New age classifications will emerge. Senior or mature adults will be those over seventy; middle maturity will range from fifty to seventy.
3. Church programs and staffing will reflect age-related concerns. The number of ministers to older adults will increase.
4. Aging will be viewed developmentally as opposed to chronologically.
5. Ministry to older adults will focus on the middle adults (fifty to seventy years).
6. Outreach to and by mature adults will receive priority.
7. The unique contributions of mature adults will be increasingly valued.
8. New churches for mature adults will be established.[38]

These eight factors alone show that a new age is approaching. New ways of engaging and involving this new generation of older adults are emerging. Churches will either prepare for this new "Age Wave" or be swept away by it. Those who are prepared will see the benefits of offering new and innovative ministry to older Americans.

Differing Senior Adult Populations

The above listing is not applicable to all senior adults. Older adults can basically be placed into three distinct categories. While the younger and middle senior adults fit the above criteria, the oldest adults are cut from a different mold.

Older Senior Adults

Our oldest adults view life differently. They are more conservative in all areas of life. Their thinking has been shaped by what they grew up with—primarily a strong work ethic that kept an eye on the basics of life. Nothing was certain for this age group, and nothing was taken for granted. In the past, The Great Depression, two World Wars, and the Korean and Vietnam wars left an impact on all of life. Later, the Iraq and Afghanistan wars left their mark on how this population views leisure. A more utilitarian approach to life is characteristic. The oldest Americans often do not want to be gone from home too long at a time and will be careful about spending money. Many are on fixed incomes because they did not have jobs that had good pension plans, or they were self-employed and did not put back enough, or they rely heavily on social security. They lived for their family and worked to provide the necessities of life. Leisure came at a price that some were not able to afford, so they did not plan on it in retirement. Neither leisure education nor leisure planning for retirement was given much thought.

The result is that the older (seventy and above) senior adult population is unprepared to cope with a leisure-oriented culture. They tend to view the younger generation as wasteful and pleasure-seeking spenders. Churches will do well to note the differences in thought patterns between the older and younger senior adults. Two or three groups may be formed within a church to meet the perceived leisure needs of each group. Some churches have several groups that meet at times convenient to them and plan activities that appeal to that particular age grouping. Their activities and outings are tailored to meet the differing needs of the various groups' membership.

Recreation Helps to Lead a Balanced and Abundant Life

Leading a balanced life is biblical and essential to well-being. A balanced life includes taking part in recreation and leisure activities. Recreation helps people recreate themselves. Often, because of the strong work ethic of older adults, they have a hard time taking advantage of their leisure. Many have not learned to say yes to fun and "recreative" activity that can enrich their lives. Scripture tells us that "Jesus increased in wisdom and stature, and in favor with God and with people" (Luke 2:52). This indicates that he was a whole person and that he needed what we all need—to grow in various areas of life. Breaking the routine and taking some time off are essential to well-being, growth, and living a balanced life. Jesus said, "I have come that they may have life and have it in abundance" (John 10:10). Recreation brings an element of joy and abundance to life; experiencing all that life has for us is good. God created us to live the abundant life. He wants us to "redeem the time" and use it to glorify him as we live. He has provided us with the capacity to play, sing, learn, converse, and to grow mentally, physically, spiritually, and emotionally throughout life. We do not stop growing just because we get older. In fact, we feel older when we stop taking advantage of the opportunities God gives us to grow in these areas.

Older adults need to have the opportunities to keep growing. Recreation provides a wonderful platform to allow the whole person's growth needs to be met. This in turn will help the person have the opportunity to lead a balanced abundant life.

Meet Needs Using Recreation Programming

Churches have unique and growing opportunities to offer leisure services that can meet the needs of all ages of senior adults. Some of these needs are:

- To be accepted by others
- To feel that they belong to a group
- To be recognized as individuals of worth
- To feel that they are contributing from their life experiences
- To have opportunities for growth in mind, body, emotion, and spirit

Perhaps nowhere in the life of the church can the senior adult as a whole person minister and receive ministry more than through recreation and fellowship. This ministry tool offers a fun, relaxed way to interact with peers in a nonthreatening way that is comfortable to members and nonmembers alike. Garner, in *Forward Together, A New Vision for Senior Adult Ministry*, states that recreation and fellowship programming should have the following characteristics:

Programming must have meaning and purpose. What is done should meet a need. To find out what is needed, a survey must be taken of the widest cross section of the senior adult population, including the homebound.

Programming should be inclusive. No one should be left out. Leaders should seek to provide ways in which all can participate. Those with disabilities, those with little discretionary money, and those with transportation problems should never be left out of program planning.

Programming should offer variety. Offer something for the goers and doers, something for the stay-at-homers, and something for those who enjoy a challenge.

Programming should be unique to the church. Adapt ideas you see, read about, or experience to your particular situation. No two situations are alike. It is OK to add to or take away something from another program and make it your own.

Programming should not be repetitive. The best way to kill the best program you have ever done is to keep doing it over and over the same way. As far as programming goes, variety is truly the spice of life. Change the way things are done once in a while. New favorites might be discovered!

Programming should offer plenty of time for fellowship. Folks like to visit with friends. Recreation programming offers the best opportunity for strengthening relationships and forming new ones. The wise programmer will intentionally build fellowship times into the overall program in order to foster relationships.

Programming should offer an intentional time of spiritual renewal. Do not be afraid of offering a time for examining one's spiritual condition. Senior adults need to assess and examine this most important aspect of their lives. Some of them may be grappling with spiritual questions. What better time to allow for introspection than during a devotional or on a retreat in a relaxed, informal setting?[39]

EXPLORING MINISTRY FOR EVERY AGE

Programming is a key ingredient to ministry effectiveness with all ages in the church. Balance should be the planning principle that assures most needs are being met. Involvement of many to plan and carry out the programming will lead to excitement and ensure participation. A well-planned, well-promoted, and well-executed program to all ages offers opportunity to impact the lives of many.

There is value in recreation and fellowship for all ages. Recreation and fellowship offer many opportunities for growth and relationship building that can enrich and enhance all of life. Churches that recognize these values and give all ages the opportunity to recreate will find that most will eagerly take advantage of it. As the differing age populations ebb and flow, the need for leisure services will increase and churches should be prepared to reach out in ministry. Recreation is a tool that can help churches meet some real needs of people. A well-planned and balanced program of leisure services will reap great benefits for participants, the culture, and the church itself.

NOTES

1. Lefrançois, G. R. *The Lifespan,* 6th ed. (Belmont, CA: Wadsworth Publishing Company, 1999), 189.
2. Cordes, K. A. and Hilmi M. Ibrahim. *Applications in Recreation & Leisure for Today and the Future,* 2nd ed. (Boston, MA: WCB/ McGrawHill, 1999), 59–60.
3. "Playorena the Original Program." http://www.playorena.com (accessed on March 5, 2002).
4. "What Makes Gymboree Play and Music Unique." http://www. gymboreehk.com (accessed on March 5, 2002).
5. Davis, L. and Janis Keyser. *Becoming the Parent You Want to Be: A Sourcebook of Strategies for the First Five Years* (New York, NY: Broadway Books, 1997). Excerpt from www.parentsplace.com/ expert/parenting (accessed March 5, 2002).
6. Lefrançois, 186.

7. Orr, T. "Babies and Books," *Christian Parenting Today,* November/December 2000. www.christianitytoday.com/cpt/2000 (accessed March 6, 2002.

8. American Academy of Pediatrics. "Prescription for Reading" (April 16, 1997). www.aap.org/advocacy/washing/readdcpr.htm (accessed March 6, 2002).

9. Lefrançois, 220–21.

10. Pellegrini, M. E. "Let Them Play: Do You OverSchedule Your Child?" *Christianity Parenting Today* (March/April 2002). www.christianitytoday. com/cpt/2002 (accessed March 6, 2002).

11. Ibid.

12. Ferguson, D., Teresa Ferguson, Paul Warren, Vicky Warren, and Terri Ferguson. *Parenting with Intimacy Workbook: A Practical Guide to Building and Maintaining Great Family Relationships* (Wheaton, IL: Victor Books, 1995), 36.

13. Cooper, K. H. *Fit Kids! The Complete ShapeUp Program from Birth through High School* (Nashville, TN: Broadman & Holman Publishers, 1999), 15.

14. Hartzell, D. *Recreation for Children* (Nashville, TN: Convention Press, 1988), 9–11.

15. Kraus, R. *Recreation Today: Program Planning and Leadership* (New York, NY: Meredith Publishing Company, 1966), 271.

16. Ibid., 270.

17. Seifert, K. L. and Robert J. Hoffnung. *Child and Adolescent Development,* 4th ed. (Boston, MA: Houghton Mifflin Company, 1997), 349.

18. Cooper, 50.

19. American Heart Association, "Obesity and Overweight in Children." www.americanheart.org (accessed March 15, 2002).

20. Bronston, B. "Fit is phat!" *The (New Orleans) Times Picayune* (January 28, 2002): E-8.

21. Ibid.

22. *A Matter of Time: Report of the Task Force on Youth Development* (New York: Carnegie Corp., 1992), quoted in Cordes and Ibrahim, 79.

23. Towns, E. L. *Successful Biblical Youth Work,* rev. ed. (Nashville, TN: Impact Books, 1973), 346–50.

24. Blum, R. W. "Lost Children or Lost Parents of Rockdale County?" www.pbs.org/wgbh/pages/frontline/shows/georgia/isolated/blum.html (accessed March 25, 2002).

25. Towns, 348.

26. Ibid., 349.

27. Ibid.

28. Black, W. *Introduction to Youth Ministry* (Nashville, TN: Broadman Press, 1991), 214.

29. Cordes and Ibrahim, 101.

30. "ACSM Releases New Position Stand on Losing Weight, Keeping It Off." www.acsm.org (accessed March 27, 2002).

31. Couey, D. and Tommy Yessick. *Fit to Serve Him Longer and Better* (Nashville, TN: LifeWay Press, 1998), 4.

32. Cooper, K. H. *It's Better to Believe* (Nashville, TN: Thomas Nelson Publishers, 1995), 38.

33. Lefrançois, 459.

34. Kovar, M. G. "Health Assessment," In *The Encyclopedia of Aging,* edited by George L. Maddox (New York, NY: Springer Publishing Company, 1995), 433.

35. "Biography of Satchel Paige." www.cmgww.com/baseball/ paige/ quote2.html (accessed March 8, 1999 and March 28, 2002).

36. Neugarten, D. A. *The Meanings of Age: Selected Papers of Bernice L. Neugarten* (Chicago, IL: University of Chicago Press, 1996).

37. Safford, F. and George I. Krell. *Gerontology for Health Professionals,* 2d ed. (Washington, D.C.: NASW Press, 1998), 18.

38. The North American Congress on the Church and the Age Wave (Colorado Springs, CO: May 1997), sponsored by L.I.F.E. (Life Living in Full Effectiveness).

39. Garner, J. *Forward Together: A New Vision for Senior Adult Ministry* (Nashville, TN: LifeWay Press, 1998), 139–40.

11

Recreation and Sports Ministry

A TOOL FOR DISCIPLESHIP

John Garner

"Discipleship is the lifelong process God uses to accomplish His transforming work in a Christian's life."

At its core, recreation and sports ministry trains coaches and leaders to multiply disciples. Recreation and sports ministry can be used to disciple a coach, a craft leader, a volunteer, and an aerobic leader or other leader, training them how to use their preferred recreational or sporting activity as a tool to bring people to Christ or a means to disciple believers. This happens as the recreation/sports ministry leader carefully chooses coaches and leaders. The most effective coaches and activity leaders have the heart first of a learner and then of a teacher. How to be a disciple and how to disciple others is a learned heart skill. The recreation and sports ministry leader helps coaches and leaders know and understand who God created them to be—as disciples—and how to disciple others. Discipleship involves all that someone is as a person and as a believer in Christ—their talents, abilities, relationships, interests and spiritual gifting. The wise recreation and sports ministry leader will choose his or her leaders carefully. Long-term success of any recreation and sports ministry will depend on: (1) Choosing the right coaches and activity leaders. (2) Training the coaches and activity leaders to be multiplying disciples. (3) Leading those who are reached to become multiplying Christians themselves. This is what Jesus did: He carefully chose His disciples, trained them, and sent them out for OJT—on the job training. They came back and reported what had happened. Jesus then taught them how to be more effective in sharing the Gospel.

But which characteristics of a disciple should recreation and sports ministry leaders have? Intervarsity Press offers four characteristics of a disciple:

1. Disciples look for knowledge. The first step of a disciple is a desire to grow in relationship to Jesus Christ.
2. Disciples are humble. A disciple submits her/himself to Jesus and His Word as the true authority for their life. They trust that Christ will lead them.
3. Disciples are willing to change. Jesus often calls the disciple to new things, leading him/her to make the changes necessary to follow Him.
4. Disciples act on what they know. Once a disciple humbles him/herself as they learn from Jesus, opening his/her heart and mind to where ever Christ may lead, they then should act on what He tells them.[1]

The recreation/sports minister must possess the same four characteristics in order to first be a disciple, then lead by multiplying him/herself as he or she teaches and leads those under their ministry to disciple others.

A coach or activity leader must desire to grow in their relationship with Christ. This should be shown through a desire to submit themselves to the authority of God's Word as the foundational authority of life. They must be flexible and willing to change as situations arise while keeping discipleship in the forefront. This could be as simple as being willing to change a coaching philosophy in order to be in line with the goals and objectives of a church or organization. All disciples must put their desires aside and let the desires of Christ dominate their thinking. A leader with these qualities is teachable, moldable, and useful to any organization. Beware the leader who must "do things his/her way."

A discipled leader wants to make a difference in the world and in the lives of others. They want to invest their lives in things that matter and impact the lives of others, using their given platform of a sport or activity to personally invest in the lives of participants, pointing them to Christ and a toward a life of discipleship.

This kind of leader is like Jason in the books of Acts "When they did not find them, they dragged Jason and some of the brothers before the city officials, shouting, 'These men who have turned the world upside down have come here too.'" (Acts 17:6, CSB) A coach or leader who teaches the precepts of Scripture is in the business of "turning his world upside down" for team or class members. Participants' lives, and perhaps the lives of their families, will be forever changed by a coach or leader who has a heart for teaching not only the sport or activity but the positive, eternal truth of Scripture as well. A transformed disciple lives an empowered life of impact because the influence of God working in a heart and life is contagious. This contagion only comes from the power of Christ. It is what He does in us! It comes by God's power not ours, for we are powerless. Romans 4:19 says: "So then, we must pursue what promotes peace and what builds up one another." Coaches and leaders must seek to be learners of Christ so they can "build up" and pass the truth of the knowledge of Christ to participants. None of this happens by itself. The leader must follow the admonition in Philippians 4:9: "Do what you have learned and received and heard and seen in me, and the God of peace will be with you."

The recreation/sports minister must be the example of a discipled leader so that he or she can disciple coaches and activity leaders. This process of "coaching up" leaders will equip them to then coach up the participants. Far too often in recreation and sports ministry, we settle for finding a willing body to fill a slot so we can offer a class or activity or field a team with no thought about our true purpose: to win people to Christ and disciple them in their journey. Some believe that is why pastors and church leaders often see sports and recreation ministry as "playtime" with no redeeming value to the church. We must understand not only what discipleship in recreation and sports ministry looks like, but also how it brings people to Christ and what we can do to facilitate the discipleship process.

DISCIPLESHIP IN RECREATION AND SPORTS MINISTRY DEFINED

We have seen that discipleship is the lifelong process God uses to accomplish His transforming work in our hearts and lives. One definition is found in "Leading Discipleship in a Church." It defines discipleship as "The lifelong journey of obedience to Christ that transforms a person's values and behavior and results in ministry in one's home, church, and the world."[2] The journey to become more like Christ lasts a lifetime. One's values and behavior are transformed or changed to reflect the precepts of Scripture, resulting in ministry. And note the context: "Church"—where we worship and learn of God (that is a given), but also "home and the world"—where we live, work, and play. That is where the Christian life is seen by others—at home and in the world, where we live, work, and play.

So, discipleship is the transformational process of becoming more like Christ. As we learn of Christ and mature spiritually, people will see Him in us, bringing God glory and making His name and salvation through His Son known by the way we live our lives. In his book *In the Arena: The Promise of Sports for Discipleship,* Dave E. Prince states:

> Our (Ed: The disciples') salt-work of preserving the culture provides us points of contact with people who do not follow Jesus or live in the light of the gospel. Sports, music, art, drama, cooking, building, creating, and countless other manifestations of culture are enjoyed by both Christians and non-Christians. The Christian's light-work is to point out how his or her appreciation and enjoyment of cultural manifestations of truth, beauty, and goodness point to the glory and grace of God. Culture always begins with God as we can only be culture makers because of his work as Creator.[3]

Coaches and leaders who live this discipled life can and do make a difference in the lives of those they lead in sports and in the surrounding culture.

DISCIPLESHIP IN RECREATION AND
SPORTS MINISTRY IS INTENTIONAL

There is nothing religious about sports and recreation events. For discipleship to happen, there must be an intentional transformational discipleship plan. That plan includes:

1. Perhaps most important—choosing the right leaders. These leaders should possess the characteristics mentioned earlier in the chapter.

2. Developing leadership materials that will enable coaches and leaders to understand the purpose of the ministry and give them transferable concepts that can be passed along to participants. These concepts include how to share the plan of salvation, how to lead a Bible study/devotional, how to look for and minister to both felt and real needs in the life of the participant, and finally, how to disciple others.

3. Providing resources that will facilitate the discipleship process. There are many such resources, some designed just for athletes and some designed for activity classes.

4. Involvement of the recreation/sports ministry leader before, during, and after the league, class, event, etc. This is crucial. The recreation/sports ministry leader must know that his/her coaches and leaders are using the training and resources they have received. It does no good for leaders to carry out their responsibilities with no oversight. This can lead to "business as usual," where the sport or activity would be primary, rather than sharing the Gospel or discipling believers. Sport-focused ministry has led to pastors and church leaders not seeing the validity of recreation and sports as ministry tools. They see a lot of activity, but no one coming to Christ, no lives changed, and little or no church growth by reaching unbelievers.

Wise recreation/sports ministry leaders will make the discipleship of coaches and leaders their personal responsibility. They will seek to pour themselves into their leaders' lives, modeling godly leadership and discipleship to those who have been recruited. The sports ministry leader may say, "I don't have time for that," but the "that" is what ministry is all about: raising up leaders who share the Gospel using recreation and sport activities, training and discipling, and thus multiplying themselves and their effectiveness. This process must be ongoing each year in the recruiting of new leaders, training these leaders, and helping them be the best they can be. If the coaches and activity leaders are successful, the recreation/sports minister will be successful. One effective model is that of recruiting Ministry Area Coordinators, as outlined in Chapter 5. The ministry leader would disciple and train the Ministry Area Coordinators; they, in turn, would do the same for coaches and leaders under them. In this model, the ministry leader is responsible for investing in a small group of leaders and not burdened by training and working with a large numbers of people all year long.

UNDERSTANDING THAT DISCIPLESHIP IN RECREATION AND SPORTS MINISTRY IS TRANSFORMATIONAL

Recreation and sports ministry, through its strategies and methodologies, addresses three stages of spiritual transformation (discipleship) in the life of a believer:

1. *Making disciples* represents the efforts to win the lost.
2. *Maturing believers* represents the efforts to disciple new believers.
3. *Multiplying ministries* represents providing opportunities for service and missions by all disciples.

The transformation process from being a pre-disciple (a person who does not know Christ), to a new disciple (a person who is young in the faith), to a growing disciple (one who is growing in their faith), to finally a multiplying disciple (one who is actively sharing the Gospel and discipling others) is important. Transformation takes time and hands-on guidance and the power of God enabling the process. Eric Geiger, in an interview with Ron Edmonson, states,

Being a disciple is simply following Jesus to a greater and greater degree. And if we are following Him, then we are through our lives becoming something different. The Holy Spirit and He alone does this transforming work in the hearts of people. What our job is, as church leaders, isn't to transform; it's to set the conditions that are most conducive for real transformation to occur.[4]

The goal for the recreation/sports minister is to put together a plan and provide resources that help the coaches and leaders become "transformed"—more like Christ—preparing them to lead a team or a class replicating the transformation process. This transformation takes time and patience. A pre-disciple may know little or nothing of Christ, so he or she may act and behave like an unsaved person in some ways. The new disciple is learning new ways of thinking and acting that may at first seem strange to them. The growing disciple is testing his faith, learning to trust God in all things—something that is hard to do in a postmodern world. The multiplying disciple experiences the joy of seeing people come to Christ and grows as a believer. The transformational process is sometimes messy—it can feel like two steps forward and one step back—but the process is necessary for spiritual growth. The mature multiplying disciple will be committed to the evangelism of the pre-disciple as well as maturing the growing disciple, helping them grow in spiritual maturity toward becoming a mature, multiplying believer themselves.

DISCIPLESHIP IN RECREATION AND SPORTS MINISTRY IS ACCOUNTABLE AND RELATIONAL

Each person, team, and class should lend itself to relational accountability. This accountability should offer positive feedback to each member of the team or class. The team or class setting should be a safe haven where concerns and problems can be shared for prayer. It should be a place where, as Scripture says, "As iron sharpens iron, so one person sharpens another" (Proverbs 27:17). Teams and classes can lift each other up. They can pray for and provide help as needed. Relationships that are mutually beneficial will bring unity and loyalty and will build a platform for teamwork. The coach or leader who is "tuned in" to his team or class will sense unspoken needs and be able to either refer the person with the need to the pastor or the recreation/sports minister or handle the need him/herself. The key is to be prepared spiritually, having a heart for team members.

DISCIPLESHIP IN RECREATION AND SPORTS MINISTRY PROVIDES OPPORTUNITY FOR SPIRITUAL GROWTH

Recreation and sports ministry provides leaders with spiritual disciplines that can enhance and promote their leadership skills. Giving a devotional, memorizing Scripture, leading in prayer, leading a small group to a deeper walk with Christ—all of these offer spiritual growth experiences to activity leaders. They learn by doing. And as they practice, they will get better, thus increasing their potential for spiritual impact. A focus on getting coaches/activity leaders involved in ever-deeper levels of ministry will provide the coach or class leader opportunities to mentor and help the participants grow spiritually and enhance their ministry effectiveness. The ultimate outcome for leaders and participants alike will be lives changed and God glorified.

BASIC DISCIPLESHIP CONCEPTS IN SPORTS MINISTRY

Being—Every participant/disciple is becoming who God wants him/her to be through the ongoing renewal work of the indwelling Spirit. This is done using gifts, talents, and abilities in a recreation/sports setting.

Knowing—The participant/disciple should learn about God as they participate. This learning comes through studying God's Word, seeing His work in the lives of others, and hearing His voice when Christ is shared in a devotional, or testimony, or team Bible study.

Doing—What the disciple does in response to what he learns about God and who he is gifted by God to be. This happens as the participant is engaged in any recreation/sports activity, resulting in spiritual growth and perhaps taking on spiritual leadership roles in church, at home, at work, or in the community.

PUTTING IT ALL TOGETHER

So what does this look like in the real world? Is discipleship in recreation and sports ministry even possible? Below are some precepts that, if taken and modified, can fit almost any church or ministry setting:

1. **Establish an assigned person as the primary discipleship leader for recreation/sports ministry. This ministry leader:**
   - Creates a vision statement that speaks to discipleship in sports ministry
   - Models the discipleship process personally
   - Becomes the champion of ministry and those involved
   - Is the teacher/encourager/discipler for leaders and participants alike
   - Sees that discipleship is integrated into the total ministry

2. **Organize a discipleship-oriented ministry leadership team**
   - The recreation/sports minister ministry leader seeks people with a heart for ministry as Area Ministry Coordinators, coaches, class leaders etc.
   - The ministry leader plans and promotes discipleship through ministry experiences/programs.
   - The ministry leader trains coaches and activity leaders to recognize and minister to the pre-disciples, the new disciples, and the growing disciples by being a multiplying disciple themselves.
   - The ministry leader provides resources to help coaches and activity leaders disciple teams/classes.

3. **Set age-appropriate spiritual disciplines as themes to emphasize yearly**
   - Choose a yearly discipleship priority (theme) on which to center each ministry/activity. Provide materials for coaches and leaders that will help them verbalize and call attention to the theme during the season, class session, etc. Examples of age-appropriate spiritual disciplines include:

Adult Spiritual Disciplines
- Spending time with the Master
- Living by God's Word
- Praying in faith
- Fellowshipping with believers
- Ministering to others
- Witnessing to the world

Student Spiritual Disciplines
- Understanding the cost of discipleship
- Building accountable relationships
- Setting godly priorities
- Studying God's Word
- Developing deeper prayer lives
- Ministering to/evangelizing others
- Following the guidance of the Holy Spirit
- Demonstrating godly character

Childhood Spiritual Disciplines
- Learning and loving God's Word
- Living godly lives
- Preparing children's hearts to receive Christ
- Memorizing Scripture
- Treating others with respect

ESSENTIAL ACTIONS AND RESULTS

From a practical point of view, effective recreation and sports ministry strategies are implemented through an ongoing process involving seven essential actions that guide its development. These actions take place in the context of a comprehensive church-wide process rather than as independent actions. This approach underscores the value of developing a holistic plan, the interrelationship of the four church practice strategies (in Chapter 1), and the collaborative spirit needed by recreation and sports ministry leaders for the good of the whole.

Essential actions for effective recreation and sports ministry as a recreation/sports ministry discipleship model include:

1. Intentionally focusing on discipleship as major goal.
2. Developing a discipleship model that is carried out through all events and sports
3. Providing leaders with resources to support the model
4. Providing leader training in the model
5. Discipling leaders so that they would have an evangelistic/discipleship mindset.
6. Having the assimilation of new people into the overall life of the church—worship, small groups/Sunday school—as a goal of the discipleship model.
7. Crafting a leadership development discipleship pathway in cooperation with other ministries in the church that will move a person from being a pre-disciple to a multiplying disciple, producing new leaders for both recreation/sports ministry and the church in general.

Discipleship in recreation and sports ministry is foundationally important. Perhaps no other ministry in the church affords the hands-on application of Christian principles in real world settings in the same way. This ministry is a true "laboratory in living" and serves as a nonthreatening entry point to the Christ life. It can be the ministry that moves a person from being a pre-disciple to a multiplying disciple by using real-world application of biblical principles to life events. Recreation and sports ministry is where the desire to use one's natural gifts, talents, and abilities intersects with spiritual giftedness in ministry to touch lives and proclaim the Gospel to a lost and dying world.

NOTES
1. "What Does It Mean to Be a Disciple." http://intervarsity.org/features/what-does-it-mean-be-disciple (accessed October 23, 2016).

2. Edgemon, R. and Steve Williams. *Leading Discipleship in a Church* (Nashville, TN: Convention Press, 1999-2000).

3. Prince, D. E. *In the Arena: The Promise of Sports for Christian Discipleship* (Nashville, TN: Broadman and Holman Publishing Group, 2016): Section 701.

4. Interview transcript. http://www.ronedmondson.com/2012/06/transformational-discipleship-how-people-really-grow.html (accessed October 25, 2016).

Epilogue

Recreation and sports ministry has been my life. God used it to reach me for Christ. I was blessed to know from high school exactly what God was calling me to do—be a recreation/sports minister. I am of all men most blessed to have been able to live out may calling all my life. They say, if you love what you are doing, it will never be work. I can testify to that statement. Doing sports ministry every day has not been work. It has been a joy and an honor—oh, yes and tons of fun! I literally got to "live the dream!" I have a full and grateful heart.

My prayer for students and casual readers of this book is that the Lord God of heaven would seize your imagination, grab your heart and open your eyes to the possibilities of serving God in recreation and sports ministry. It is the absolute most challenging work you will ever do. But it is also the most rewarding.

Now, go. Go use what you have learned to impact a world that is dying and going to hell. As God leads, use sports and recreation to capture the imaginations of people who may think that all they need to do is play on a team or take a class. Provide intentional ministry touch points in that league or class to meet their real need—to know Christ or to walk closer with Him. Ask the Holy Spirit to work in the participant's life. Help them see their need for Christ and give them a chance to respond. That is all God expects. Do your part with excellence and leave the results up to Him. You will be amazed—lives and families will be changed for eternity, people will be discipled to become mature multiplying believers and the church built up.

Then you will say like me: "Yes, I love this work!"

—John Garner, 2017

Selected Book List for Sports and Recreation Ministry

This list is not at all comprehensive but it is representative of books and writings that have impacted recreation and sports ministry. I am indebted to Steward Weir (a leader in sports ministry in the UK) for compiling a most comprehensive bibliography of books, articles research and other writings on the subject. The reader can find his excellent 78 page (and growing) work at:ttp://www.veritesport.org/downloads/Sports_Bibliography_shorter.pdf.

This is a list, not an official bibliography. However, the reader should have enough information to find the resources online or in bookstores. It is an alphabetical list, not a ranking.

Of particular interest to the author is the last section listing books of historic value. We must never forget those who came before, paid the price, and paved the way.

SELECTED BOOK LIST:

- *A Brief Theology of Sport,* by Lincoln Harvey, 2014
- *A Strategy for Implementing Biblical Principles Within a Sports Ministry,* by Shawn DeMoss, 1995
- *Beyond the Gold: What Every Church Needs to Know about Sports Ministry,* by Bryan Mason and Milton Keynes, 2011
- *Born to Play,* by Graham Daniels and J. Stuart Weir, 2004
- *Character That Counts—Who's Counting Yours?: Growing Through Accountability,* by Rod Handley, 2012
- *Credentialing Sport Chaplains: An Idea Whose Time Has Arrived,* by S. Waller, L. Dzikus and R. Hardin (International Journal of Sports & Ethics)
- *Christian Paths to Health and Wellness,* by Peter Walters and John Byl, 2013
- *Christmanship: A Theology of Competition and Sport,* by Greg Linville, 2014

- *Christianity and Leisure,* by G. Van Andel and P Heintzmann, 2006
- *Christianity and Leisure: Volume II,* by G. Van Andel and P. Heintzman, 2014
- *Coach them Well: Fostering Faith and Developing Character in Athletes,* by D. D. Brown, D. Cutcliffe, K. Herrmann, and T. J. F. Welsh, 2006
- *Contemporary Christian Ethic of Competition,* by Greg Linville (available from Overwhelming Victory Ministries, Canton, OH)
- *Competition,* by Gary Warner, 1979
- *Competition and the Christian,* by Rodger Oswald
- *Devotions from the World of Women's Sports,* by Kathy Hillman and John Hillman (Cook Communications Ministries International), June 2000
- *Disability in the Christian Tradition: A Reader,* by B. Brock and J. Swinton, 2012
- *Fair Play—Sports, Values and Society,* by Robert L. Simon, 1991
- Faith on the Field: A Cultural Analysis of Sports Ministry in America, 2003
- *Fit to Serve Him Longer and Better: Physical Fitness and Nutrition,* by Dick Couey, 1999
- *Focus on Sport in Ministry,* by Lowrie McCown and Valerie J. Gin, 2003
- *Game Day for the Glory of God,* by Stephen Altrogge, 2008
- *Glory of the Games,* by Chad Bonham, 2012
- *Good Game: Christianity and the Culture of Sports,* by Shirl James Hoffman, 2010
- *Handbook of Athletic Perfection,* by W. Neal, 1981.
- *How to Build a Church Intramural Sports League,* by Chip Tudor, 2016
- *In the Arena: The Promise of Sports for Christian Discipleship,* by David Prince, 2016
- *Intentional Outreach: A Guide to Simple Church Sports Ministry,* by Steve Quatro, 2009
- *Into the Stadium: Active Guide to Sport Ministry in the Local Church,* by Mason and Bryan, 2003
- John Wooden One-on-One, by John Wooden and Jon Carty, 2004

- *John R. Wooden, Stephen R. Covey and Servant Leadership,* by S. Jenkins (International Journal of Science and Coaching), 2014
- *Keeping Faith in the Team: The Chaplain's Story,* by Stuart Wood, 2011
- *Leisure and Spirituality Special Edition,* by Paul Heintzman, 2009
- *Local Church: A Vision for a Recreation Ministry,* by Marvin Rickard
- *Meditations for Athletes,* by B. Sessoms, 1987
- *Muscular Christianity,* by Tony Ladd and James Mathisen, 1999
- *Playing for God: Evangelical Women and the Unintended Consequences of Sports Ministry* (North American Religions), by Annie Blazer, 2015
- *Practical Ethics in Sport Management,* by Angela Lumpkin, Sharon Kay Stoll, Jennifer Marie Beller, and McFarland, 2011
- *Prayers Out of Bounds,* by Shirl Hoffman in Good Game: Christianity and the Culture of Sports, 2010
- *Redeeming the Time: A Christian Approach to Work and Leisure,* by Leland Ryken, 1995
- *Religion and Sport,* by Charles S. Prebish, 1993
- *Religion and Sports in American Culture,* J. Scholes and R. Sassower, 2013
- *Religion and Sports in American Culture,* by Jeffrey Scholes and Raphael Sassower, 2014
- *Sport and Christianity: A Sign of the Times in the Light of Faith,* by Kevin Lixey, C. Hübenthal, D. Mieth,and N. Müller, 2012
- *Sport at the Beginning of Christianity,* by Tomas Emilio Bolano, 2008
- *Sports and Christianity: Historical and Contemporary Perspectives,* by Nick Watson and Andrew Parker, 2012
- *Sport and Recreation and Evangelism in the Local Church Leonard Browne,* Grove Booklets, 1991
- *Sport and the Christian Religion: A Systematic Review of Literature,* by Nick J. Watson and Andrew Parker, 2014
- *Sport and Religion,* by Shirl J. Hoffman (Editor), 1992
- *Sport and the Spiritual Life: The Integration of Playing & Praying,* by A. M. J. Maranise, 2013
- Sport and Spirituality: An Introduction, by Jim Parry, Simon Robinson, Nick J. Watson, and Mark Nesti, 2007

- *Sports Chaplaincy: Trends, Issues and Debates,* by Andrew Parker and Nick J. Watson, 2016
- *Sport in America: From Wicked Amusement to National Obsession,* by David K. Wiggins (Editor), 1995
- *Sports Ministry for Churches,* by Tommy Yessik (Editor), 1998
- *Sports Outreach,* by Steve Connor, 2003
- *Sports, Religion and Disability,* by Nick J. Watson and Andrew Parker (Editors), 2014
- *Sports Theology: Playing Inside Out,* by Greg Smith, 2010
- *Teamwork, Fellowship of Christian Athletes,* 2009
- *The Contribution of Sports Ministry to Growth in Church Membership,* by Cheri-Lynn Wyman, 2010
- *The Games People Play: Theology, Religion and Sport,* by Robert Ellis, 2014
- *The Ministry of Recreation,* by Ray Conner, 1993
- *Touching Lives Through Your Sports Program,* by Byron D. August and Krystal L. Bell, 2007
- *What the Book Says About Sport,* by Stuart Weir, 2000
- *Why Sports Morally Matter,* by William J Morgan, 2006
- *Winning,* by Grant Teaff, 1985

BOOKS WITH HISTORIC VALUE

- *A Handbook for Church Recreation Leaders,* by T. B. Maston, 1937
- *Church Recreation,* by Agnes D. Pylant, 1959
- *Reaching People Through Recreation,* by Frank Hart "Pogo" Smith, 1973
- *Recreation and the Church,* by Herbert Wright Gaines, 1917
- *Recreation and the Church,* National Recreation Association, 1961
- *Recreation for Churches,* Bob Boyd, 1967
- *Recreation Leadership for Church and Community,* Warren Thomas Powell, 1923
- *The Church and the People's Play,* Henry Atkinson, 1915
- *The Church at Play,* Norman E. Richardson, 1922
- *The Recreation Leader,* E.O. Harbin, 1952

Appendix 1
Qualifications for the Person who is Called into Recreation and Sports Ministry

1. Be a mature, practicing, committed Christian.
2. Have a concept of using recreation as a ministry tool.
3. Have a broad-based knowledge of recreation and ministry in general.
4. Be able to impart vision to one's church as to the ministry and evangelism opportunities of recreation and sports ministry for that community.
5. Be a people person who understands the needs of the many ages that will be ministered to.
6. Have a heart for ministry.
7. Understand recreation and sports as tools that can offer those in the community a non-threatening introduction to the Christ-life and church participation.
8. College degree in a related field. A seminary education is helpful but not always necessary—requirements vary from church to church.
9. Be a team player. Good staff relationships with other ministry area staff are important for smooth cooperation and coordination of overall ministry efforts.
10. Have good organizational/administrative skills. Juggling schedules, working with maintenance personnel, working to keep the ministry functioning as a part of the overall church ministry, scheduling volunteers, working with budgets, keeping up with finances, and if a facility is involved: handling facility scheduling, contacting prospects who visit the facility, and doing other ministerial duties that come up are many of the requirements of his ministry position.
11. Understand how the church works and what its mission is.
12. Be an educator, seeking to teach the Kingdom value of recreation and sports used as ministry tools.

Appendix 2
Recreation and Sports Ministry: Positioning for Impact

1. Any ministry that impacts culture will have the following characteristics:
2. Defined uniqueness identified in the vision statement
3. An articulated Christian worldview
4. Focus on evangelism and discipleship in its kingdom vision
5. A focus on quality and hospitality
6. Developed strategy to use the unique giftedness of members to demonstrate Christianity in action
7. Articulated beliefs as outlined in a mission statement
8. A place for people to sense "'community"
9. A comprehensive promotion plan
10. A plan to meet needs with quality and services
11. Quality, quality, quality!
12. Focus on people
13. Show world concern
14. Set of incremental goals
15. Empowered staff and volunteers
16. Recognition that ministry is effective when multiplied in others

Appendix 3
Sources for Lifelong Learning and Networking for Recreation and Sports Ministers

FAITH BASED TRAINING CONFERENCES/ PROFESSIONAL ORGANIZATIONS

Christian Camping International

www.cciworldwide.org

Church Sports and Recreation Ministers Conference

www.csrm.org/

Christian Camp and Conference Association

www.ccca.org/

International Sports Federation

www. eamisf.com/

Upward Sports

www.upward.org/

SECULAR TRAINING CONFERENCES/ PROFESSIONAL ORGANIZATIONS

Amateur Athletic Union

www.aausports.org

American Alliance for Health, Physical Education, Recreation and Dance

www.shapeamerica.org

National Association for Sport and Physical Education

www.aahperd.org

American Camping Association

www.acacamps.org

American Mountain Guide Association

www.amga.com

National Outdoor Leadership School

www.nols.edu

Association for Challenge Course Technology

www.acctinfo.org

National Recreation and Park Association

www.nrpa.org

Association for Experiential Education

www.aee.org

North American Society for Education Sport Management

www.nassm.org

National Alliance for Youth Sports

www.nays.org

Outward Bound

www.outwardbound.com

Project Adventure

www.pa.org

National Intramural Recreational Sports Association

www.nirsa.org

Appendix 4
Sources of Information on Recreation Equipment, Management, Trends, and Programming

The wise recreation and sports minister will keep up with what is happening in the secular field of recreation and sports. Why? Because management is management, games are games and equipment is equipment—there is nothing "religious" about those things. Good management is good management—whether at the city park and rec department or in the church sports ministry. Each of these organizations will do conferencing, have continuing education credits and offer memberships that can be a source of expertise. There are many more than this, but these are the ones that are best known.

National Recreation and Park Association (NRPA)

www.nrpa.org

Association of Outdoor Recreation and Education

www.aore.org

American Camping Association

www.acacamps.org

National Intramural—Recreational Sport Association (NIRSA)

www.nirsa.org

North American Society for Sport Management (NASSM)

www.nassm.org

National Institute for Fitness and Sport (NIFS)

www.nifs.org

International Health, Racquet, & Sports Club Association (IHRSA)

www.chs.ihrsa.org

Appendix 5
Buyers Guides

Buyer's Guides are sponsored by professional organizations or publishers. They will be divided into sections helping the buyer find the equipment or service they are searching for quickly. Each guide will list providers of equipment and services. They are found online or as printed catalogues. If online, key word: "Buyer's Guide." These guides can save time and money.

Athletic Business Buyer's Guide

www.athleticbusiness.com/buyers_guide

Camp Business

www.campbusiness.com

Parks and Rec Business

www.parksandrecbusiness.com

www.**Parks and Recreation Magazine Field Guide**

www.fieldguide.org

Recreation Management

www.recmanagement.com

International Health, Racquet & Sportsclub Association (Ihrsa)

www.ihrsa.org/fit-buyers-guide

Appendix 6
General Recreation and Sports Equipment Suppliers

Bison Inc.

www.bisoninc.com

BSN Sports

www.bsnsports.com

Flaghouse

www.flaghouse.com

Gopher Sports

www.gophersport.com

Jaypro Sports

www.jayprosports.com

S & S Worldwide

www.ssww.com/sports-pe-recreation

Sports Chalet

www.sportchalet.com

Appendix 7
Sample Liability Release Form

Do not copy this form. It is strictly for the purpose of example. Seek guidance from your local legal counsel to create a personalized form.

SPORTS CLINIC MEDICAL FORM

Name _____

Age _____ Grade _____

Parent's Name _____

Phone _____

Address _____

City_____ Zip _____

Email_____

I give my permission for _____
to participate in the Sports Clinic. Furthermore, I give consent for medical treatment, should it be needed. I release the Sports Clinic, its sponsors, and coaches from liability as they seek medical attention should it be needed.

_____
Parent or Guardian Signature

_____
Date

Appendix 8
Sample Medical Information Form

Do not copy this form. It is strictly for the purpose of example. Seek guidance from your local legal counsel to create a personalized form.

SPORTS CLINICAL MEDICAL INFORMATION FORM

Name _____

Age _____ Grade _____

Parent's Name _____

Phone _____

Address _____

City_____ Zip _____

Email_____

List any medical information that a Doctor or Emergency Medical Team would need to know should they treat your child _____

_____

_____

_____

Doctor's Name _____

Phone _____

I give permission to the Sports Clinic personnel to obtain medical help for my child in case of an emergency during the clinic.

_____
Parent/Guardian Signature

_____
Date

Appendix 9
Participant Information Card

_____Church

Name _____

Grade Completed/Age _____

Address _____ Zip _____

Home Phone _____Birth Date _____

Mother's Name _____

Work Phone _____ Cell Phone_____

Father's Name _____

Work Phone _____ Cell Phone_____

If parents cannot be reached, in an emergency call:_____

Phone _____

Family Doctor_____ Phone _____

Hospital Preference _____

Insurance Carrier_____

My child will arrive at _____ a.m. and be picked up at _____

p.m. by_____

(name of person to pick up child)

Does your child take daily medication? _____

Does your child have allergies or any other special problems that the camp staff should be aware of? _____

_____

Should (child's name) need emergency treatment and neither of the parents or our family doctor can be reached, we hereby give permission for our child to be transported to the nearest doctor or hospital, and the attending doctor has our permission to render any treatment he/she feels is necessary.

_____
Mother/Guardian   *Date*

_____
Father/Guardian   *Date*

Appendix 10
Incident Report Form

Date _____

Child's name _____

Parent's name _____

Address _____

Phone _____

Emergency contact_____

Time of incident _____

Place of incident _____

Type of incident _____

_____

Nature of incident/injury _____

_____

_____

When and how parents were notified_____

_____

_____

Who was present when incident occured _____

_____

Name of person handling incident_____

Explanation of how incident happened_____

_____

_____

Action taken _____

Treatment given on site _____

by whom _____

Where and how transported (if taken to doctor/hospital) _____

_____

Date _____ Time_____

Result of follow-up with parents/guardian _____

_____

Appendix 11
Permission Form

Child's name _____

Parent/guardian _____

Address _____

Phone number (work) _____ (cell) _____

Email_____

Emergency contact name _____

Address _____

Phone _____

Brief medical history _____

_____

_____

Allergies_____

_____

Medications _____

_____

PERMISSION TO TREAT

My permission is granted for _____
(name of caregiver) to obtain necessary medical attention in case of
sickeness or injury to my child while participating in _____
(name of program/activity).

Family doctor _____

Medical insurance _____

Appendix 12
Abuse/Neglect Reporting Form

Report made to _____

Date _____

Child's name _____

Age _____ Sex _____

Child's address _____
_____

Name of parents _____
_____

Address of parents _____
_____

Names, addresses of other care givers_____
_____

Physical indicators observed and when_____
_____
_____

Behavioral indicators observed and when _____
_____
_____

Other indicators observed/known _____
_____
_____

If known, name and address of person responsible for abuse_____
_____

Source of report_____

Action taken by reporting source _____

Parents informed of report being made?   Yes   No

Reporter's name and position_____

Appendix 13
Event Cost Projection Worksheet

Event_____ Year _____

Program/Committee _____ Budget _____

Date(s) _____ Participant Goal _____

	Total $	Jan	Feb	Mar	Apr	May	Jun	Jul	Aug	Sep	Oct	Nov	Dec
EXPENSES/PROMOTIONS													
Printing													
Newspaper Ads													
Mail/Postage													
Other													
EVENT/PROGRAM													
Registration													
Tickets													
Materials													
Supplies													
Decorations													
Meals													
Lodging													
Transportation													
Child Care													
Wages													
Other													
LEADERS/GUESTS													
Travel													
Contract Fees													
Honorariums													
Other													
Total Expenses													
INCOME													
Amount to be received: $						per person:							
Registrations													
Tickets													
Fees													
Other													
TOTAL INCOME													
Net Cost/Budget													

Appendix 14
Non-Event Cost Projection Worksheet

Year_____

Program/Committee _____ Budget # _____

Person in Charge _____

PLEASE LIST THE AMOUNT TO BE SPENT EACH MONTH

	Total $	Jan	Feb	Mar	Apr	May	Jun	Jul	Aug	Sep	Oct	Nov	Dec
EXPENSES (Please list the items to be paid - one per line)													
Total Expenses													

Appendix 15
Total Cost Projection Worksheet

Year _____

Program/Committee _____ Budget # _____

Person in Charge _____

PLEASE LIST THE MONTH IN WHICH THE COST IS ANTICIPATED

	Total $	Jan	Feb	Mar	Apr	May	Jun	Jul	Aug	Sep	Oct	Nov	Dec
EXPENSES (Please list the items to be paid - one per line)													
Total Expenses													

Appendix 16
Recreation and Sports Ministry
Budget Accounts

Budget Area _____

Monthly Account Total _____

Acct #	Acct	Jan	Feb	Mar	Apr	May	Jun	Jul	Aug	Sep	Oct	Nov	Dec

Appendix 17
The Programmer's Cube

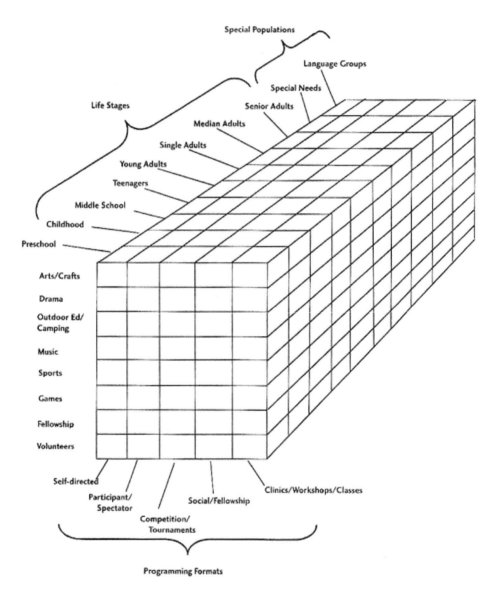

*Adapted from Patricia Farrell and Herberta M. Lundegren, *The Process of Recreation Programming: Theory and Technique*, 3rd ed. (State College, Pa.: Venture Publishing, 1991.)

Appendix 18
Recreation Ministry Programming/ Event Possibilities

Camping and Outdoors
Sailing
Senior Adults:
 Chautauqua
 Conferences
 Historic Places
Sightseeing
Snow Skiing
Sporting Events:
 College
 High School
 Professional
Swimming
Tennis Tournament
Tubing
Water Skiing
Zoo

**Activities Away
from Church**
Bike Hikes/Trips
Bird Watching
Boating
Camps: Trip, Day
Canoeing
Cycling
Camps:
 Family
 Resident
 Sports
Deep-Sea Fishing
Diving
Family Camp-Out
Fishing Tournament
Float Trip
Golf Tournament
Hiking

Horseback Riding
Horseshoes
Hunting/Hunter Safety
Ice Skating
In-Line Skating
Mission Ideas:
 Concerts
 Craft at Park
 Day Camp
 Mobile Rec Unit
 Volleyball
Nature Study
Play Day Picnic
Playgrounds
Putt-Putt Golf
Retreats

Gymnasium Activities
Aerobics
After-School Program
for Children
All-Night Parties
Archery
Associational Youth Rally
Badminton
Banquets
Basketball:
 Clinics
 Christmas Tournament
 Free-Throw Contest
 Intramurals
 League
 On Skates
 Wheelchair
 Hot-Shot Contest
 Three-Man League
Bike Rodeo

Cheerleading Class
Dinner Theatre
Dodge Ball
Elementary Fun Day
Fellowships
Fencing
Football:
 Flag
 Touch
Four-Square
Frisbee Fun/Golf
Game Night
Golf Clinic
Gymnastics
Handball
Hockey on Skates
Indoor Track Meet
Jogging
Judo/Karate
Lock-Ins
Men's Noonday Exercise
Mother's Day Out
Movies
Officiating
Peanut Patch Olympics
Ping Pong
Preschool Recreation
Racquetball
Recreation for
Children's Choir
Missions Organizations
Relays
Roller Skating
Roller/In-Line Hockey
Self-Defense Class
Shuffleboard
Skateboards

Sports Clinics
Basketball
Soccer
Volleyball
Cheerleading
Baseball
Football
Tennis
Superstar Olympics
Tennis:
  Lessons
  Leagues
  Doubles Tournament
  Mixed Doubles
  Tournament
  Singles Tournament
Volleyball:
  Clinics
  Intramurals
  League
  Sunday School
  Three-Man
  Blind
Walking Club/Program
Weight Training
Wiffleball
Wrestling

Craft Ideas/Classes
Banners
Brass Rubbings
Bread Dough Art
Cake Decorating
Calligraphy
Candle Making
Ceramics
China Painting
Christmas Decorations
Coin Collecting
Cooking Classes
Craft Fair
Creative Stitching

Crewel Embroidery
Crocheting
Decoupage
Dip and Drape
Drawing
Floral Arranging
Fly Tying
Gun Safety
Home Decorating
How to:
  Auto Repairs
  Furniture Refinishing
  Plumbing Repair
Hunter Education
Jewelry Making
Knitting
Lace Darning
Leather Craft
Macramé
Model Building
Needlepoint
Oil Painting
Party Foods
Photography
Pine Cone Wreath
Pottery
Puppet Construction
Quilting
Rag Baskets
Recipe Clinic
Scrapbooking
Sculpture
Sea Shell Collecting
Self Defense
Sewing Class
Silk Flowers
Sketching
Smocking
Stained Glass
Stamp Collecting
Stenciling

Taxidermy
Tennis Shoe Art
Tole Painting
Tying Scarves
Wallpaper-hanging Class
Weaving
Woodworking

Family Night Ideas
All-Church Activities
Children's Cookie Bake
Church-Wide Picnic
Covered-Dish Supper
Crafts Fair
Dinner Theatre
Drama Classes
Family Camp-Out
Field Day Activities
Game Night
Health Services Night:
  Diabetes Test
  Medical Screening
  Blood Donations
  Blood Pressure Check
Hobby Show
Homemade Ice Cream
Cake Bake Contests
Movies
Musical Drama
Pet Show
Pizza Party
Senior Adult Luncheons
and Monthly Meetings
Skating
Video Night

Social
All Church:
  Banquet
  Fellowship
  Picnic
Breakfasts

Covered-Dish Supper

Family Night at the
Church

Food Truck Festival

Hayride

Talent Night

Team Sports

Basketball

Soccer

Softball

Team Handball

Volleyball

**Ideas Not
Listed Elsewhere**

Computer Classes

CPR Classes

ESL Classes

First-Aid Classes

Health Services

Blood Pressure Checks

Weight Monitoring

Health Fairs

Nutrition Counseling

Language Classes
(Sign/Foreign)

Life Guarding Classes

Mother's Day Out

Officiating Class

Getting On-line Classes

Sports Banquet

Tax Preparation Seminar

Appendix 19
Seven Rules of Gamesmanship

Everyone likes to play games. Children and teenagers like games; and the wilder, crazier, and messier they are, the better they like them. Adults like games too—a little more sedate, but they still like games.

Games for any age group must constantly be updated and adapted to be effective. All games can be adapted to fit the occasion or the age group, from preschool to senior adults. The secret is how the leader comes across in the introduction and instruction of the game to the group. Leaders should convey excitement about the activity.

RULES FOR GAMESMANSHIP

1. **No one should be hurt.** When playing games, you should consider the possibility of persons getting hurt. Ask yourself, "Can anyone get hurt doing this?" If so, modify or change the game to lessen the possibility. If you are playing in a rocky field, perhaps you should move to a grassy area. Use your head!

2. **No one should be humiliated.** The idea is to foster togetherness, fellowship, and goodwill. The days of humiliating someone for a laugh are long gone. Youth ministers who humiliate kids soon don't have any to work with. To keep the more athletic from running over the "nonathletes" and humiliating them, change the rules to level the playing field. Adapt some games so athletic ability is not a factor. Everyone will have a great time— even the athletes.

3. **No one should be forced to play.** Making people play a game they really don't want to play is like making someone pray. You risk loosing that kid. If the game is fun and everyone is enjoying playing, the one who is sitting out usually ends up choosing to give it a try. This is better for everyone.

4. **Games should fit the occasion.** You don't do a really messy game at an event where everyone is dressed formally (like a banquet). Be sure your games are appropriate for the occasion.

5. **Don't mix ages too widely.** Seventh graders usually don't mix well with seniors, and the seventh graders might get hurt. Consider age and ability differences.

6. **Games should not be divisive.** Competition is OK if it does not get out of hand. Watch for signs of a "win at all costs" mentality as your kids participate. Games should foster fellowship and unity. If you get an "us against them" thing going, it can destroy the group.

7. **Know the game.** Know the rules and how you are going to adapt the game before you start playing. It is best if the leader has played the game. The game leader needs to make games come alive and be inclusive.

Appendix 20
Recreation and Sports Ministry Best Practices

It has been shown that recreation and sports ministry best serves the church if the following are characteristic of its mission and actions.

I. Definition and Purpose

Definition: Recreation and Sports Ministry provides opportunities for the sharing of the gospel and discipleship through social interaction, sports and games, camping, retreats, recreational music, arts, crafts, hobbies, fitness/wellness, lifelong learning opportunities, therapeutic recreation, and leisure ministries for all age groups.

Purpose: The purpose of Recreation and Sports Ministry is helping people become aware of their need for a relationship with Christ, His role in their lives and their place in His Kingdom's work.

II. Biblical Foundations

The Recreation and Sports Ministry in any church, by the empowerment of the Holy Spirit and obedience to the Great Commandment and Great Commission; is to use every means possible to reach all ages with the message of salvation for the lost and discipleship of Christians (1 Cor. 9:22-23; Matt. 28:19-20; Matt. 22:36-40).

III. Strategic Principles

A. The Recreation and Sports Ministry is led by God-called servant minded individuals who strive to provide recreation/sporting events and resources and training that will advance the Kingdom of God.

B. The Recreation and Sports Ministry is led by church staff (volunteer, part-time or full-time) whose Christ-like character is a model for the congregation and who sense a call of God to minister using recreation and sports.

C. Recreation and sports ministry leaders are gifted by God with the competencies, character and vision necessary to accomplish the work that God has called them to do.

D. In any Recreation and Sports Ministry, creative programming and congregational involvement will be key to accomplishing its goals.

IV. Other Best Practices:

A. The successful Recreation and Sports Ministry will have pastoral and staff support as they validate the ministry with their verbal and attendance support.

B. The Recreation and Sports Ministry is coordinated by a Recreation/Sports Ministry Team/Committee or Leadership Team.

C. The Recreation and Sports Ministry supports and under girds church ministries by providing assistance to all other ministries.

D. The Recreation and Sports Ministry at times is a leading tool to capture the imagination of an unseeded (with God's Word) culture using recreation/sports as a non-threatening entry point for the lost into the life of the local church. This affords a first point of contact and a place for cultivation of the unchurched.

E. The Recreation and Sports Ministry trains church leadership to use recreation as a reaching and discipling tool.

F. The Recreation and Sports Ministry provides an environment for the fostering of fellowship among all ages.

G. The ministry of recreation provides services, events and resources through the church as it implements its mission in the community.

V. Relationships with Other Ministry Organizations

Note: (1) For all church ministry organizations the recreation/sports ministry will serve as a first touch for the overall church as it represents each ministry area. (2) The recreation/sports ministry will help prepare future church leaders by providing opportunities for discipleship through leadership opportunities within the ministry.

A. The Recreation and Sports Ministry of seeks to establish and maintain effective working relationships with ministry leaders by participating in the Church Council/Church Leadership Team.

B. Sunday School/Small Groups—The Recreation and Sports Ministry assists Sunday School/small groups with all ages in carrying out their fellowship actions including social events, intramural sports, and retreats.

C. Discipleship Ministry—The Recreation and Sports Ministry works with the Discipleship Ministry leaders in providing lifelong learning opportunities and the opportunity to gain leadership experience through the Recreation and Sports Ministry activities.

D. Senior Adult Ministry—The Recreation and Sports Ministry works with Senior Adult Ministry in providing fellowship and lifelong learning opportunities for senior adults including clubs, health and wellness activities, and travel opportunities as called upon.

E. Collegiate Student Ministry—The Recreation and Sports Ministry assists the Collegiate Student Ministry leaders in providing college students recreational and sports related opportunities.

F. Single Adult Ministry—The Recreation and Sports Ministry assists the Single Adult Ministry in providing recreational and sporting opportunities including retreats, outings, social events, leagues, mission/service opportunities and interactive learning opportunities.

G. Men's Ministry—The Recreation and Sports Ministry assists the Men's Ministry in providing recreational and sporting opportunities including retreats, outdoor education, leagues/tournaments mission/service opportunities, and continuing education events.

H. Women's Ministry—The Recreation and Sports Ministry assists the Women's Enrichment Ministry in providing recreational and sporting opportunities including retreats, social events, health and wellness information, fitness opportunities, leagues and creative events.

I. Family Ministry—The Recreation and Sports Ministry assists Family Ministry leaders by providing recreational opportunities for families including intergenerational retreats, outings, family wellness information, and helps on families having fun together.

J. Evangelism Ministry—The Recreation and Sports Ministry assists Evangelism leaders by providing recreational opportunities which can be used as entry points for lost people into the church family.

K. Local Mission Ministry—The Recreation and Sports Ministry assists the Mission Team with recreational opportunities as mission projects such as sports evangelism teams, block parties, or sponsoring a booth at a community event.

L. Missions Ministry—The Recreation and Sports Ministry assists the mission education organizations with recreation/sports mission opportunities including retreats and opportunities to participate in recreation/sports missions.

M. Music Ministry—The Recreation and Sports Ministry assists the Music/Worship Ministry with recreation/sporting opportunities.

N. Christian Life and Citizenship Ministry—Recreation and Sports

O. Ministry offers creative alternatives that can help people make decisions for the use of their leisure time. Providing opportunities and events to church members and persons in the community that will strengthen and enhance a moral lifestyle could do these alternatives.

P. Pre-school/Children's Ministry—Recreation and sports Ministry assists the preschool/children's ministry in providing support to planned activities and expertise in activities such as: play days, outings, games for VBS, gym or outdoor activities, sports leagues/camps/clinics for older children and where organization and experience with recreation is needed.

Q. Middle school and High School—Recreation and Sports Ministry partners to provide assistance with sports leagues, camp recreation, retreat recreation. Assistance is also given in providing leadership training as older students are trained to be leaders in areas of skill and interest.

Appendix 21
Reaching a Leisure-Oriented Culture with Intentional Sports and Recreation Ministry

Churches today have more opportunity than ever to capture the imaginations of people caught up in our leisure-oriented culture. Any church can reach people for Christ using a well-organized and intentional recreation and sports ministry.

This is not about having numerous recreation/sports events on your church calendar. It is a recreation/sports ministry that has at its center the intention of fostering relationships, sharing the gospel, or developing disciples.

Think what it might mean in your community to have individuals or teams who will share the gospel in a natural, non-threatening way each time a team, group, club, or class meets at or away from the church campus during a recreation/sports event.

Here is a plan you could follow to develop an intentional recreation and sports ministry in your church family.

1. Seek the support of your pastor, church staff, and key leaders

Help your pastor, staff, and key leaders understand that this is a ministry and more than "play-time" for a few athletes, teenagers, or children. Provide articles and resources so they can familiarize themselves this ministry. It is vital that your pastor understands the usefulness of recreation and sports as an evangelistic and discipleship tool.

2. Find the right ministry leader

Seek someone with a vision for use of recreation and sports as intentional ministry tools. It may be a volunteer, a part-time staff member, a staff member who has a "combination" role, or a dedicated full-time recreation and sports minister.

This person should have the ability to communicate, educate, and lead the church in this evangelistic and discipling effort. The person must be a good motivator, mentor, recruiter, teacher, administrator and minister. This individual does not have to be an expert in sports or any other recreationally oriented activity.

3. Develop a simple organization for the ministry

Once you have the support of your church leadership and the buy-in by your congregation, it is vital to get organized.

4. Create new ministry teams/committees

Depending on your organization and polity, your church may vote to set up a ministry team or a committee with a Lead Team sub-structure. You might consider a recreation ministry team made up of persons who are willing to serve for a one to three year term as a policy making/advisory/planning group.

Lead teams are made up of small groups of people who serve for a short term to help with an event or activity and then are disbanded. This group is usually made up of people who have a deep interest in the activity or sport.

5. Develop a philosophy/mission statement

Here is a sample mission statement:

Recreation and Sports Ministry seeks to make God's name and salvation through is Son, Jesus known by using recreation and sports as ministry tools. This ministry seeks to "become all things to all men that we might by all means win some" (1 Cor. 9:22-23). We will use these tools to evangelize the lost, disciple believers, minister in Christ name, facilitate worship, and encourage fellowship.

6. Provide ongoing education and vision casting for this ministry

Your pastor might preach on reaching people for Christ through recreation/sports ministry.

A guest speaker with experience in this field and success stories to share will encourage your church family to become involved.

When someone joins the church after being first touched by the recreation and sports ministry, share this with your church family.

Take a survey to discover recreation/sports interest of your church family and community. Find a posted a sample survey at http://www. lifeway.com/recsports

7. **Provide consistent quality in all aspects of your ministry**

People will come to events when they perceive strong "value" for the time spent in attendance. From your promotion, to the registration process, to the "walk up" experience as they are greeted, to the way the event is run, to how it ends are key to the success of your ministry.

Reaching people using well-organized and intentional recreation and sports ministry can honor God and be rewarding.

Appendix 22
Working with Volunteers

ADVANTAGES OF USING VOLUNTEERS:

1. Allows for wider participation and inclusion of more people
2. Allows facilities to be open longer hours
3. Allows for a wider variation of programming
4. Allows money that would have been spent on wages to spent on other areas of ministry
5. Provides the individual with opportunities to minister.
6. Gives the volunteer a chance to move outside themselves in ministry to others
7. Volunteering leads to loyalty
8. Gives the minister the freedom to minister (follow his calling)

POSSIBLE VOLUNTEER RESPONSIBILITIES:

1. Greet people that participate in programming
2. Answer the phone
3. Hand out equipment
4. Referee/Supervise events
5. Register guests
6. Leading classes
7. Coaching teams
8. Making phone calls
9. Share their faith
10. Register participants for events
11. Repair equipment
12. There could be many more listed depending on the situation

TEN WAYS TO KEEP VOLUNTEERS:

1. Train them
2. Help them see a need that is being met
3. Recognize them
4. Reward them

5. Listen to and act on their suggestions
6. Verbally show appreciation
7. Do some of their work yourself - see what they put up with
8. Always let them know where they can find you in case they need you
9. Train them again
10. Love them—you can't do without them!

Appendix 23
Recreation for Families

Types of Programming for Families
- Crafts
- Sports
- Fitness
- Hobbies
- Camping/Outdoor Education
- Special Days/Holidays
- Leisure Education
- Continuing Education
- Fellowship Opportunities with Other Families
- Games/Tournaments
- Family Enrichment Emphasis
- Others?

Family Programming Ideas
- Tailgate Party (During football season)
- Family Pet show (Smallest, ugliest, biggest, ETC.)
- Family Talent Show (Songs, skits, drama, make it light and fun)
- Family Fun Night (Activities for all ages interacting)
- Family Circle Cycle Trip (short or long, include everyone)
- Kamp-Out Kapers (Camp-out with all the trimmings)
- Great Shirts! It's a Family! (Create family shirts for each person)
- This is Us Fair (Pictures, hobby items for each family mbr.)
- Creek Walking (Skip stones, count creatures, enjoy nature)
- Canoe Trips (Half day, all day, multiple days)
- Family Fun Run (Walk or run set distance)
- Family Health Fair (Health care professionals invited to screen)
- Sock-It-To-Me Softball (softball with a twist – played with a sock ball)
- Fast Food Progressive Dinner (Just what the kids want)
- Fishin' Families and Fun (Catch and release or catch and eat)
- There's a Gorilla in My Soup! (A trip to the zoo and picnic)
- Ye, Ha! Ride'em Cowboy! (Attend a rodeo or do your own)
- Family Fest! (Bible study, interaction, and fun stuff retreat)
- Adventure Recreation Family Style (Learning to trust)
- Fun For All Play Day (Games, activities and more games)
- Family Album (Make a Photo or Music Album)
- It's Up To Us (Service Project and fun)
- The Great Leaf Hunt (Hike and picnic)
- Family Line Dancing Classes (Square Dancing)
- The Great Ornamentation Night (Make Christmas Decorations)
- Hey! Look What We Made! (Give 'em the stuff and let 'em go)
- Family Night at the Videos (With a Video Projector)
- Hot Dogs, Hay and Horses (Old fashioned Hay Ride)
- Fine Feathered Friends (Building Bird houses and Feeders)
- The Thrill of Playing! (Family Game night)
- Family Fun Renewal (Revival centered around fun and food)
- A Portrait of . . . (Seeing the Church as family)
- Mystery Ramble (Into the bus and off we go)

Appendix 24
Recreation and Sports Ministry

APPLICATION FOR COMMUNITY SPORTS TEAM

Contact Person _____ H _____ C _____

Email_____

Chaplain _____ H _____ C _____

Email_____

Organization responsible for league_____

Location _____ Deadline for signup _____

Desired sport _____ League fees _____

Equipment requested _____

_____

Please return this form to the Recreation office and we will contact you concerning your request. Please complete a different form for every request.

- These are the policies for representing the church on a community sports team:
- For participation in community leagues the team contact person must pick up an application from the Recreation Office. Return the completed form to the Recreation office, and receive approval from the Recreation Ministry Team.
- All participation fees related to the league will be absorbed by the team members.
- Fees will be collected by the Team Contact Person.
- All fees must be collected prior to registration and turned into the Recreation Office. The Recreation staff will request a check cut for the amount of the league.
- All team members must sign a Pinelake Players Code of Ethics to be on file in the Recreation Office. Violations to the Code of Ethics will be evaluated by the Recreation Ministry Team.
- No refunds given to players after registration is completed.
- Every team must have a team contact person to handle application, collection of fees and other administrative duties.
- Every team must have a person that serves as the Sports Chaplain of the team. This person is responsible for team devotionals to be held either at practice or before the game. This person is also responsible for leading the team in prayer prior and after all meetings. The contact person and Chaplain can be the same person if so desired.

If you agree to the above policies, please sign below.

_____

Team Contact Person

_____

Team Chaplain

Appendix 25
Ten Commandments for Recreators/Sports Ministers

Written by Frank Hart "Pogo" Smith who is now walking the streets of gold, this is great advice for any minister. It first appeared in the Rec Lab Notebook and later in Church Recreation Magazine. Thanks, Pogo.

1. **Thou shalt be a recreated and a re-created recreator.**
   - Be involved in recreation yourself
   - Grow in other areas of your life: relationships, religion, politics, etc.
2. **Thou shalt be aware of the worth of the individual.**
   - Others worth as well as your own worth
   - Expect the best of others
3. **Thou shalt experience the excitement of ordinary encounters.**
   - Always see the best in others
   - Walking the second mile when needed
4. **Thou shalt be a "lazy" leader.**
   - Lazy…don't do anything you can get someone else to do for you. Delegate
   - Empathetic…look at situations from every possible angle
   - Adaptable…roll with the punch—if it can go wrong it will
   - Daring…but have it okayed by superiors
   - Enthusiastic...enjoy your work
   - Resourceful…don't need to know it all, but know where to get it
5. **Thou shalt water not the spark.**
   - "Fan the spark and water the seed"
   - Don't destroy someone's excitement or enthusiasm
   - Build creativity in others
6. **Thou shalt realize the necessity for integrity.**
   - Be professional
   - Be honest, your word is your bond
   - Be above board, no hidden agendas
   - Give receipts, be able to prove all monetary actions

- Abide by copywrite laws
- Dress appropriately

7. **Thou shalt appreciate the staff.**
    - Utilize the gifts of those that work under you
    - Be a good supervisor, communicate, guide
    - Take your day off!!!
    - If something is programmed on your day off, take another day
    - Plan and use your vacation days

8. **Thou shalt be a family first.**
    - Whether single or married, childless or not take the time to be with those closest to you.
    - Don't let work be the ugly monster that keeps mommy or daddy away
    - When you are "off" be "off"—not distracted from putting family first
    - Your work is other people's play—so give yourself permission to play with your family

9. **Thou shalt know the value of organization.**
    - Be self-motivated, be a professional, get your act together before you approach others
    - Follow proper channels

10. **Thou shalt study trends and continually learn.**
    - Work hard at seeing what is going on around you
    - Take opportunities for conferences and conventions

Appendix 26

Five Leadership Principles For Sports Ministers

1. **The Sports and Recreation Minister Must Work with Church Leadership**

   The sports and recreation minister must work proactively with their senior/lead pastors, administrative staff, and church elders/deacons to not only establish foundational theological and biblical precepts but also to determine agreed upon practical guidelines that will assist the sports/recreation minister if an incident should ever arise. Churches that don't do the work of establishing their ministries on theological and philosophical foundations open themselves up to disappointed (even angry) people, or even worse—paralyzing lawsuits that cripple any present or future ministry.

2. **Learn from Denominational, Christian University and Parachurch Sports Ministry Leaders**

   Sports and recreation ministers (whether professional or volunteer) would be wise to suggest to their congregational leadership that the congregation should reach out to the broader Church for help in determining a way forward. Astute denominational leaders have already wrestled with these issues and should be able to provide excellent leadership, counsel, and resources. Church-based (and thus assumed, biblically based) universities have completed or may be in the midst of helpful research on these issues, and most parachurch ministries have either encountered similar kinds of pressures and/or exist to provide counsel to local churches on issues such as the ones discussed in this chapter.

3. **Build Significant Relationships**

   The best advice for a local church sports and recreation minister may well be what has long been an industry standard of wisdom: seek to have an amiable relationship with everyone who walks into your gym or onto your fields. This opens the door to opportunities to share the life-changing message of the Gospel. Rather than trying find reasons to keep people out of your sporting or recreational activities, work hard to love people unconditionally and seek to be inclusive in every sensible and biblical way.

4. Research and Network

There are many denominational, as well as para-church organization, resources available designed to help churches determine their theological foundations and philosophical principles. From these resources can emerge biblically based core values, vision, and mission statements. It is highly recommended that local church sports and recreation ministers should read the books, study, and be knowledgeable. It is also wise to keep abreast of the latest research and to reach out to other sports and recreation ministers in the field to learn from them. Part of this networking can include taking part in various webinars, conferences, and connection groups.

5. Determine and Communicate Your Core Values and Specific Principles

Once the church (and recreation/sports ministry) has determined its theological and philosophical foundations and its core values, it should put them in writing and then strategically make them available. Good places to display them would include social media and physical brochures, especially a church's constitution and by-laws. Communication, however, goes well beyond electronic and hard copy circles. There is nothing better than personal face-to-face communication, and a piece of paper cannot communicate acceptance or provide the warmth of a smile or the excitement of engaging eyes. Remember another long-standing sports outreach maxim: Jesus is more caught than taught!

CPSIA information can be obtained
at www.ICGtesting.com
Printed in the USA
BVHW050337260123
657104BV00005B/833